[illegible] ON EGYPT AND CHALDAEA

[illegible] Religion [illegible]

[illegible] Magic [illegible]

[illegible]

[illegible] Religion [illegible]

[illegible]

[illegible] III.—Book of the [illegible]

[illegible]—History of [illegible]

[illegible]—The Decrees of Memphis and Canopus
The [illegible]

[illegible]—The Decrees of Memphis and Canopus
[illegible]

[illegible]—The Decrees of [illegible]

[illegible]

[illegible] Book of [illegible]

[illegible] Book of [illegible]

[illegible]

[illegible] The Book [illegible]

[illegible]

[illegible]

[illegible]

[illegible]
The Dead

[illegible]

[illegible]

[illegible]

BOOKS ON EGYPT AND CHALDÆA.

Vol. I.—**Egyptian Religion.**

,, II.—**Egyptian Magic.**

,, III.—**Egpytian Language.**

,, IV.—**Babylonian Religion.**

,, V.—**Assyrian Language.**

Vols. VI.—VIII.—**Book of the Dead.** Translation. 3 vols.

,, IX.—XVI.—**History of Egypt.** 8 vols.

Vol. XVII.—**The Decrees of Memphis and Canopus—The Rosetta Stone.** Vol. I.

,, XVIII.—**The Decrees of Memphis and Canopus—The Rosetta Stone.** Vol. II.

,, XIX.—**The Decrees of Memphis and Canopus—The Stele of Canopus.**

Vols. XX—XXII.—**The Egyptian Heaven and Hell.** 3 vols.

Vol. XXIII.—**The Book of Kings.** Vol. I. Dynasties I-XIX.

,, XXIV.—**The Book of Kings.** Vol. II. Dynasties XX-XXX.

,, XXV.—**The Liturgy of Funerary Offerings.**

,, XXVI.—**The Book of Opening the Mouth.** Vol I.

,, XXVII.—**The Book of Opening the Mouth.** Vol. II.

Vols. XXVIII.—XXX.—**Book of the Dead.** 3 Vols. Egyptian Hieroglyphic Text

Vol. XXXI.—**Hieroglyphic Vocabulary to the Book of the Dead.**

Full Prospectus on Application.

KEGAN PAUL, TRENCH, TRÜBNER & CO., Ltd.,

Dryden House, Gerrard Street, London, W.

Books on Egypt and Chaldæa.

VOL. XXXI OF THE SERIES.

HIEROGLYPHIC VOCABULARY

WITH AN INDEX
TO ALL THE ENGLISH EQUIVALENTS
OF THE EGYPTIAN WORDS.

Books on Egypt and Chaldæa.

A

HIEROGLYPHIC VOCABULARY

TO THE THEBAN RECENSION OF THE BOOK OF THE DEAD

WITH AN INDEX TO ALL THE ENGLISH EQUIVALENTS OF THE EGYPTIAN WORDS

BY

E. A. WALLIS BUDGE, M.A., LITT. D., D. LITT., D. LIT.

KEEPER OF THE EGYPTIAN AND ASSYRIAN ANTIQUITIES IN THE BRITISH MUSEUM.

VOL. XXXI.

NEW EDITION. REVISED AND ENLARGED.

LONDON

KEGAN PAUL, TRENCH, TRÜBNER & CO. LTD.

DRYDEN HOUSE, 43, GERRARD STREET, W.

1911

PRINTED BY
ADOLF HOLZHAUSEN,
19-21 KANDLGASSE, VIENNA.

PREFACE TO THE SECOND EDITION.

THE following pages contain a Hieroglyphic Vocabulary to all the texts of the Chapters of the Theban Recension of the Book of the Dead which is printed in this Series (Vols. XXVIII—XXX), and also to most of the supplementary Chapters of the Saïte and Graeco-Roman period which are appended thereto. The whole work has been comprehensively revised, and in the case of characters to which the values given in 1897, when the first edition was compiled, are now obsolete, special care has been taken to place them in the order in which they have since been proved to belong. The arrangement of the words and their various forms is usually alphabetical, and it is hoped that the few exceptions to this rule will cause the reader no difficulty. A very considerable number of words and forms have been added to this edition, and it was necessary, for reasons of space, to omit all references.

A new feature of this edition of the Vocabulary is the Index to all the English equivalents of Egyptian words printed herein. This was prepared in answer to the requests of many who had used the first edition of the Vocabulary.

For the care which Mr. Adolf Holzhausen has given to the printing of this work my sincere thanks are due.

E. A. WALLIS BUDGE

BRITISH MUSEUM,
February 4th, 1911.

VOCABULARY.

 A.

aatā, atitā 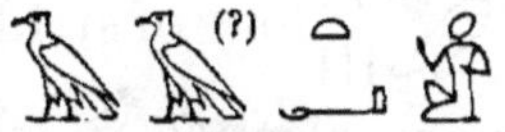 ministrant, celebrant, a kind of priest.

aár  to bind, tie together, to put under restraint, to coerce, to persecute, to oppress.

au  to make a gift or offering, to present.

ait  bread-cakes, loaves of any shape offered for funerary oblations.

aut 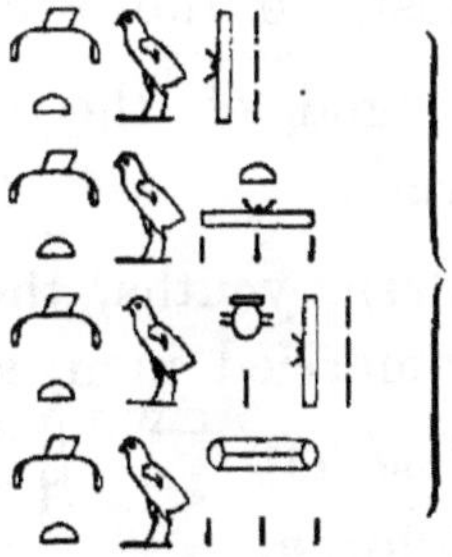 offerings of meat and drink, sacrifices, bread-cakes, etc.

aut  light, radiance.

au  to be long, length, the opposite of  *usekh* breadth, to extend, be extended, *e. g.* extended (*i. e.*, lavish) hand, length of the back, extended of years, long of strides; compare also , .

au — to expand, to dilate (of the heart), hence , joy, gladness, pleasure, delight.

au — fully, exceedingly, to the utmost, to the full extent.

Au-ā — the "god of the extended arm".

au — children, youths, the young, unmarried men, synonym of *sheriu* children.

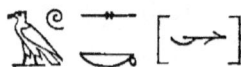

ausek — stick, staff, sceptre, symbol of high position and dignity.

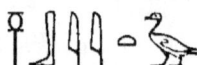

abit — an insect which brought the deceased into the Hall of

Osiris, identified with the praying mantis. A variant gives *bai* .

abu — cessation ceaselessly, unremittingly.

Abu — Elephant-city. The Island of Elephantine and the town and district of Syene. The region of the First Cataract.

abka — to shine.

abtu — maternal and paternal ancestors. Heb. אֲבוֹת.

Abt-ṭesi-ruṭu-neter — a proper name.

apṭu — geese, ducks, water-fowl in general, and finally birds of any and every kind offered for sacrifices.

afiu — fish offered at funerary feasts.

afu — to injure, to harm.

Amm — flame, fire, heat, blaze, to scorch, to burn, to shrivel up. Var. .

Am[m]u — the Fire City of the Other World.

amm  to grasp with the hand, to hold in the fist, to seize, take by violence, snatch at, fist, grasp.

amu 

ames  the name of a sceptre, or staff, associated with Àmsu, or Menu, the god of generation and fertility.

Ani  a scribe and treasurer of holy offerings.

Arthikasathika 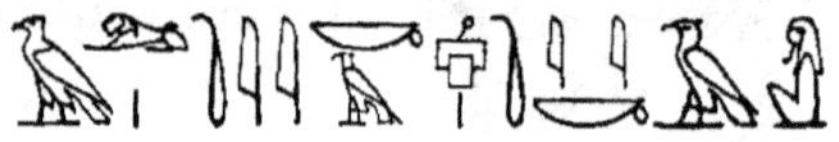 a proper name.

ah  to be troubled, injured, suffering.

aha  evil, injury, harm.

Ahat  an ancient goddess, who was identified with Hathor, and appeared in the form of a cow or a woman.

Ahit  a goddess who supplied the dead with food.

Aḥu	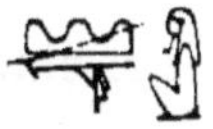	a god who was connected with offerings.
Aḥui		the name of a canal (?).
aḥu	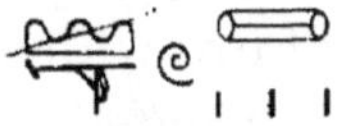	food, bread-cakes, offerings of all kinds.
aḥet	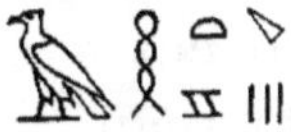	fields, estates, farm, cultivated land.
akh		to bloom, to blossom, flower, bloom.
akhakh		flowers of the sky, *i. e.*, stars.
akhi		reed, water-plant, rushes, marsh flowers.
akhet		the first season of the Egyptian Year.
akhaā		to enter, to penetrate.
akhab		to give to drink.
Akhabiu		a class of divine beings, or gods, who were associated with the Akeru-gods .
akhetu		*i. e.*, , things, objects, food, bread-cakes.
Aseb		the name of a Fire-god in the Other World.

asbiu  sparks of fire, flames, fiery spirits.

Aseb-ḥer-per-em-khetkhet  a god with a face of fire which advanced and retreated alternately.

askh  to cut a crop, to reap.

asta 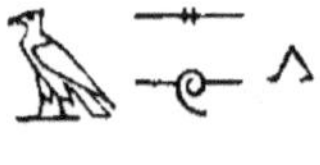 to hasten, to hurry, be swift or rapid.

asta ȧb 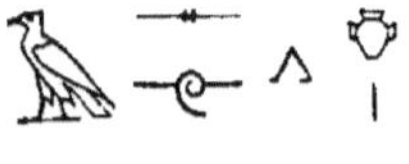 to hurry the heart, to arrive at a hasty judgment.

astu  water in motion, a stream or canal.

Ashu 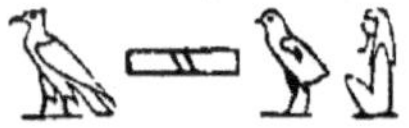 name of a god.

Ashbu  name of the warder of the 5th Ārit.

Asher 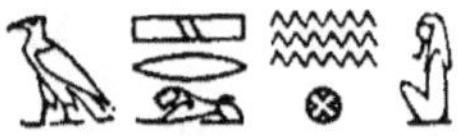 name of a city, or temple district, or god.

ashert 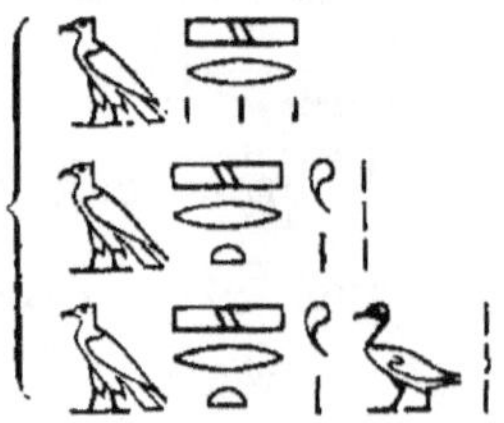 roasted flesh of animals, or birds, grilled meat, steaks, joints, etc.

akit  a chamber, or hut, or small house.

Aker  a very ancient name of the Earth-god.

Akeru  The two gods who guarded the western and eastern ends of the tunnel through the earth which the Sun-god passed through nightly. They were the ancestors of the Akhabiu gods, 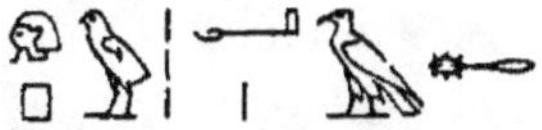 , and also of Rā 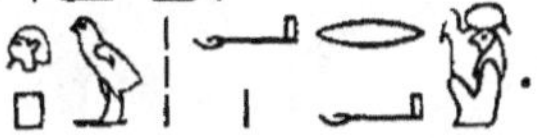.

Akeriu  a group of earth-gods who appeared in the form of serpents.

aqa  *i. e.*,  dirt, filth, what is filthy.

Aqeṭqeṭ  one of a group of seven gods or spirits associated with Osiris.

Aḳab
Aḳb  the great celestial ocean and the god who presided over it, water, flood, celestial Nile.

Aḳbȧ	the great celestial ocean and the god who presided over it, water, flood, celestial Nile.
at ***atu***	injury, assault, attack.
at	a support of a god, a perch for a bird, etc. The word is also written with a wrong determinative.
at	the vertebrae, back, the middle of something.
at	not
at	moment, a period of time, season.
Ati	The ninth nome of Lower Egypt; its capital was Per-Ȧsȧr (Busiris).
atiu	evil beings, fiends, enemies.
atutu	a kind of wood.
atep	a load, a burden, something carried on the head, to carry, to bear, to support.

'atef  name of one of the principal crowns of Osiris.

.atefu 

Atef-ur  a proper name.

aṭ 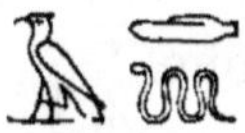 to be wounded, injured.

atȧu  a ceremonial garment with • magical properties.

aṭu  crocodile, or water lizard. Plur. 

Ȧtes ḥer-mer (?)  a proper name.

aṭet  the vertebrae, back. Also written .

 Ȧ.

A  The god Thoth . The form is common in the later period.

ȧ  Personal pronoun. I, me, my.

ȧ  O! Hail!

ȧ  praise, acclamation.

ȧa  boat.

ȧa  standard, perch for a sacred bird.

ȧaa  plants, flowers, growing crops.

ȧaau  he of the two feathers, plumed one.

ȧaat  standard, perch for a sacred bird.

ȧau, **ȧaut**  aged one, old age, old man, senior; plur. .

ȧait 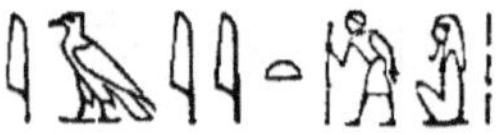 aged gods, divine old men.

ȧau  to praise, to applaud, to ascribe glory to, to acclaim, to rejoice.

ȧaiu 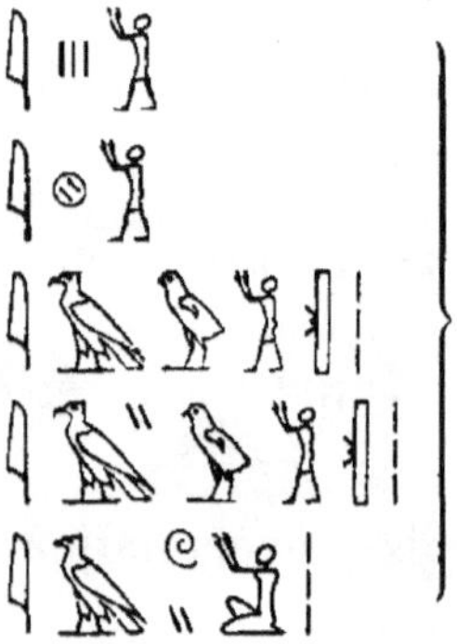 praise, praises, acclamations, rejoicings, glorifyings.

àaiu 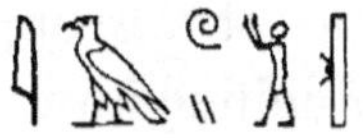

àaut  praise, praises, acclamations, rejoicings, glorifyings.

àait  tombs, or funerary domains under the charge of priests, sepulchres.

àaiti  the gods who preside over the Àats; see Chapter CL.

aamḥet  see 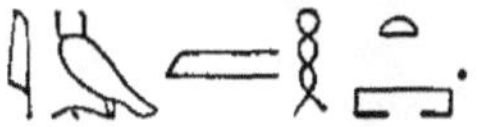.

Àaru   a region in the Other World which formed a portion of the abode of the blessed.

àarret  eyes (?).

àarret  milk.

àaret  vine, vineyard.

Àaheṭ 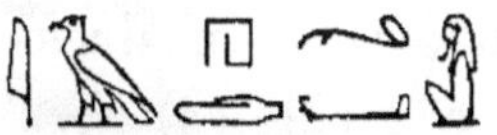  a god whose functions are undefined.

àakhu  light, splendour, radiance, brilliance, rays, the god of light or splendour.

Àakha-bit  the name of a goddess.

Àaku the name of a group of gods or of deified human beings.

àakebi, ***àake-bit*** women who wail and pluck out their hair, professional wailing women or mourners.

àakebu groans, lamentations, mourning, wailings. Another form is .

àaqet flowers, grass, herbs.

Àaqeṭ-qeṭ "He who revolves", name of a god.

àat dignity, rank, grade of honour, position, preferment. Plur. .

àaat things possessing a bad or strong smell.

àat an article of dress, part of a girdle (?).

àat the vertebrae, back.

àat to split, to cleave asunder, to break.

àat standard, perch, pedestal.

Åat ent Vp-uat "Standard of Åp-uat", name of the lower deck of the magical boat.

åat domain of a god, tomb of a god, funerary district; plur. . The kingdom of Osiris contained 14 Åats :—

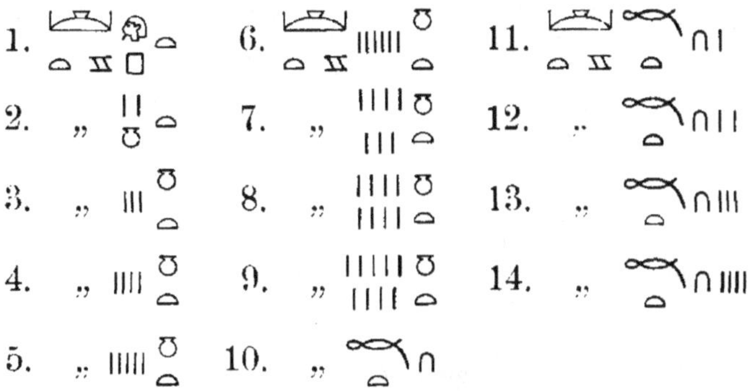

1.   6.   11.

2. „ 7. „ 12. „

3. „ 8. „ 13. „

4. „ 9. „ 14. „

5. „ 10. „

åat Åmentet the funerary domain of the West (Åmentet).

åat khu the Åat of blessed souls.

åat en khet the Åat of fire.

åati The two Åats, *i. e.*, the Åat of Horus and the Åat of Set, or the two Åats of Osiris.

Åat-urt the god of the Great Åat.

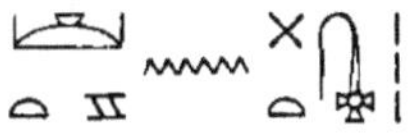

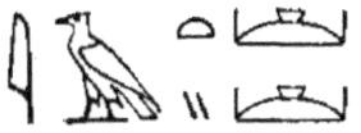

Åat ent Kher-āḥa  The Åat of Kher-āḥa, *i. e.*, the ancient Egyptian city which stood near Old Cairo (Fusṭâṭ).

åatu  praise, praisings, adorations.

åati  slaughter houses, chambers of tortures; places where the enemies of Rā and Osiris were punished.

åatu

åaṭ 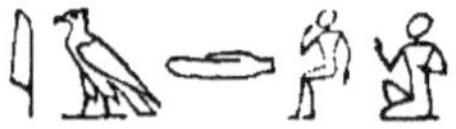 child, male or female, youth.

åaṭeb  flood, storm, rush of water.

åaṭet  net for snaring birds or fish, the net in which the Enemy snared souls.

åaṭet 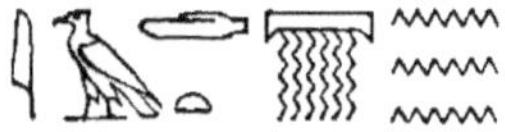 rain-storm, dew, moisture.

åaṭti  oppression, injury, oppressor.

åā 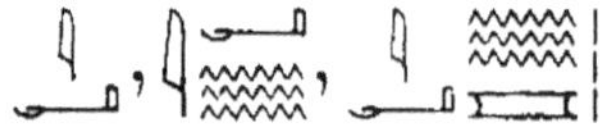 to wash, to cleanse, purify,  to wash the heart, *i. e.*, to cleanse the heart by taking vengeance.

ȧāu a washing, a cleansing.

ȧā a sinful act. to sin against the god.

ȧāāu apes, incarnations of the spirits that praised the rising sun.

ȧāb to come towards, to meet, to present an offering, one opposite, an offering.

ȧāb, **ȧābet** an offering, oblation, ceremonial gift, a vessel of offerings.

ȧāb an offering of a libation.

ȧānu praise, adoration, words of glorification; plur.

ȧār, **ȧārt**, **ȧārtu** serpent, snake, cobra. The Greek form is οὐραῖος, uraeus.

ȧārāt snake goddess; plur.

ȧārti the Two Snake-goddesses, *i. e.*, Isis and Nephthys; the Four Snake-goddesses .

ȧārtu ānkhu the "living uraei" which lived on the cornice of the shrine of Osiris.

ȧāḥ, ȧāḥu , the moon.

ȧāḥu the Moon-god, in later times called Khensu .

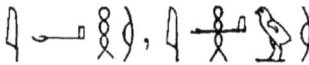

ȧātu ent khert name of a part of the magical boat (Chap. XCIX).

ȧu praises, rejoicings.

ȧu = old man.

ȧu used in later times for *er* from, to, into, for, at, in, etc.

ȧu to be, to exist; I am, thou art, he is, we are, she is; as an auxiliary , etc., and see *passim.*

àu  to be shipwrecked,

 the shipwrecked man.

àu  offence, sin, crime, iniquity, wickedness, defect, breach of the Law.

àui 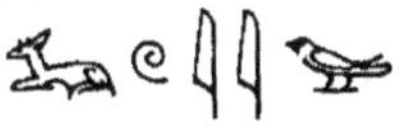

àuit 

àut 

} evil, harm, injury, defects, deceit, to commit wickedness, or sin.

àu  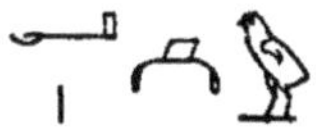 } to speak, cry out, utter words.

àu  to conceive a child, be pregnant.

àua 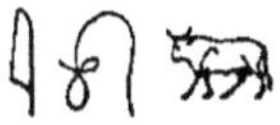  } ox (of the Earth-god Seb).

àuai  roof of a building.

àuàu  dogs, jackals.

Àuu-ba  a proper name.

ȧuāu  the living body.

ȧuā
ȧuāu  flesh and bone, joint of meat, haunch of an animal, carcase.

ȧuā
ȧuāā
ȧuāu 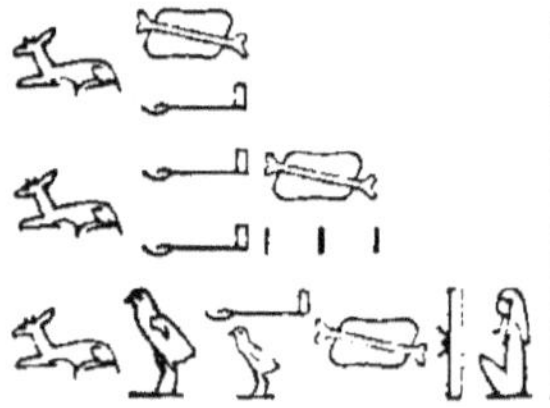 to be flesh and bone of some one, to be the heir, inheritance, the divine Heir.

ȧuāu  heir.

ȧuāt  heirship, inheritance.

ȧuāu  heirs, kinsfolk, people of one's own flesh and blood.

ȧuiu  those who lacerate or cut.

àuur  to conceive, conception, pregnant.

àuurt  a pregnant goddess.

 heir.

àuf  flesh, limbs, members.

Àuf-ānkh  a proper name.

àumes  false or deceitful speech, exaggeration in speech, lies.

àun 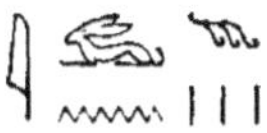 colour, skin, hair.

àuna  certainly, assuredly.

àunt  a garment, clothed, dressed.

Àuràu-àaqer-sa-ànqrebathi   a proper name.

àuhet  to utter words.

åuheṭ name of a god or divine being.

åuḥ to be submerged, sprinkled, steeped in something.

åukhemu a group of gods, stars.

åukhemu urṭu stars which never rest.

åukhemu seku circumpolar stars which never set.

åukhemu Pen-ḥeseb (?) stars of the god Pen-ḥeseb.

åukhekh night, evening, darkness.

åusu scales, balance.

Åuḳer, ***Åuḳert*** the name of the Other World of Heliopolis (Ånnu).

Åuḳeru  the gods of the Heliopolitan Other World.

Åuḳert  the goddess of Åuḳert.

Åuḳert-khentet-åst-s  name of one of the seven sacred cows.

åuṭ   to travel.

åu-t  thou art.

åu-ten 
åu-then  ye are.

åuti   fiends, enemies, foes.

åb  desire, wish.

åb  pegs, stakes.

åb  thirst.

åb  thirsty man.

Ȧb  = Abtu 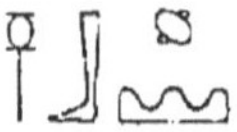 Elephantine.

ȧb  name of a fish.

ȧb 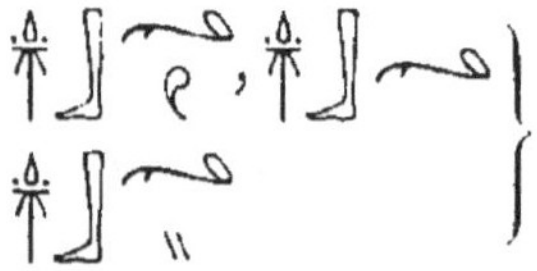 left side.

ȧb  cessation.

ȧb  the physical heart, will, wish, love, desire; plur. 

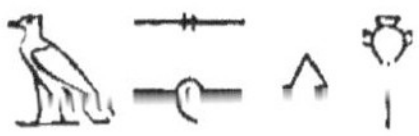 to judge hastily.

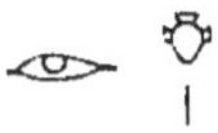 to do as one pleases.

 "great of heart", bold, brave, arrogant, boastful.

 of joyful heart.

 to eat the heart, *i. e.*, to lose the temper, be sorry.

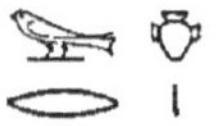 valiant.

 be brave.

 to fill the heart, to satisfy, be satisfied.

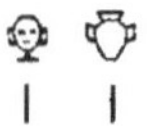 within.

	[hieroglyphs] with [hieroglyphs]	heart's desire.
	[hieroglyphs] with [hieroglyphs]	prompting of the heart, desire.
	[hieroglyphs]	the amulet of the carnelian heart.
àba	[hieroglyphs]	heart-soul.
àbu	[hieroglyphs]	drink.
àbu	[hieroglyphs]	the desired one.
Àbu-ur	[hieroglyphs]	a proper name.
àbu	[hieroglyphs], or [hieroglyphs]	to stop, to cease.
	[hieroglyphs]	cessation.
10 **àbui**	[hieroglyphs]	left side.
àbi	[hieroglyphs]	panther or leopard skin.
àbit	[hieroglyphs]	the praying mantis.
àber	[hieroglyphs]	a kind of unguent.
àbḥu	[hieroglyphs]	tooth. Plur. [hieroglyphs] [hieroglyphs]

ȧbekh — to penetrate, to make a way through.

ȧbsit — hull of a boat.

Ȧb-ka, **Abt-ka** — a proper name.

ȧbku — grief, to grieve, to weep.

ȧbt — middle hall, or chamber, of a house.

ȧbt — coffer.

ȧbt — thirst.

ȧbt — left hand side, the east.

ȧbt, **ȧbti** — east wind.

ȧbt, **ȧbti** — eastern country, or region. eastern sky, east of heaven;

àbti 

àbtet (**àbti**) 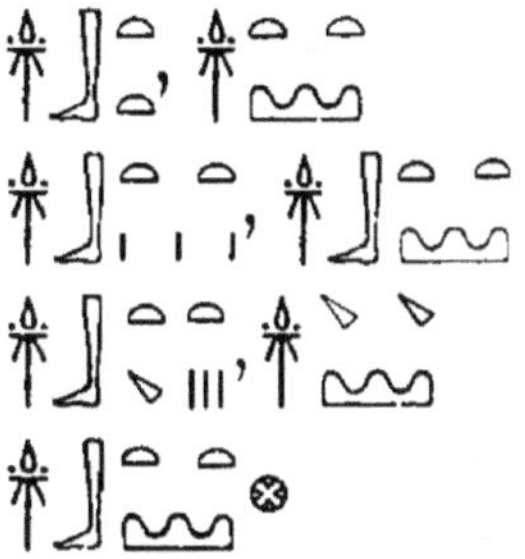 east, eastern country, or region.

àbtet 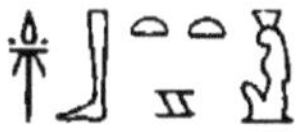 goddess of the east.

àbtiu  gods of the east, eastern deities.

àbt 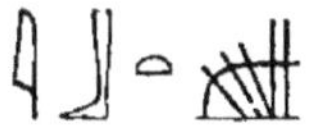 net.

àbtu  slaughter, slaughterings.

Àbṭ 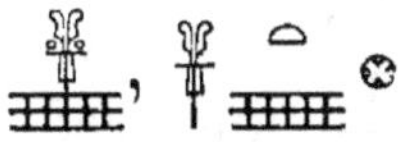 the nome of Abydos.

Àbt 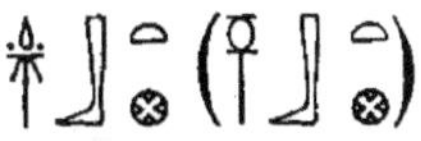 the city of Abydos.

Àbṭu  the city of Abydos.

Ȧbṭu 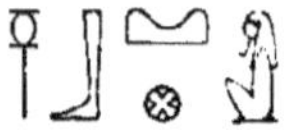 the city god of Abydos.

ȧbeṭ 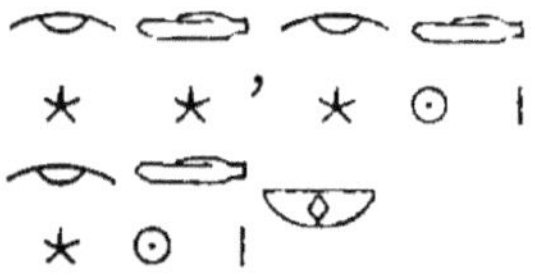 the month of thirty days, plur. 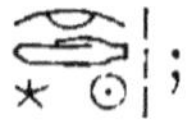; the monthly festival, plur. .

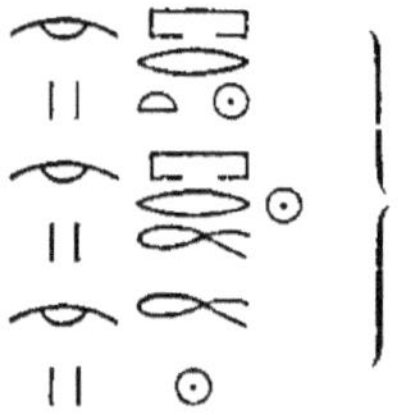 the second month of the season Pert, the last day of the second month of this season.

ȧbṭ 

ȧbṭu  a mythological fish which swam before the Boat of Rā; its companion was the *ȧnt* fish.

ȧp 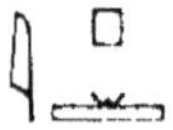 to count up, to reckon, to consider, a reckoning, a counting,  reckoner of years,  counter, 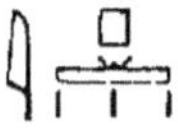 numbered, counted.

ȧppet  reckoning, account.

ȧp  to judge, to be judged, to decree, be decreed, judgment.  great judgment.

ȧp — judge of dooms.

judged. judge.

ȧp, **ȧpu** — to judge, to dispute or argue with someone, to award, be awarded, to bring a message, to announce tidings. a judge of words or affairs, *ȧp maāt* righteous judge.

ȧpt — decree, judgment, sentence of doom.

ȧput mitu — sentence of death.

ȧp, **ȧpu** **ȧpi** **ȧpt** — to open. open! , opened.

ȧp re **ȧpu re** **ȧpt re** — the ceremony of "opening the mouth".

Ȧp-uat
Ȧp-uati
Ȧp-uatu  "Opener of the roads", a name of a wolf-god who was supposed to conduct the deceased over the roads which lead to the Sekhet Ȧaru, or Elysian Fields. Ȧp-uat was a companion of the jackal-god Ȧnpu, with whom he is sometimes confounded.

Ȧp-uat meḥt sekhem pet  The god Ȧp-uat of the north as guide to the roads of heaven.

Ȧp-uat resu sekhem taui 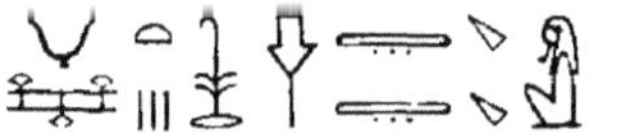 The god Ȧp-uat of the south as guide to the roads of earth.

Ȧp-ur  "great opener", name of a god.

ȧp ḥer  except. 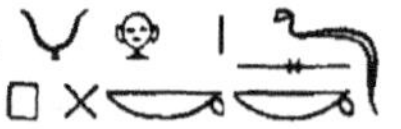 except thyself.

Ȧpu  A city, the Panopolis of the Greeks, the Akhmîm of the Arabs.

ȧpu
ȧpiu  these,  these gods, 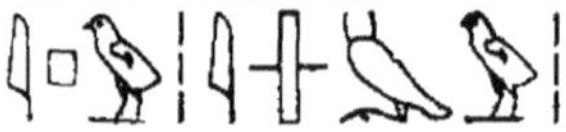 these who dwell in.

àpiu  openers, those who make a way.

àputi  messenger, envoy, ambassador; plur. .

 two envoys.

àppiu 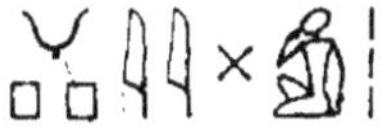 judges.

àpen  (see ) these.   these gods who dwell in.

Àpsi  a name or title of a god.

àpt 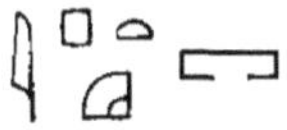 sacred chamber of a temple, private apartments of a house, sacred or profane *ḥarîm.*

àpt 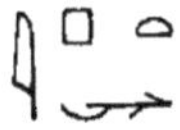 stick, staff, sceptre.

àpt àst  name of a portion of Eastern Thebes, Karnak (?).

àpt  message, envoy.

àpt  messengers.

ȧpt  brow, forehead, top of the head (?).

 the hottest part of the fire.

 top, surface (?) of the waters.

 brow of the god Qaḥu.

ȧptu 
ȧpten  } these.

Ȧp-shāṭ-taui 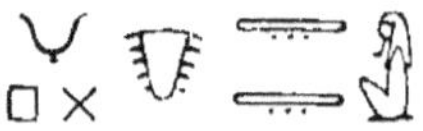 a name of Osiris.

ȧf, afu  flesh, limbs, members.

ȧfṭ 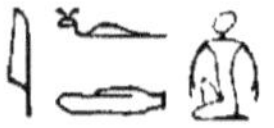 to rest, to sit down.

ȧfṭu 
ȧfṭet 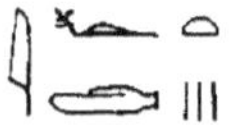 } four.

ȧfṭi  a kind of cloth or garment.

ȧm  in, into, inside.

ȧm (?) 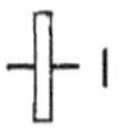 a standard.

ȧm  a boat.

ȧm  to arrive in safety.

ȧm	flax, a kind of cloth.
ȧm	not, do not.
ȧm **ȧmu**	to eat, to consume, swallow up, devour.
ȧmi	eating, eater; plur.
ȧmti	eater.
ȧm baiu	eater of heart-souls.
ȧm besku	"Eater of Livers", or intestines.
ȧm sāḥu	"Eater of mummies".
ȧm snef	"Eater of Blood"; one of the Forty-two Judges in the Hall of Osiris.
ȧm (un)	to eat, to consume.
ȧm	bread-cakes, food.
?	drink.

Ȧm-ḥauat-ent-pehui-f  "Eater of the offal of his body"; the name of the doorkeeper of the Third Ārit.

ȧmt, **ȧmtu** 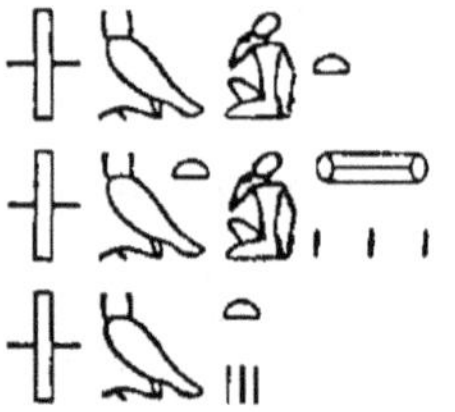 food, something fit or used for food.

ȧm, **ȧmt** 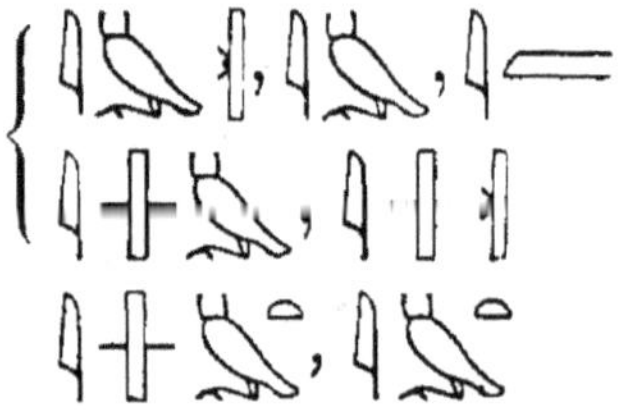 in, among, with, through, upon, by, around, there, therein.  in it (or him),  in it (or her), 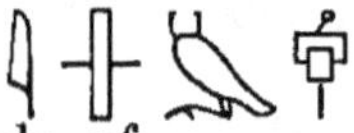 by the back of.

ȧm, ȧmt 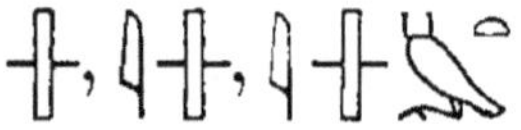 dweller in.

ȧmi 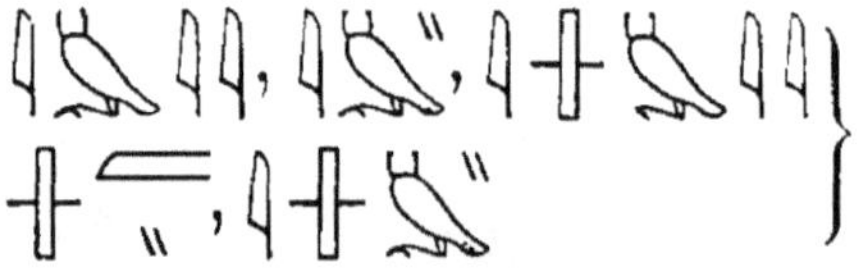 he who is in, dweller in; plur. , 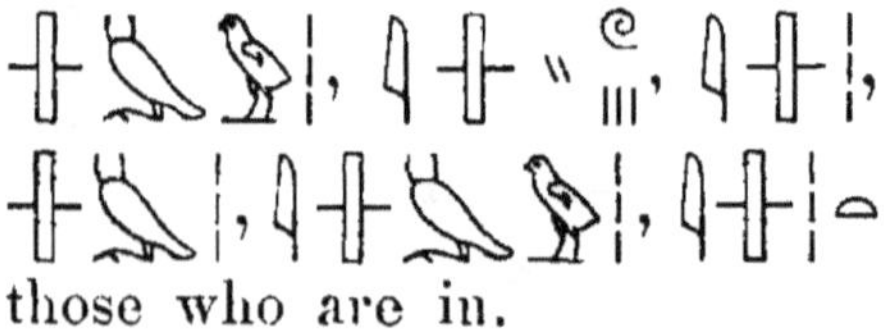 those who are in.

ȧm-ā — a title of a priest or ministrant.

ȧm ȧst-ā

ȧm-~~uḥet~~ (?) neb ta Tchesert — "he who is in the embalmment chamber, Lord of Ta-tchesert", a title of Anubis, the divine physician and embalmer.

ȧmi-at — one in, or at, the supreme moment.

ȧmi ȧb — he who is in the heart.

ȧm-ȧten-f — he who is in his disk, *i. e.*, Rā.

ȧmi-uȧa-f — he who is in his Boat, *i. e.*, Rā.

ȧmi mu — he who is in the water, *i. e.*, Sebek.

ȧmi unnut-f — he who is in his hour.

Ȧmi-meḥen-f, **ȧmi-meḥent-f** — he who is in his Meḥen serpent, *i. e.*, Rā, or Ȧf; plur.

àmi-ha-f  he who is in his time, or place.

àmi-hem-f  he who is in his fiery serpent, *i. e.*, Rā.

àmi-khet  he who is in his fiery disk.

àm-khet
àmi-khet  he who is in the following of.

àmi-suḥt
àm-suḥt  he who is in his egg, *i. e.*, Rā.

àmi-mer-nesert (?) 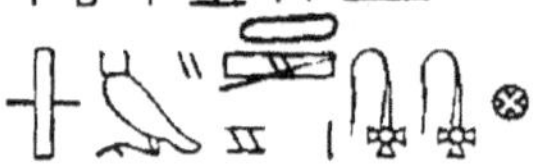 he who is in his fiery Lake, *i. e.*, Rā.

àmi-karà-f  he who is in his shrine, *i. e.*, Rā or Osiris.

àmi-ṭebtu  he who is in his coffin, *i. e.*, Osiris.

àmi-tchetta  he who dwelleth in eternity.

àmiu-àat-sen  the gods in their domains.

àmiu Àbṭu  those in Abydos.

ȧmiu-Ȧnu  the gods in Ȧnu (Heliopolis).

ȧmiu-ȧḥ-ur 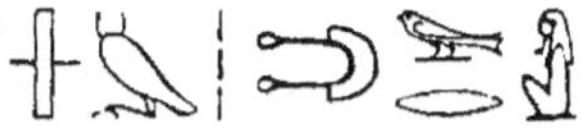 those in the Great Field.

ȧmiu-āāui  those in the hands.

ȧmiu-bah  the gods who are in the presence.

ȧmiu-beḳa  those who are in a weak state.

ȧmiu em-baḥ  the gods who are in the presence.

ȧmiu-hru-sen  those who are in their days.

ȧmiu-Nekhen  those who dwell in Nekhen.

ȧmiu Kher-neter  those who are in the Other World.

ȧmiu Neṭet  those who dwell in the city of Neṭet.

ȧmiu khet, **ȧmiu khet-**  those who are in the following of.

ȧmiu khuti  those who are in the two horizons.

ȧmiu sāḥu — those who are in their mummied forms.

ȧmiu-sut-sen — those who are in their hair.

ȧmiu seḥu-sen — those who are in their halls.

ȧmiu-shems, ***ȧmiu-shemsu*** — those who are in the following of.

ȧmiu-karȧ-sen — those who are in their shrines.

ȧmiu-ta — those who are in the earth.

ȧmtu, ***ȧmth***, ***ȧmith***, ***ȧmithu*** — among, between; Chap. CIV. 1, CIV. 1.

ȧmt — in

ȧm ȧb — what is in the heart, thought? prayer?

ȧm khent — title of a priest.

ȧma  tree.

ȧmam  date-palm.

ȧmakh 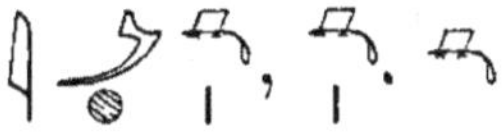 serf, servant, one who venerates another, or is venerated, a beatified being, 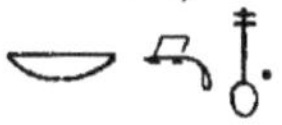.

ȧmakhi  partic. masc.  partic. fem.; plur. , 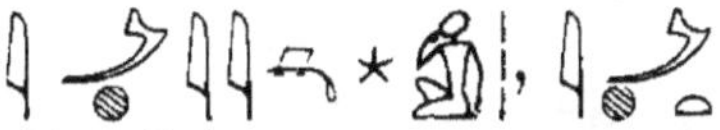 . A late form is .

ȧmu  divine beings.

ȧmu  trees, plants.

ȧmu  flames, fire.

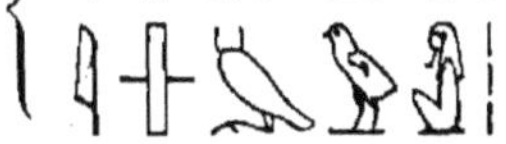 gods of fire.

ȧmu  colour, pigment.

Ȧm-urt  a proper name.

ȧmi shrine, chamber.

ȧmuhettu, ***ȧmihettut*** apes, incarnations of the spirits of the dawn.

ȧmuti image, figure.

ȧmem palm-tree.

ȧmem to putrefy.

ȧmem skin, hide.

ȧmmā grant, give, let there be, prithee, give I pray, open I pray, give water and air, give thy hand, let me pass, give (*i. e.*, incline) thy face.

ȧmmu beams, rays of light, splendour.

ȧmmu  boats.

ȧmmeḥet  a portion of the Other World of Seker.

ȧmm ḳeḥu  those who are in a state of weakness.

Ȧmen 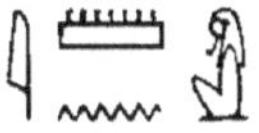 a god of generation and conception, who symbolized the invisible creative forces of Nature.

 "Ȧmen which art in heaven".

 "Ȧmen the prolific Bull".

Ȧmen-nathk-ruthi-Ȧmen 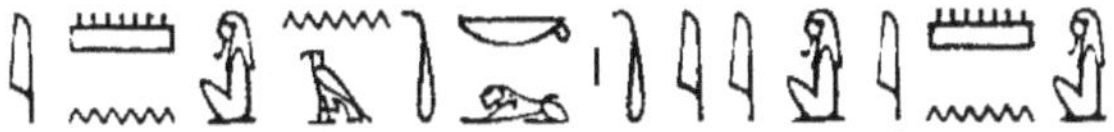 A Sûdânî form of Ȧmen.

Ȧmen-nau-ȧn-ka-entek-Sharu  A Sûdânî form of Ȧmen.

Ȧmen-Rā 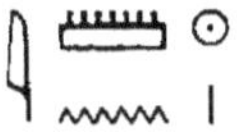 the great god of Thebes, chief element in the triad Ȧmen-Rā, Mut and Khensu.

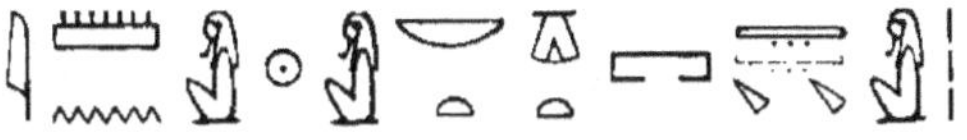 "Ȧmen - Rā, Lord of the throne of the Two Lands".

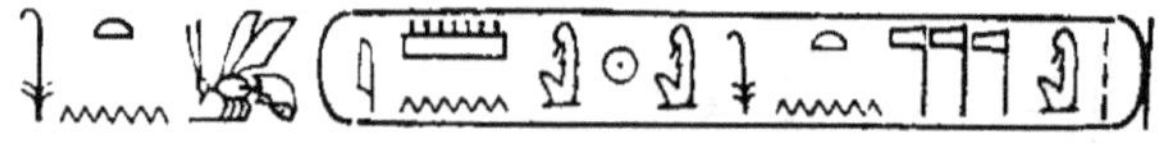 "King of the South and North, Ȧmen-Rā, king of the gods".

Ȧmen-Rā Ḥeru-khuti  Ȧmen-Rā Harmachis.

Ȧmen-ruti  Ȧmen and the two lion-gods Shu and Tefnut.

ȧmen 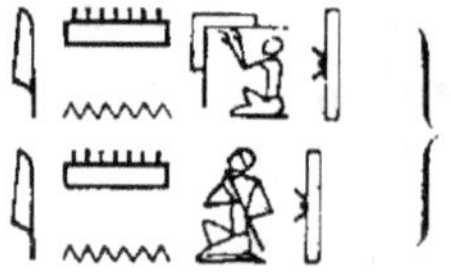 to hide, be hidden, hidden one, something hidden. 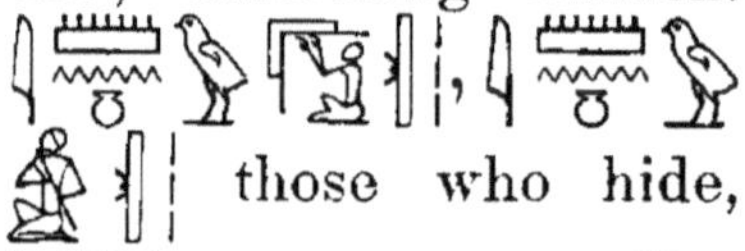 those who hide, 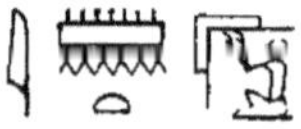 hider,   secrecy, in secret,  the hidden gods.

ȧmenu-ā  those whose arms are hidden.

 he whose name is hidden.

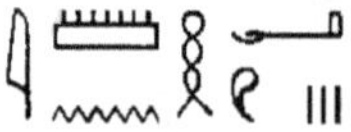 those whose bodies are hidden.

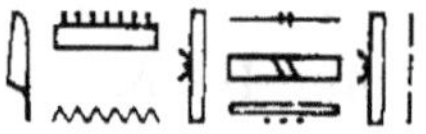 those whose mysteries are hidden.

ȧmenḥiu 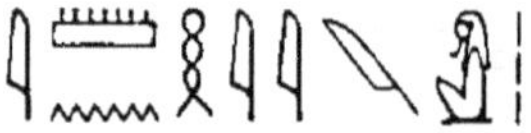 the divine butchers, or gods of slaughter.

Ȧmen-ḥetep 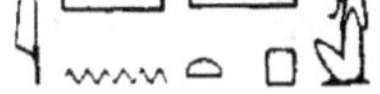 a proper name.

Ȧment, **Amenti**, **Ȧmentet**  the "hidden" place, or land, the West, the abode of departed spirits, the name of the first division of the Other World. A late form of the name is .

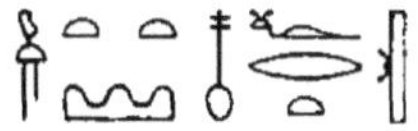 the "beautiful Ȧmentet".

Ament 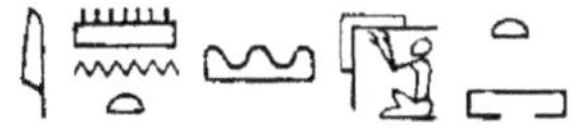 hidden place; plur. .

ȧmentiu  divine beings who live in Ȧmenti, or the West;  Ȧmenti deified, 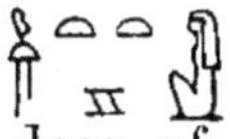 the goddess of the West, or Ȧmenti.

ȧmenti  the west wind.

àmsi 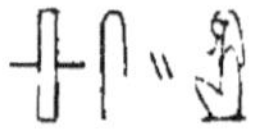 a god of generation, fertility, fecundity, etc. Probably a form of Menu .

Àmseth 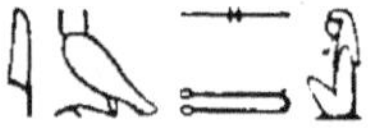 one of the four sons of Horus. The reading appears to be a mistake made by the Egyptians in reading 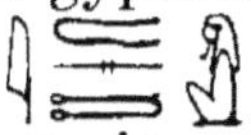 *Àmseth* instead of *Àḳesth*. See Ḳesthà.

àmt 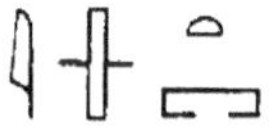 chamber, house, abode.

àmt  possessions, goods of a house.

àmt  the title-deeds of a house or property.

àmt  tree (?), or tent, camp.

àmt  light, radiance, splendour.

àmt 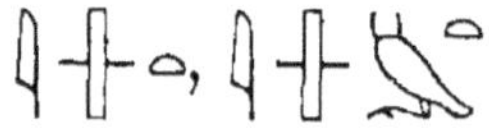 that which is in. 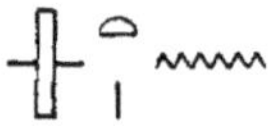  what is in the waters. 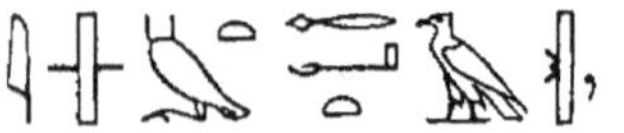, etc.

Àmt-ṭehen-f  a proper name.

àmtiu  . . . .

ȧn — a mark of emphasis or interrogation, used sometimes as a preposition, behold! lo! cf.

ȧn ḳert — lo moreover.

ȧn (*n*) — no, not, mark of the negative. most certainly there cannot be done. I am not.

ȧn ȧs — except, unless.

ȧn ȧbu — ceaselessly.

ȧn urṭ — unresting.

ȧn petrȧ — unobserved.

ȧn maa }
ȧn maa-n-tu } unseen, invisible.

ȧn maa-n-tu  ***ȧn maatu***  unseen, invisible.

ȧn mu 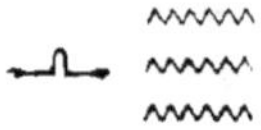 waterless.

ȧn meḥ 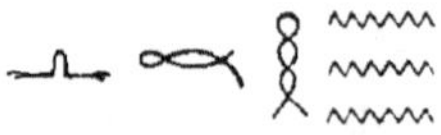 ***ȧn meḥ-f***  undipped (?), unwashed (?). Also 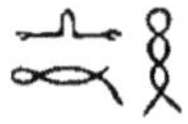 .

ȧn nifu  airless.

ȧn netchnetchet 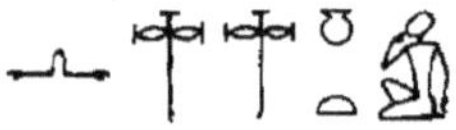 not to be discussed or gainsaid.

ȧn rekh 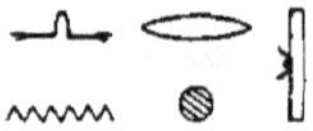 ***ȧn rekhtu***  unknown.

ȧn kheper  never was.

ȧn sep 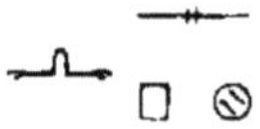 at no time.

ȧn smȧ 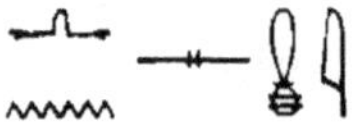 untold.

ȧn sek  indestructible,

ȧn seṭ 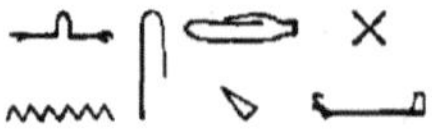 unsplit.

ȧn shenārtu  unturnable.

Ȧn ȧruṭ-f | **Ȧn ȧarruṭ-f** — the place where nothing grows.

Ȧn-erṭā-nef-bes-f-khenti-heh-f — name of one of the Seven Spirits with Osiris.

Ȧn-ḥeri-ertisa — name of a god.

ȧn | **ȧnu** — to bring, to bear, to carry. to bring, bringing, brought, those who bring; something brought.

ȧnu — what is brought in, gifts, increase.

ȧntu — offerings; peace-offerings.

Ȧniu — name of a god.

Ȧn — name of a god.

Ȧn- { ***ṭes*** / ***ṭemt*** } a proper name.

ȧnit a dwelling, chamber, house.

ȧnuk I.

Ȧnu On, Heliopolis.

ȧnnu skin.

ȧnnuit skin, hair, plumage.

Ȧn-ȧtef-f "Bringer of his father", a proper name.

Ȧn ā-f "Bringer of his arm"; the name of one of the Forty-two Judges in the Hall of Osiris.

Ȧn-urt-emkhet-uas name of the mast in the magical boat (Chap. XCIX).

ȧnb to dance, to rejoice.

ȧneb wall; plur.

åneb 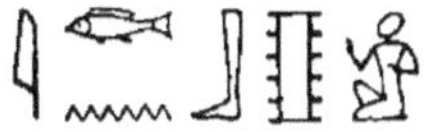 mason.

ånep  region, estate, ground.

Ånp
Ånpu  The god Anubis, son of Set and Nephthys, a jackal-god who embalmed the dead, and guided the souls of the blessed to the Other World. Titles: , .

Ån-mut-f  "The pillar of his mother", title of a ministrant or priest.

ånem 

 skin, hide.

ånemsit  a kind of garment.

ånenit 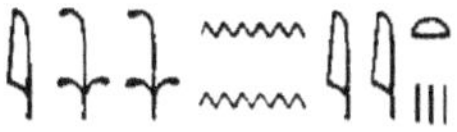 a proper name?

Ån-ruṭ-f  the god of the place where nothing grows.

Ånreruṭ-f  the place where nothing grows.

åner 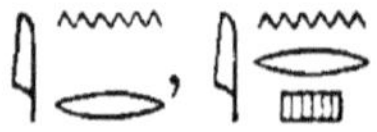 stone.

 "Stone of Maāt", a proper name.

åner 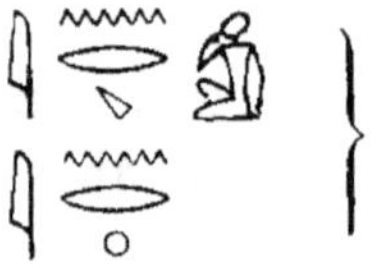 a proper name.

ånhetet 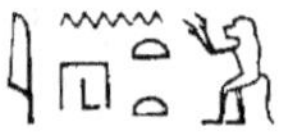 ape.

ånḥui 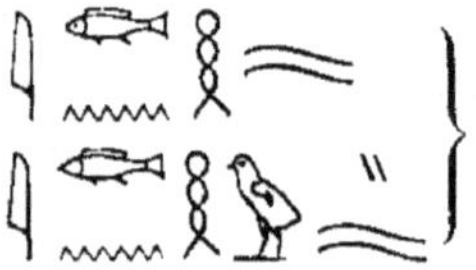 the two eye-brows.

ånḥu-tu  surrounded.

Ån-ḥer  "Bearer of the sky"; an ancient god of Upper Egypt who is often associated with .

Ån-ḥer  name of the warder of the Sixth Ārit.

Ån-ḥetep  one of the Forty-two gods in the Hall of Osiris.

ånes
ånsi 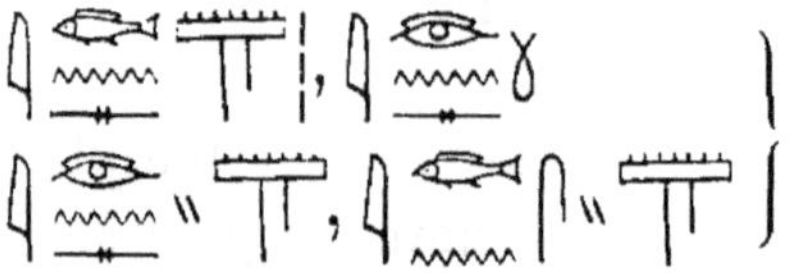 name of a ceremonial garment.

ånset 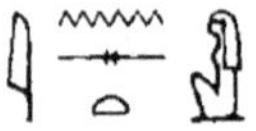 a goddess (?).

àneq — to bind, tie on, to fasten.

ànqet — to embrace, to surround.

ànqet — name of a tool, or instrument, "clincher", rope (?).

ànt — name of a mythological fish which swam before the boat of Rā.

ànt — name of a solar boat.

ànt, ***àntet***, ***ànti*** — a valley, especially a funerary valley.

ànti — pillars, columns.

Ànti — the hill-folk who lived in the Eastern Desert of Ta-sti, or Nubia.

ànti — a hindrance, obstruction.

àntiu — those who have nothing, the destitute, those who are not, or do not exist.

àntet — to go back.

ȧntet  cord, fetter, chain.

Ȧn-ṭebu  the name of a god.

ȧnetch  to incline, to bow.

ȧnetch ḥer  to incline the head to a suppliant, to turn the face towards.

ȧr  to tie together.

ȧr  if, now.

ȧr sa 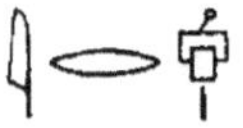 if after, now as for.

ȧr ḳert 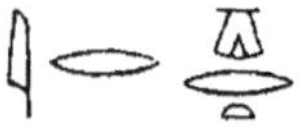 if moreover, however.

ȧr, **ȧru**, **ȧrit** 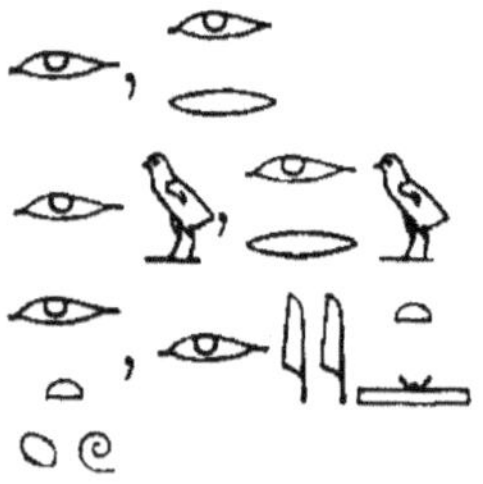 to do, to make, to create, to form, to fashion; ,  doing, making, creator;  made, wrought,  made;  make ye;  things done.

àrit 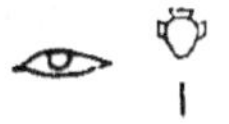 to work the heart, to think.

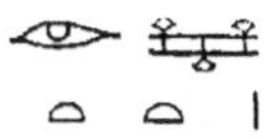 to make or prepare a path or road.

 to prepare food.

 to celebrate the Haker festival.

 to keep festivals.

 to make protection, to perform ceremonies for the protection of some one.

 to work for successful results, to strive for peace.

 to perform a transformation.

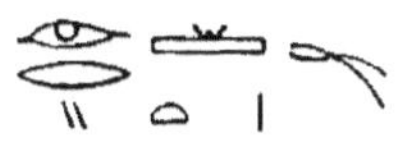 to make, or write, or recite, a book.

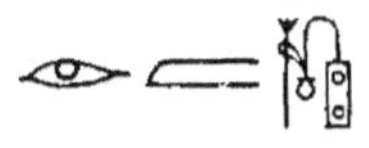 to do into writing, to make a copy, to write.

àriu 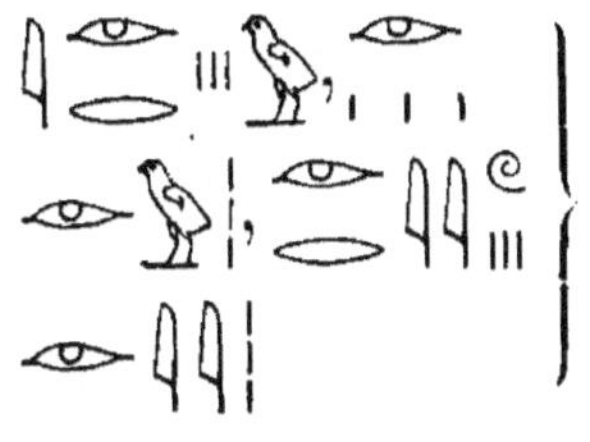 doers, makers, workers.

àriu  workmen; fem. 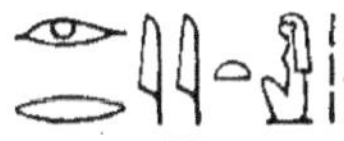.

àrit — work, something done.

— actions, deeds, labours, works, things done or to be done.

àr, àri — used as an auxiliary verb, see *passim*.

àri-Maāt — "Maker of truth, or righteousness", a title of Osiris, Hathor, and other gods.

Àri-em-àb-f, **Àri-en-àb-f** — the name of one of the Forty-two Judges in the Hall of Osiris.

Àri-nef-tchesef — name of a plank or peg in the magical boat.

Àri-entuten-em-meska-en-Mer-ur uṭebtu-en-Suti — name of the leather bands in the magical boat.

Àri-ḥetch-f — a proper name.

Àrisi — a proper name.

àru — form, attribute, figure, image; plur.

àri 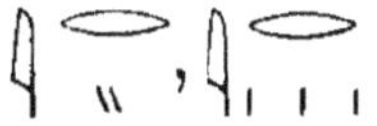 belonging to:  their name; 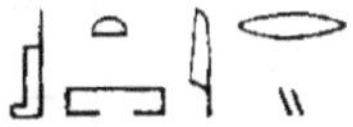 their seat;  their bull (var. 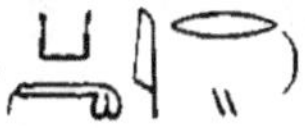);  their length.

àri   a person in charge of, or belonging to, or attendant upon something, watcher, porter, guardian.

 guardian of my flesh.

 guardian, or guardians, of the sky.

 keeping watch about, or around.

 keepers of my mouth.

 watching the limbs.

 keeping guard over the neck.

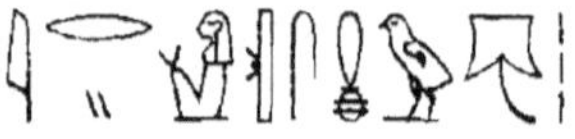 belonging to the leathers.

 guarding the earth.

ȧri āa  porter, doorkeeper, guardian ; plur. 

 porter of the door of Ȧmentet.

ȧriu ārrtu 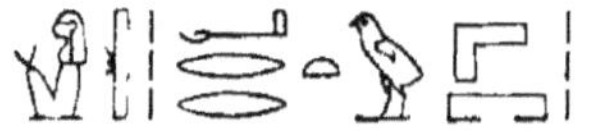 warders of the Ārits.

ȧri mākhait  warder of the Scales.

ȧri ḥemit  warder of the oar, *i. e.*, steersman.

ȧri ḥenbiu  warder of the cultivated lands.

ȧru khut  guardians of light, *i. e.*, beings of light.

ȧri sȧpu 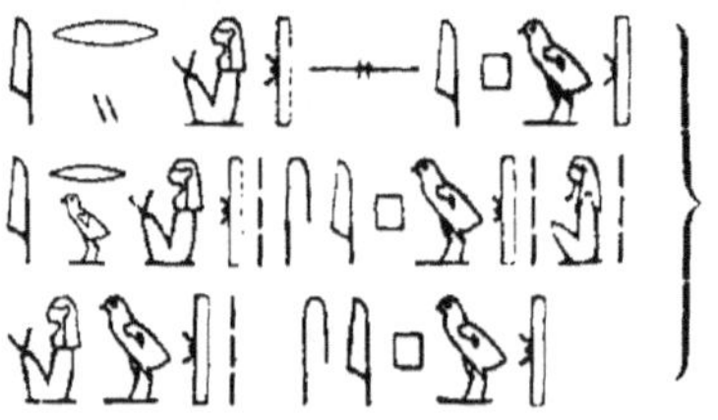 keepers of the records, or books of doom.

ȧri sebkhet-f 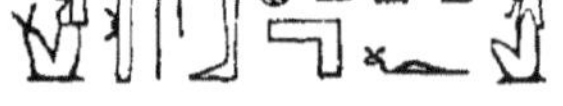 keeper of his pylon.

ȧri qeb en meru en khet 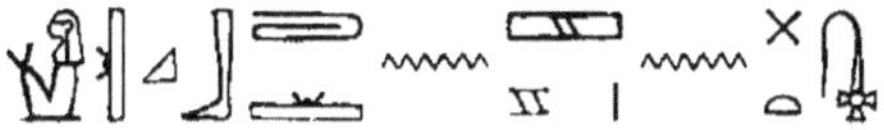 keeper of the Bend of the Lake of Fire.

ȧrārti 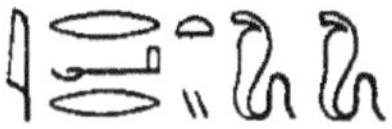 two uraei.

Ȧruhut  a proper name.

ȧrp  wine.

ȧrpu  ... Chap. CLXIX. 1.

ȧref  an emphatic particle.

ȧrmā  with.

ȧrek  a particle.

ȧrt 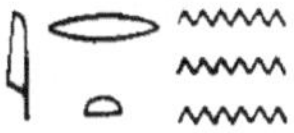 to flow, what flows.

ȧrt  Chapter LB. 1.

ȧrtet 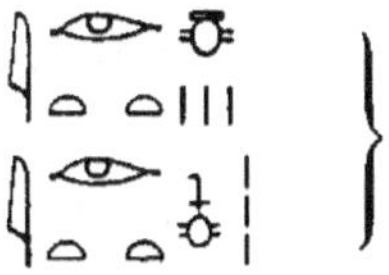 milk.

ȧh  calamity.

ȧhabu  joy, gladness, cries of joy.

ȧhen 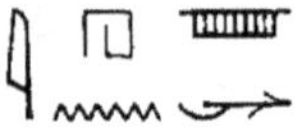 a kind of wood.

ȧhehi  rejoicings, cries of joy.

Ȧḥ  the Moon-god,

ȧḥ  ... Book of Breathings II. 22.

ȧḥ  collar, embrace, to ward off.

ȧḥ, ȧḥu  ox; plur.  oxen, .

ȧḥai  a sistrum bearer.

ȧḥāu 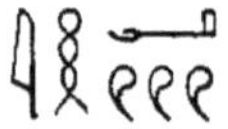 members.

ȧḥi 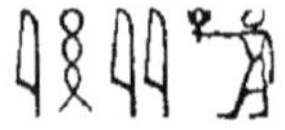

ȧḥu  the name of one of the Forty-two Judges in the Hall of Osiris; a proper name; 

ȧḥu  fields (?), measuring cords.

ȧḥu  wooden tools or instruments.

ȧḥui  the two *ȧḥui* gods = 
.

Ȧḥibit name of a god.

ȧḥunnu youth, child.

ȧḥemu (?) ... Chap. XCII. 13.

ȧḥti throat.

Aḥti a name of Osiris.

Ȧkh O!, would that, O tell me.

ȧkhabu grain.

ȧkhib to speak.

ȧkhemu urṭu a class of stars.

ȧkhekhu, **ȧkhekhui** darkness, night.

Ȧkhsesef a proper name.

Ȧs a proper name.

ȧs — behold, to wit, namely,

ȧsu — intestines.

ȧsu — winds.

ȧsu (?) — ... Chap. CXXVII B. 17.

ȧsi, ȧsu — tomb, sepulchre.

ȧsu — recompense or in return for, in place of.

ȧs — to pass forward, to advance.

ȧsu, **ȧsi** — to decay, to rot, destruction. decay,   incorruptible.

Àsàr 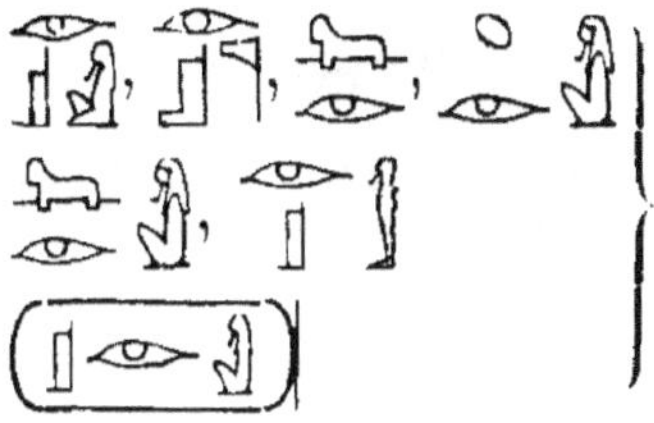 the god Osiris, son of Seb and Nut, husband of Isis, and father of Horus. The deceased is usually identified with Osiris and is called by his name.

Àsàr Ànpu 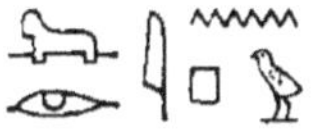 Osiris-Anubis.

Àsàr ānkhti  Osiris the Living One.

Àsàr Unnefer  Osiris Un-Nefer.

Àsàr Utetti  Osiris the begetter.

Àsàr-ba-erpi 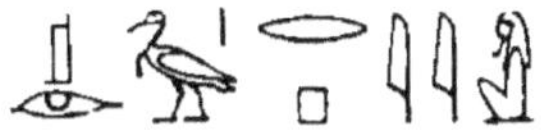 Osiris, soul of the divine Image.

Àsàr-bati-erpit  Osiris, twin soul of the divine image.

Àsàr Ptaḥ neb ānkh  Osiris-Ptaḥ, Lord of Life.

Àsàr-em-pesuru  Osiris in Pesuru.

Àsàr em pesṭ ent nut-f 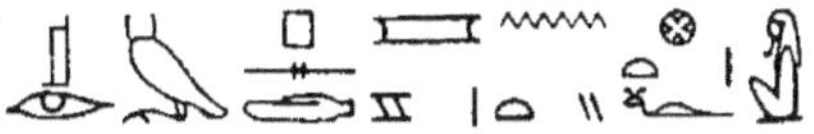

Àsàr em Seḥnen 

Àsàr em Ṭenit

Àsàr nub ḥeḥ Osiris, gold of eternity.

Àsàr neb ānkh Osiris, Lord of Life.

Àsàr neb er tcher Osiris, Lord to the boundary, *i. e.*, of All.

Asàr Netchesti Osiris the Less.

Àsàr Ḥenti Osiris of the two crocodiles.

Àsàr Ḥoru Osiris-Horus.

Asàr Ḥeru-khuti Tem Osiris-Harmachis.

Àsàr ḥer àb semt Osiris in the funerary mountain.

Àsàr ḥer shāu-f Osiris on his sand.

Àsàr khent Àbṭu Osiris, President of Abydos.

Àsàr khenti Àmenti Osiris, President of Amenti, or the Other World.

Åsår khenti Åmentiu		Osiris, President of those who dwell in the Other World.
Åsår khent Un		
Åsår khenti	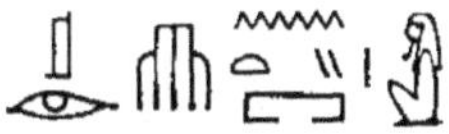	
Åsår khenti Nefer (?)		
Åsår khenti nut-f	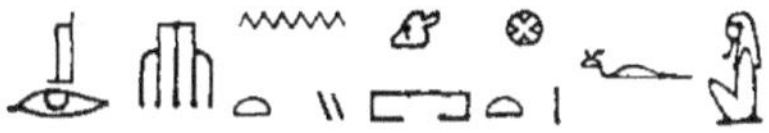	
Åsår khenti nestu	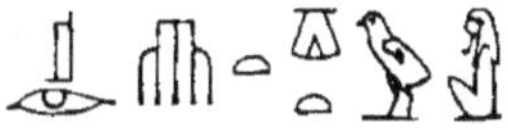	
Åsår khenti Ru-stau		
Åsår khenti seḥ ḥemt	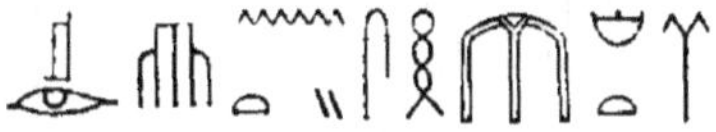	
Åsår sa Nut		
Åsår saa	 	
Åsår Sab (or ***Ḳeb***?)		
Åsår Saḥ		

Åsår Sekri 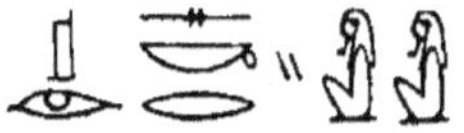

Åsår Taiti 

Åsår tua 

Åsår Ṭem ur 

Åsår Teḳaiti 

Åsårtiu  beings like unto Osiris.

åsi  who?, what?

åsp  grief (?), misery, wretchedness.

åsfet 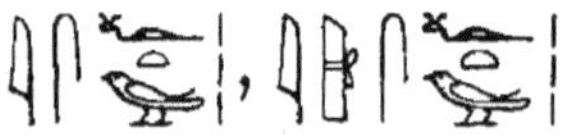
åsfeti  faults, sins, evil deeds, sinners, evil ones.

åsfetiu  evil fiends, sinners.

åsentu 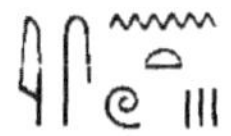 cords, ropes.

åser  tamarisk (?),  plants, herbs, grass.

Åsert  name of a city.

åsha  linen, some kind of woven stuff.

Åses / **Åsest** 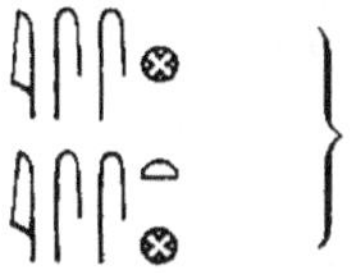 a city in the seventh Åat.

åses  to rope in, to bind.

åsstu  a rope.  those whose heads are tied.

åsk  behold, lo!

åst, åstu / **åsth**  behold.

Åst 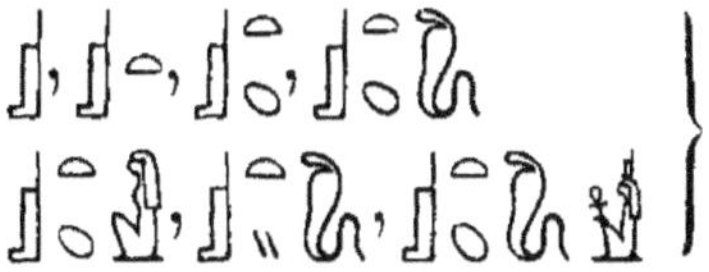 the goddess Isis.

åst 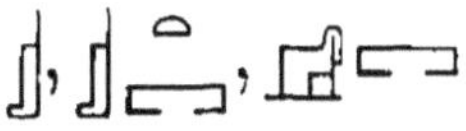 seat, place, habitation, abode, shrine; plur. 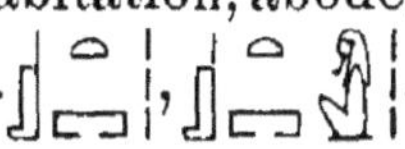.

åst åb 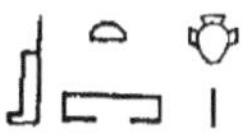 place of the heart, heart's chosen place.

åst āāui  place of the two hands.

àst urt  great place, *i. e.*, the sky.

àst utchat 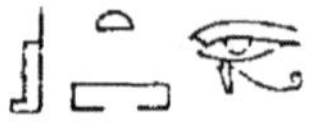 seat of the Utchat, resting place of the Eye of Rā.

àst maāt  the place where the Law is administered.

àst ḥert  heaven.

àst ḥeḥ 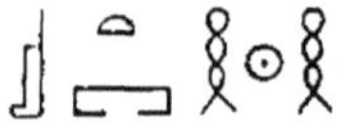 everlasting abode.

àst Ḥeqet  shrine of Ḥeqet.

àst ḥetep 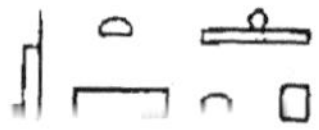 place of repose.

àst ḥetep àb 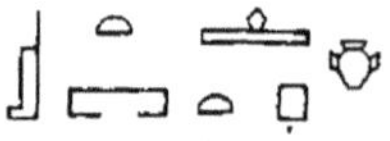 seat of rest of the heart.

àst shetau en Ḥeru 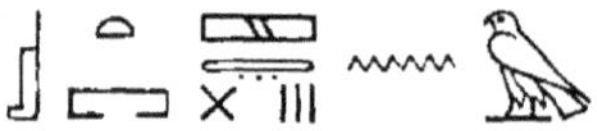 the secret abodes of Horus.

àst qebḥ  place of cool water, bath.

àst taa  place of fire in the Other World.

àst tchesert 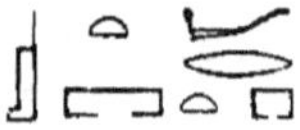 shrine, sanctuary, holy place.

àsṭ 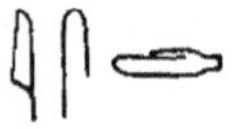 to tremble, make to shake.

Àsṭenu  name of a god.

ȧsteḥ (?) — **ȧstheḥt** (?) — to beat down.

Ȧsṭes — name of a god.

Ȧstcheṭet — name of a district.

ȧshāt — knife, slaughter.

ȧshep — light, radiance.

ȧshpit — chamber, hut, house.

ȧsheset — see ȧqeset.

ȧshesh — to be carried away.

ȧshet — subsistence, oppression, oppressor (?).

ȧshta — tree.

ȧsheṭ — persea tree, trees, plants.

ȧk — injury.

àkebu hair.

àkeb, àkebu, ***àkebet*** lamentation, wailing, weeping.

àkebit wailers, mourners.

Àkeniu a proper name.

Àkentaukha-kheru the porter of the Sixth Ārit.

Àkenti a proper name.

Àksi a city of the Ninth Àat.

Àqen name of a god.

Àqeh name of a god.

àqer perfect, strong, complete, skilful; plur. a skilful scribe.

Àqrit a goddess.

Àqert-khenti-ḥet-set the name of one of the Seven Cows.

àqḥu to enter.

àqeset who, what, where,

àqet wine, beer.

àqeṭu builders, masons, architects.

àqeṭs bad, wicked, evil.

Àḳau name of a god.

àḳap
àḳep } rain-storm, tempest.

Àḳeru
Àḳeriu } gods of the Other World.

Àḳert
Àḳertet } the name of the Other World of Heliopolis.

Àḳert-khent-Àset-s the name of one of the Seven Cows.

àḳeḳit a kind of garment, robe.

àt father.

àt (for **ànt**)
àti (for **ànti**)
àtet

negation, no, none, not, cannot, without, impotence, plur. 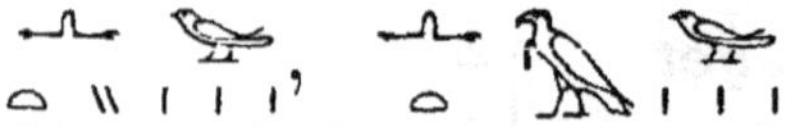 things which are not, evil beings;  without, destitute, abjects.

àti ākhem  unquenchable.

àti uteb  immutable.

àti men 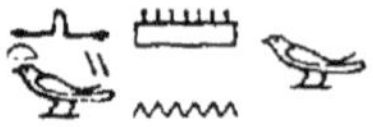 painless.

àti maa  invisible, not seeing, blind.

àtu rekh  unknown.

àtu khesef 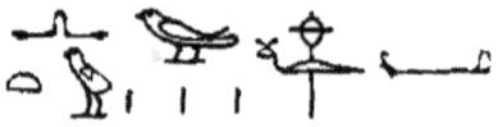 irresistible.

àtu àsi 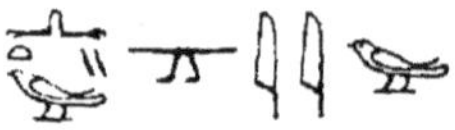 incorruptible.

àti sek 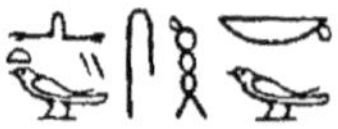 undecaying.

àti shes  impassable.

àt 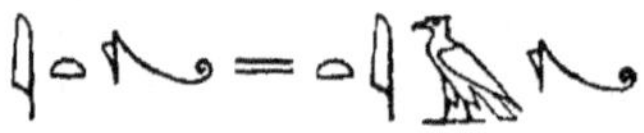 emanation.

Àtaru-àm-tcher-qemtu-renu-par-sheta   a proper name.

áteb territory, region.

átef father; dual , ; plur. , father gods , Father Osiris , Father Kheperá .

Átem see under Tem, Temu.

áten the solar disk.

the god of the solar disk.

the two-horned disk.

átennu appellations.

áter
átru river, canal, water-flood, stream; plur. .

átert one half of the sky, or world.

àtert meḥt 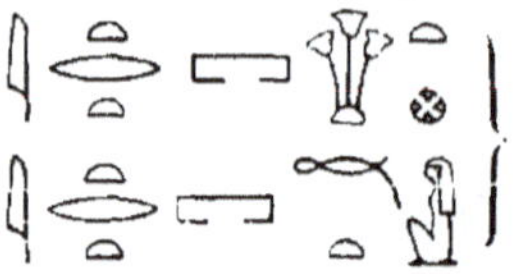 the northern half of the sky.

àtert shemā 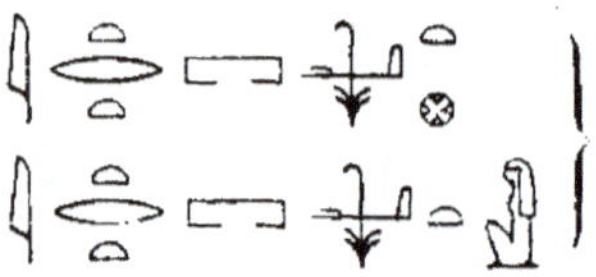 the southern half of the sky.

àterti

àturti  the two halves of the sky.

Àthabu  name of a city.

àtḥu 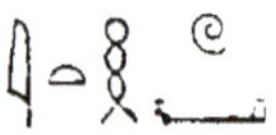 to drag, pull, draw.

Àtektaukehaqkheru 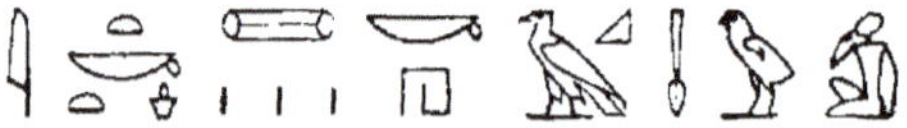 a proper name.

àṭ  oppression, oppressed one.

àṭ  to be deaf.

Àṭu  a city of the Eleventh Àat.

àṭu  children.

ȧṭeb  region, domain; plur. 

ȧṭmȧ 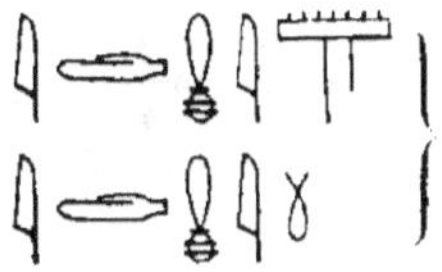 a kind of cloth, a ceremonial garment.

ȧṭen  deputy, vicar, chief?

ȧṭent 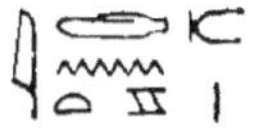 division, a separation.

ȧṭerit  misfortunes, calamities.

ȧṭḥu  papyrus swamps, the Delta generally.

ȧṭeṭiu  those who injure.

ȧthi (ȧti)  prince, sovereign, king.

ȧthen 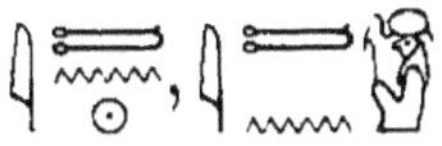 the solar disk, the god of the solar disk.

ȧtheth 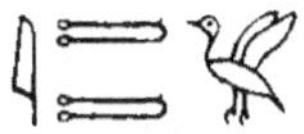 to hover, to alight.

ȧtcha  robber, man of violence, violence.

Ā.

hand, arm, paw of an animal; dual , , ; plur. , power ; at once, straightway, immediately, ancestor (see ṭep ā); "Eater of the Arm", name of a god, a flight, action of battle, place of yesterday, before.

Āāiu, etc. the name of the posts of the magic net (Chapter XCIX).

ā, āa house, dwelling.

āa , to advance, journey onwards.

āa , , door, gate; plur. , , , , ; the two leaves of a door , , .

āatu

gods of the doors.

the two doors of the sky.

the two doors of truth.

the two doors of the sky.

the two doors of Ta-qebḥ.

āa, **āat** great, large, mighty, to be great; great one, great god, great goddess; plur.

āaui, **āaāa** twice great.

āati two great goddesses.

āa-ȧb great of heart, *i. e.*, proud, arrogant.

great forms, *i. e.*, possessing many forms.

āat ur sep sen  most exceedingly great.

āa *baiu*  great of souls, *i. e.*, most valorous.

āa *mertu* 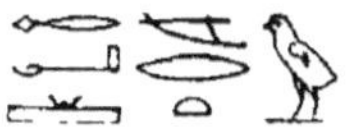 greatly beloved.

āa *neruȧ*  greatly victorious.

āa *rennu*  possessing many names.

āa *khāu*  possessing many crowns.

āa *kheperu*  of many transformations.

āa *senṭ* 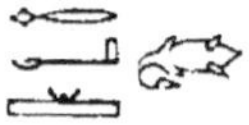 he who is greatly feared.

āa *sekhemu* 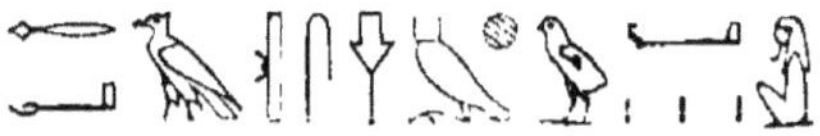 great one of powers.

āa *sheps*  most holy.

āa *shefshefit*  most terrible, or awful one.

Āa-kheru  "mighty of speech", the warder of the Seventh Ārit.

Āat-em-khut  "great one in the horizon", a proper name.

āā 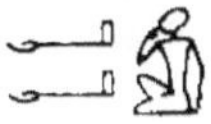 to eat?

āā 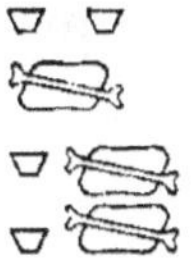 heir, inheritance, heritage, to inherit.

āat 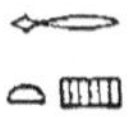 stone amulet, plur. 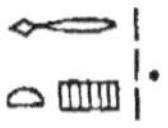.

āt, āāt 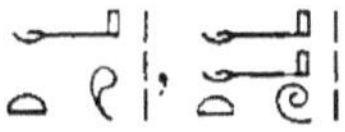 members, limbs, body.

āātu-pu-ent Kher-neter 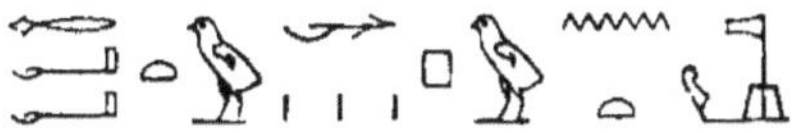 name of the oar-rests in the magic boat (Chap. CXIX).

Āaṭi 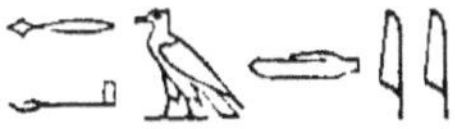 the name of one of the Forty-two Judges in the Hall of Osiris.

āu, āāu  ass.

āān, ***āānā***, ***āānāu***  ape, monkey.

āu, ***āut*** 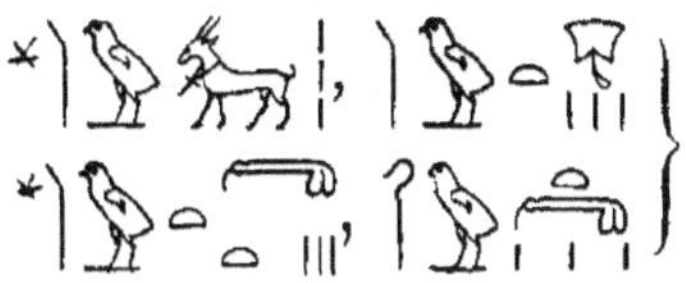 animals, quadrupeds.

āu  sins, offences (vol. II, 148, 4).

āua, **āuau** to be strong, to act violently, to plunder, to rob, to oppress, vanquish, etc. , violence, wrong, evil act, evil doer, robber; ill treated, oppressed; (Chap. XVII, Nebseni, l. 25).

āuai violence.

āun, **āunu** to be strong, violent, fierce.

āun-àb (?) to be of a fierce disposition, violence.

āuq pool, marsh, watery ground.

āb , with , opposite, before, in front of, thus; , , , , , , .

āba (**uba**) opposition.

āb 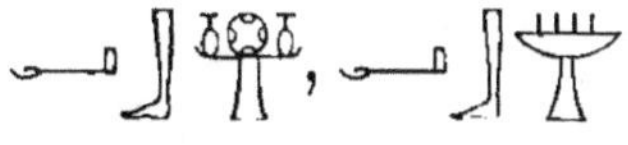 altar, table of offerings.

āb 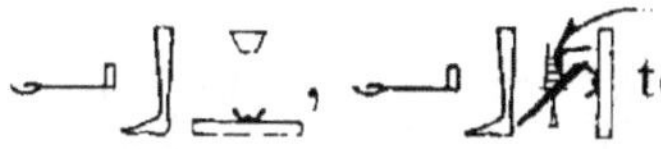 to present offerings, to offer up a sacrifice.

ābuaa  to bring before, to present.

āab
āabet, ābet 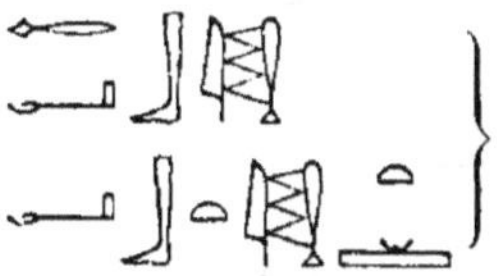 offering, sacrifice; plur. 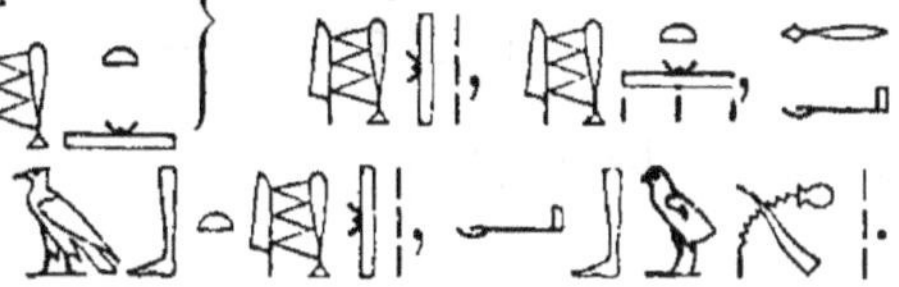

ābai (**āabai**)  sacrifice, offering, 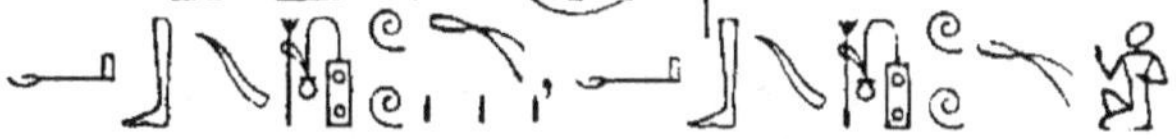 a priest who read the Liturgies.

āb (**uāb**)
ābu (**uābu**)
ābet (**uābet**) 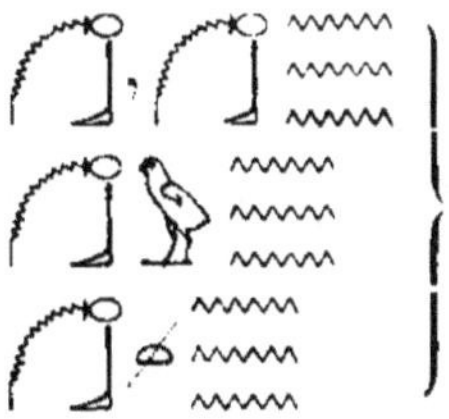 clean, pure, holy, to be pure, to purify, to sprinkle or wash ceremonially.

āb (**uāb**)  libation, purification; plur. 

āb (**uāb**) 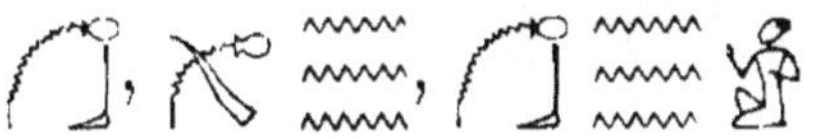 libationer, a man ceremonially pure.

āb (*uāb*) 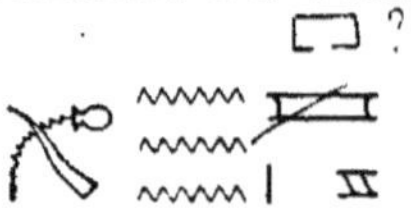 ~~pool~~ of water used for purificatory purposes.

ābu (*uābu*)  clean raiment, holy apparel.

ābet (*uābet*)  water-house, bath, clean place; plur. 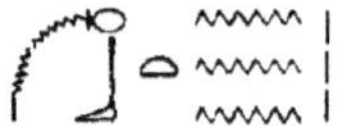; great pure place 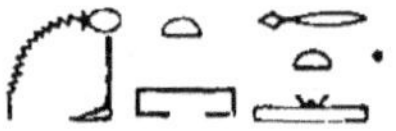

ābti (*uābti*) 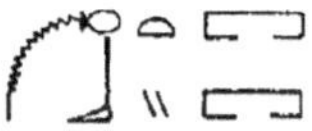 double holy place.

āb (*uāb*) **āāui** , 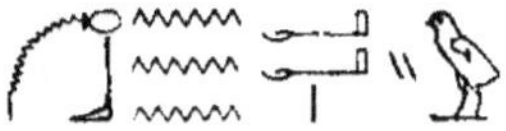 clean-handed.

āb (*uāb*) **ru**  clean-mouthed.

āb (*uāb*) **ḥeru**  clean-faced beings.

ābu (*uābu*)  propitiatory offerings.

Āb-ur (*Uāb-ur*) 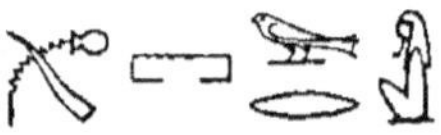 a title of Osiris.

āba (*uba*)  to open or force a way, or passage, through something.

āba (*uba*) **ru**  to open the mouth.

āb altar, table of offerings.

āb to present offerings, to offer up a sacrifice.

ābuaa to bring before, to present.

āab
āabet, ābet offering, sacrifice; plur.

ābai (āabai) sacrifice, offering, a priest who read the Liturgies.

āb (uāb)
ābu (uābu)
ābet (uābet) clean, pure, holy, to be pure, to purify, to sprinkle or wash ceremonially.

āb (uāb) libation, purification; plur.

āb (uāb) libationer, a man ceremonially pure.

āb (**uāb**) 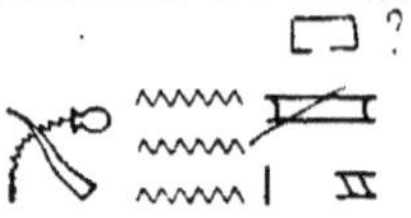 pool of water used for purificatory purposes.

ābu (**uābu**)  clean raiment, holy apparel.

ābet (**uābet**)  water-house, bath, clean place; plur. 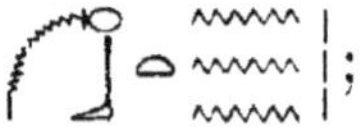; great pure place 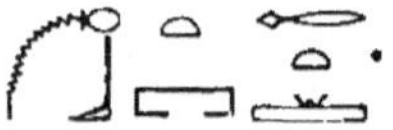

ābti (**uābti**) 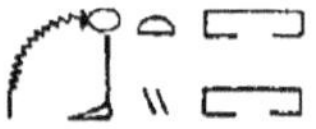 double holy place.

āb (**uāb**) **āāui** 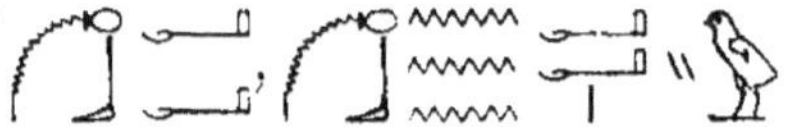 clean-handed.

āb (**uāb**) **ru**  clean-mouthed.

āb (**uāb**) **ḥeru** 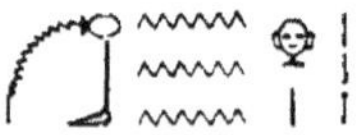 clean-faced beings.

ābu (**uābu**)  propitiatory offerings.

Āb-ur (**Uāb-ur**) 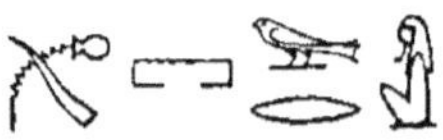 a title of Osiris.

āba (**uba**)  to open or force a way, or passage, through something.

āba (**uba**) **ru**  to open the mouth.

āba (*uba*)
ābet (*ubet*)
ābata (*ubata*) } entrance, opening.

āba to see.

ābat (*ubat*) } fore-court of a temple.

Āba-ta (*Uba-ta*) "Opener of the Earth", a name of a god.

Ābau-taui the name of a god.

āb horn; , two-horned; plur. ; broad-horned; *neb ābui* "lord of two horns" = Dhu 'l-Ḳarnên, a title of Alexander the Great.

ābiu divine ancestors.

ābeb to see.

āp (*āap*) , to fly.

Āpep — the arch-enemy of Rā. Copt. ⲁⲫⲱⲫ "giant".

Āpef — name of a fiend.

āper — to be equipped or provided with, furnished with: provided.

Āper, **Āpert** — the name of a city and city-god.

āpesh — tortoise, turtle.

āpshait — a kind of beetle. Perhaps the weevil, the Muta Jambi, or "head of God", of the Bakuba of the Kasai District in the Congo Free State. (See T. A. Joyce in *Man*, vol. IX, No. 1, p. 3.)

āfa — filth.

āfau — food.

āfent — wig, headdress; plur.

āftet — place, abode, chest.

āfṭet place, abode, chest.

ām to eat, consume, devour; eaters.

āmām ~~to eat~~, to understand, to comprehend.

āmt what is eaten, food.

ām àb "to eat the heart", *i. e.*, become angry and rage.

āmam-àrit "Eater of the Eye"; name of a god.

Ām-āu "Eater of the Ass"; name of a fiend and enemy of Rā.

Ām-àsfetti "Eater of Sinners"; name of a god.

Ām-baiu "Eater of souls"; name of a fiend.

Ām-ḥeḥ "Eater of eternity".

Ām-khaibitu  "Eater of Shades"; the name of one of the Forty-two Judges in the Hall of Osiris.

Āmām 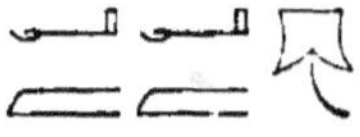 "Devourer"; the name of the Eater of the dead.

Ām-mit  "Devourer of the dead".

Ām-mit  a consuming serpent goddess.

Ān  a proper name.

ān 
āni  } tablet, board, writing palette.

ān  to turn back. Partic. plur.
 those who turn away, or return.

ānu  a mythological fish.

Ānpet  a name of the city of Mendes.

ānkh 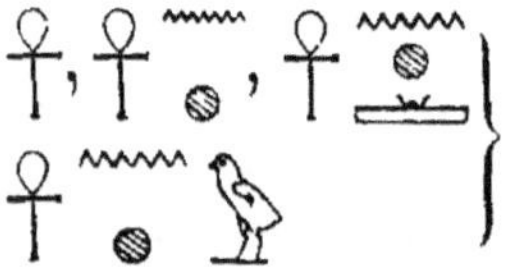 to live, to live upon, to feed upon, life, living one, living; , 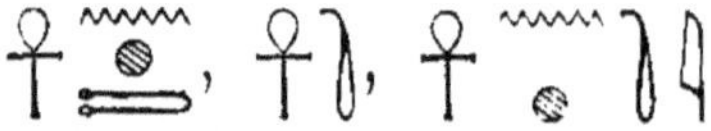 alive. Copt. ⲱⲛϩ.
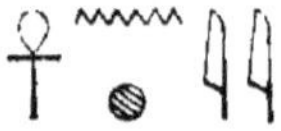 the living one, a name of Osiris.

ānkhu,
ānkhiu

the living, men and women, title of the blessed dead.

ānkh tchetta 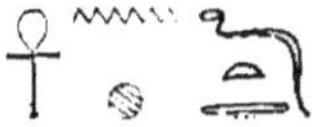 the living for ever. 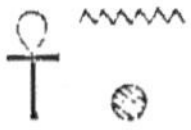 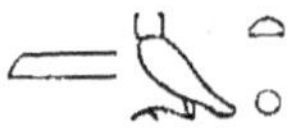 life from death.

ānkh user  life and power.

ānkh utcha senb  life, strength and health.

ānkhet  life.

ānkhet 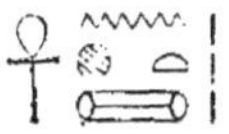 victuals.

Ānkhti 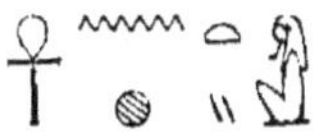 a name of Osiris.

ānkh  a kind of unguent.

Ānkhet pu ent Sebek neb Bakhau 

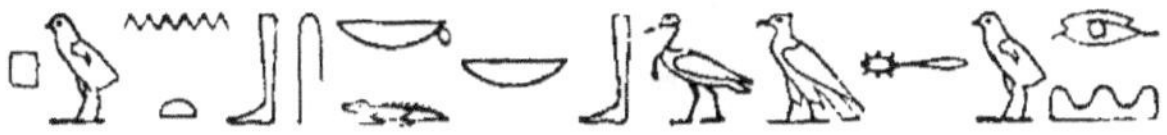

a proper name.

Ānkh-em-bu  "Eater of abominable things".

Ānkh-em-fentu  "Eater of worms"; name of the warder of the Fifth Arit.

ānkhui  the two ears.

ānkhȧmu  flowers, or aromatic plants.

ānt  ring.

ānt 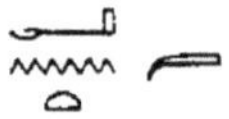 to be covered with something.

ānt  claw, talon, hook, nail of the hand or foot,  "Claw of Ptaḥ"; a proper name.

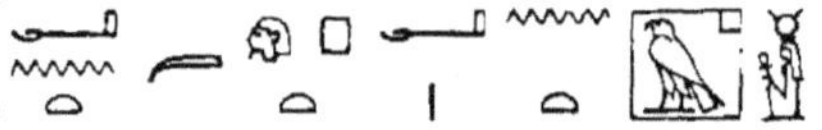 "Claw on the hand of Hathor"; a proper name.

ānti 

ānṭ 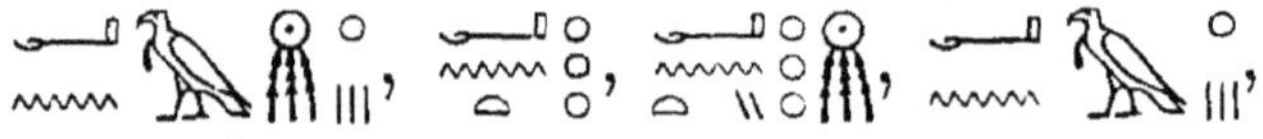

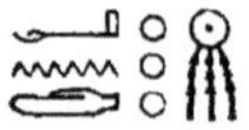 myrrh, unguent (?).

ānti a preparation of myrrh used by women.

ānṭu light, radiance.

ānṭ evil.

ānṭu darkness.

Ānṭi the name of one of the Forty-two Judges in the Hall of Osiris.

ār an animal of the goat species.

ār to approach, to bring, to come, to arrive; ; divine beings who approach.

ārȧ to find (?).

ārār jawbone.

ārārt uraeus.

ārāti two uraei goddesses.

two very large uraei.

the living serpent goddesses.

ārit tool, lintel of a door.

ārit hall, chamber; plur.
The Seven Ārits

ārfi bundle, purse.

ārrt, **ārrit** hall, mansion; plur.

Ārq to bind, to tie, girdle, to be completed.

ārq to swear.

Ārq-ḥeḥ name of a city.

ārq end; end of the earth.

ārqi last day of the lunar month.

ārt jaw, jawbone.

ārti the two jaws.

ārtu houses, abodes, mansions.

āḥ moon.

āḥ  to surround, embrace.

āḥa, **āḥau** 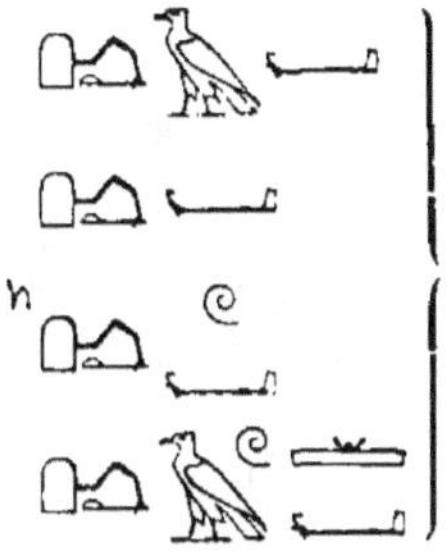 to fight, do battle, wage war:  fighter,  fightings.

āḥa-ā  to fight bravely (?).

āḥa-tu 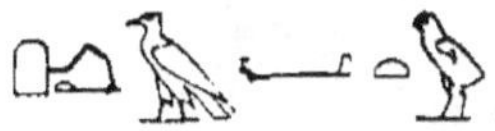 fight, contest, struggle.

āḥau  fighting implements, weapons.

āḥaui  the two Fighters, *i. e.*, Horus and Set.

Āḥau ḥeru  "Fighting faces", a name of certain gods.

āḥāt 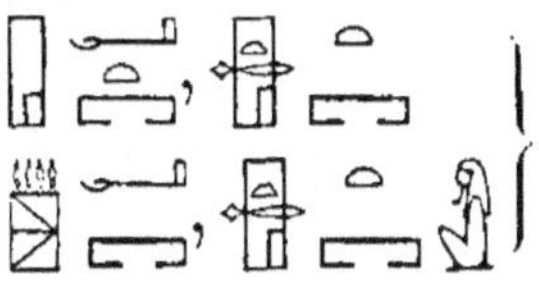 great house, palace.

āḥā 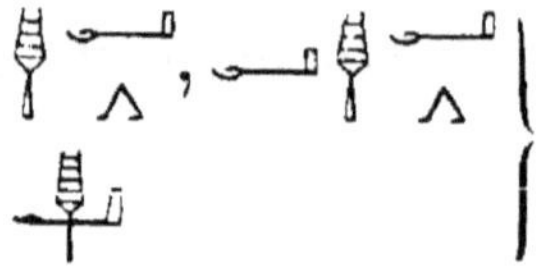 to stand up, to withstand. 

āḥā  as an auxiliary verb: 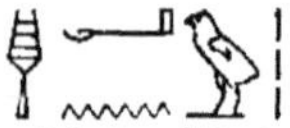 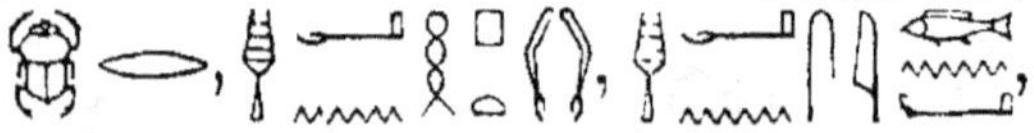 and see *passim*.

āḥā  stability.

āḥāu  condition, state, position.

āḥā
āḥāu
āḥāt 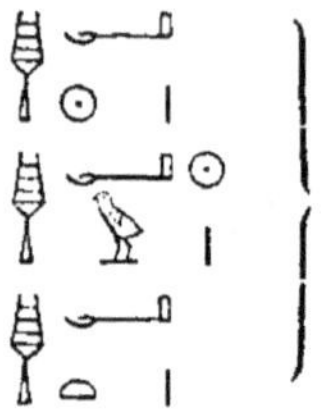 time, season or duration of life, life, a contemporary. 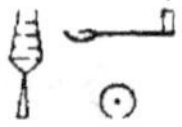 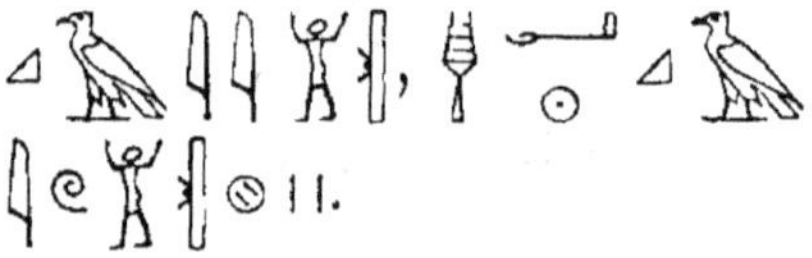

 period from life, or in life.

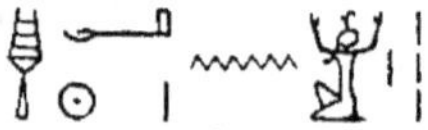 period of eternity.

āḥāu  noon-day.

āḥāu  supports.

āḥāu  stores, food, provisions.

 folk who are provisioned.

āḥāit boat.

āḥāt tomb.

ākh to spread out the heavens, or sky.

Ākhtuset a class of divine beings. The variants are:
ākhmiu.
àukhu-seku.
ākhsemiu.

ākha to fly, to soar; *ākhai* flying.

ākha to sleep.

ākhan
ākhanet } to close the eye.

ākhu } fire-altars.

ākhem
ākhemu } to quench, to extinguish; quenched.

ākhemu, **ākhmiu** — quenchers, those who extinguish.

ākhem — figure of a god.

ākhemu — figures of gods.

ākhmet — river banks.

Ākhen-ȧriti(?)-f — a proper name.

ākhekhau — serpent-fiends, monsters.

ākhekhu — "Darkness"; a proper name.

āsha — to be much or many, manifold.

many reeded.

of multitudinous festivals.

of many forms.

loud voiced to speak

āshau, **āshat** — crowd, multitude.

āshat  crowd, multitude.

āsh  to call, to invoke, to cry out.

āshu 

 evil speech.

āsh 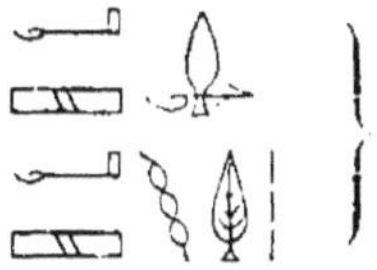 cedar, or acacia, tree, cedar gum.

āshāsht 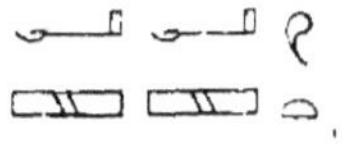 part of the body.

āshāt  knife.

āshem  the forms in which the gods appear upon earth.

āshemu
āshemiu  crocodiles. A variant gives  

āshashat  gullet.

Ākesh  name of a city.

āq 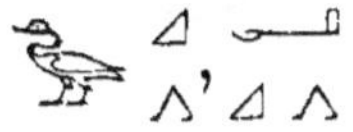 to enter, go in.

āqiu those who enter.

aqet things which enter.

āq pert entrance and exit.

Āq-ḥer-àmi-unnut-f "He who enters in his hour"; a proper name.

āqu cakes, loaves of bread.

āqa to present bread (?). Chap. XCIX, 3.

āq maāt (?) exact truth (?), just.

āqa to keep the mean, right, exact, true, just, truth, to be in the middle.

to be exactly over the heart.

āqau truth, right, justice.

Āqan the name of a god.

āqi part of a boat.

āq, āqa — rope, cordage, tackle of a boat.

Āqennu — the name of a city.

āḳa — unguent.

āḳu — to be burned.

āt — domain.

āt — hall, palace.

āt — member, limb; plur.

Āti — name of the ninth nome of Lower Egypt.

āteptu — grain, seeds.

āter — provisions.

āṭ (ānṭ) — pole of a net with curved ends.

Āṭ (Ānṭ) — name of a god.

āṭ (ānṭ) — domain, territory, soil.

***āṭ* (*ānṭ*)** to split, to divide.

***Āṭ* (*Ānṭ*)** the morning boat of the sun.

āṭu name of a mythological fish.

āṭurtu (a mistake ?)

Ātch-ur "Great splitter"; name of a god.

***ātchet* (*āntchet*)** fixed, firm.

U.

. . . . Chap. CLXVIII. Circle X, 14, 2.

u they, them, their.

u district, region.

Ua a proper name.

ua, ***uau*** to depart, go away, be afar off; remote.

ua
uau — way, path, road; plur.

uau — waterway, stream.

uauau — radiance, light.

uau — flame, fire.

uau — chains, fetters.

uauu — to speak evil, blaspheme.

uauiuait — hair.

uai — to destroy, overcome, gain the mastery over.

Uaipu — a cow-goddess.

uab — flower, blossom.

Uamemti — the name of one of the Forty-two Judges in the Hall of Osiris.

uart — ropes, cordage.

Uarekht (?) — a mythological region.

Uart-neter-semsu a proper name

uaḥ to place, to set, to fix, to add to permanent, abiding.

to add to something.

uaḥit libation vessels.

uaḥuu mummy bandages.

uaḥtu to mummify.

uakh
uakhet "Green"; the name of a poo in the Elysian Fields.

uas sceptre.

uas contentment, happiness.

Uast Thebes.

uash to worship, be adored two-fol worship.

Uaḳ the name of a festival.

uat way, road, path; plur. , ; great roads, good roads, all roads, ways of the dead; the two roads.

eastern roads.

western roads.

northern roads.

southern roads.

uatch ~~sceptre, staff,~~ stick.

uatch tablet of green faïence, amulet.

uatch unguent, sulphate of copper eye-paint.

uatchu sulphate of copper.

uatch shemāt sulphate of copper of the south.

uatchet a kind of linen.

uatch  to make to flourish, be green, vigorous, to blossom, be new, fresh.

uatchet  green.

uatchet  green things, plants, herbs.

uatchu 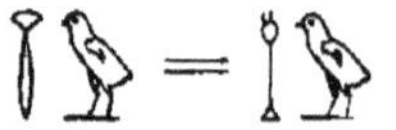 *q. v.*

Uatch-àriti (?) 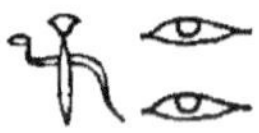 "Green Eyes"; a proper name.

Uatch-ur 
Uatch-urà  "Great Green Sea"; *i. e.*, the Mediterranean.

Uatch-nesert 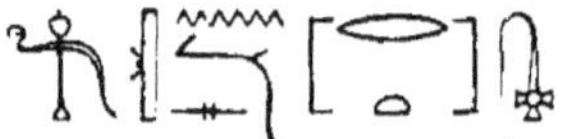 "Green Flame"; the name of one of the Forty-two Judges in the Hall of Osiris.

Uatchit  a goddess of fire.

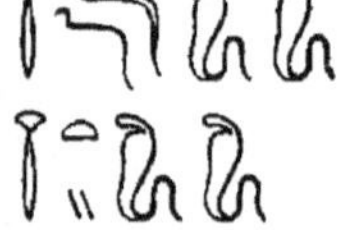 the two fire-goddesses, Isis and Nephthys.

uatchit  abode, house.

uà  I, me.

uȧa — boat, boat of Rā.

uȧaui — the two boats of Rā, the boats of morning and evening.

uȧa en Maāti — the boat of Maāt.

uȧa en ḥeḥ — "Boat of Millions of Years".

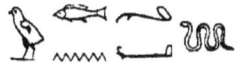

uȧn — to become worms.

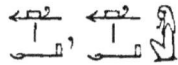

uā — One, the One, *i. e.*, God.

uāu — One of the gods;

One God (Osiris); One (fem.).

uā — one; fem. ; , being one, or alone; to be one .

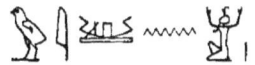

uā—ki one ... the other; one embraced the other; fem. ... ; one in one; one of one.

uā = indefinite article ,

uā neb any one, each one, every one.

uā uāu one alone, only one.

uāu alone. Also and .

uāuti solitude.

uā with at once, all at once; and compare , .

uāt in a piece of cloth.

Uāau the herald of the Third Ārit.

uār passage.

uār to depart.

uārt 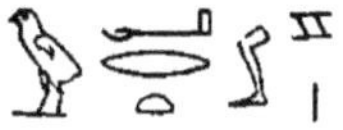 passage, the name of a place.

uārt 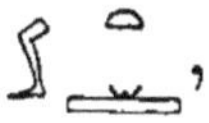, 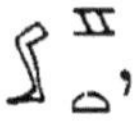, 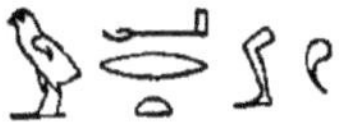 thigh; 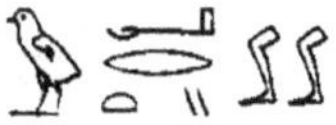 the two thighs.

 "thigh" of water.

 "thigh" of the lake.

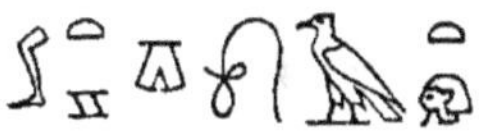 "thigh" surrounding.

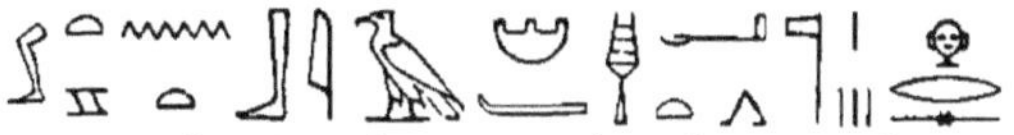 "thigh" of iron whereon is the station of the gods.

 that "thigh" of Kher-āḥa.

 that "thigh" whereon is the House of the Moon.

uārt  stream.

uu  evil, evil one.

uu  region, district; 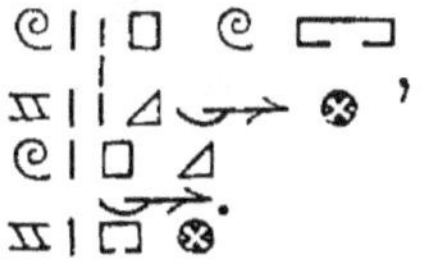

ui  sign of the dual.   two very mighty gods.

Ui — a proper name.

uit — chamber.

uben — to rise (of a luminary), to shine; rising and setting;

ubennu, *ubentu* — rays of light.

ubennu — to flow.

ubekh, *ubekht* — to shine, light up, shining, blazing.

ubes — water-flood.

ubesu — beings of fire, sparks (?).

Ubes-ḥer-per-em-khetkhet "Fiery face, coming forward in retreating"; a proper name.

ubeṭ — to be scalded, to set fire to, to burn up.

ufa to chance on, to light upon.

umet a garment.

umet the middle (?).

umet walls, fortifications, building.

un lightness, defect,

un, unen to be, being, existence, to become, to exist; as an auxiliary verb see *passim*.

unt
unent being, existence; , ; plur. , ; those who are, things which are.

uniu human beings.

un maā , in very truth.

un , , to open, opener, opening; , opened.

uniu, *uneniu* — openers, scatterers.

un ḥer — to open the face, *i. e.*, show the face, to appear; — ; to open the mouth — , — .

un — shrine.

un — shaved.

un, *unnu* — to pull out the hair.

un, uni, unt — , — , — to walk, run, rise upright; — runners.

unun, *unn-unn* — , — , — to run, stand up.

unun — to sow seed.

Unȧset — name of a city.

unām — unguent.

Uniu, or *Unniu* — name of a city.

unini light.

uni light, defective.

Unen-em-ḥetep a division of the Sekhet-Åaru.

unb flower, bloom; plur.

unpet flowers, blossoms.

Unpepet ent Ḥet-Ḥeru

"Flower of Hath

unef to rer
unl

unem

unemi the right side, the right as opposed to left.

unemt

unem to eat, see *Åm*.

unnu evil, wrong, defect.

Unnu Hermopolis, the city of Thoth.

unnuiti sacrificer.

unnut a brief space of time, a moment, an hour, a season, interval. Plur.

Unnut goddess ~~of the~~ hour.

Un-Nefer
Unen-nefer
Unen-Neferu
Unen-Neferu
A title of Osiris, meaning something like "the well-doing Being". Coptic forms of the name are ⲟⲩⲉⲛⲉϥⲣⲉ, ⲟⲩⲉⲛⲟϥⲣ, ⲟⲩⲉⲛⲟϥⲣⲓ, ⲱⲛⲟⲫⲣⲉ, etc.

Un-Nefer-Rā.

Un-Nefer, son of Nut.

Un-ḥāt a proper name.

unkh
unkhu
to dress, to array oneself, to put on a garment.

unkh ~~to tie, untie, set loose.~~

unkh a garment.

Unes — the metropolis of the XIXth Nome of Lower Egypt.

unshu — wolves.

Unt — a city of the Twelfth Àat.

Unti — the name of a god.

un tini — be ye.

unṭu — mankind, people, kinsfolk, relatives.

Unth — name of a district or country.

ur — to be great, great, mighty, supreme, powerful.

ur, uru — great one (God); plur.

urt — great one (fem.), goddess.

uru — dual masc. "two great".

urti dual fem. "two great goddesses".

two very great goddesses.

ur great man, chief, prince, nobleman, master; princess. Plur. masc. ; plur. fem.

ur sep sen doubly great.

ur as comparative, ... greater than.

ur as superlative, greatest of 5 gods.

ur in titles etc.:

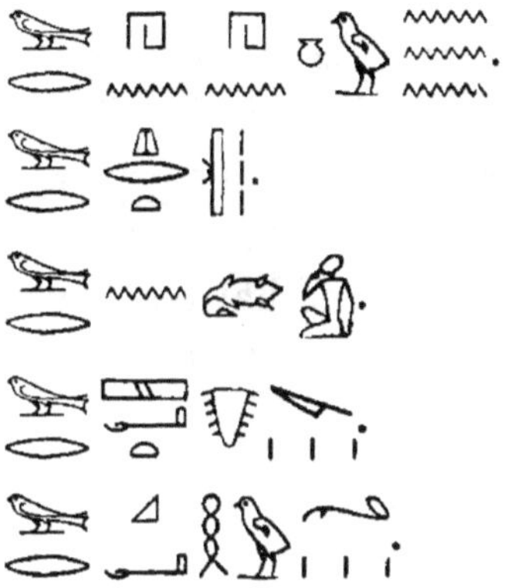

ur  a joint of meat, haunch, carcase; 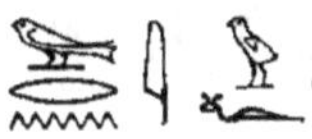, 

Ur-at  "great of moment", a proper name.

Urit  name of a city.

urit 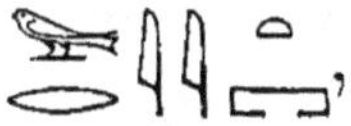, 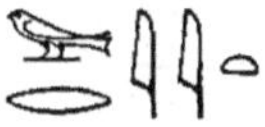 hall, house, room.

Ur-ȧrit-s 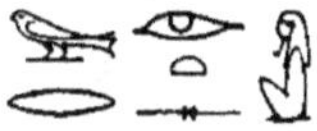 a proper name.

Ur-peḥui-f  a proper name.

Ur-ma  title of the high-priest of Heliopolis (?).

Ur-maat  a proper name.

Ur-mertus-ṭeshert-shenu

Ur-mertis-ṭeshert-shenu "The red-haired one who is greatly beloved"; name of one of the Seven Cows.

Ur-ḥekau a deity who is mighty in words of power, a god or goddess of magic.

Ur-kherp-ḥem "chief master of the blacksmith's tool"; a title of the high-priest of Memphis.

Ur-senu chief of the physicians.

urer

urert the name of a crown. the gods who wear the *urert* Crown.

urertu

urḥ

urḥu to smear or rub with unguent, to anoint.

Urḥetchati two goddesses of Heliopolis.

urs  a pillow, head-rest.

ursh 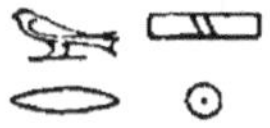 to pass the day, to watch; 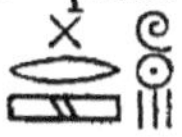 watchers.

Urek 

urt 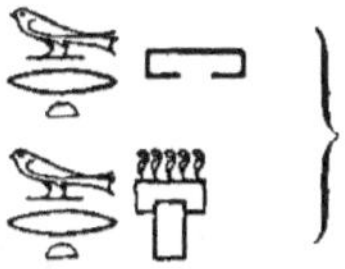 hall, palace.

urt  funeral chest, or coffer.

urt 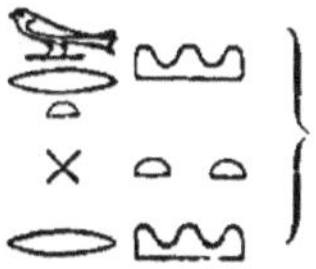 funerary mountain, cemetery.

urt  flood.

urt 

Urt-urt  a proper name.

urṭ, urṭu  to be inert, motionless, helpless, to rest.

Urṭ-àb  "He whose heart is still"; a title of Osiris.

urṭu , see .

uh to be troubled?

uhau to supplicate.

uhaȧu to fail.

uhem

uhemu to repeat, to report, to narrate; , ;

uhemm to repeat; .

to speak again.

to renew life, live again.

a new form.

to renew protection.

, with , a second time, again.

uhem-ā anew, afresh.

Uhem-ḥer a proper name.

suhen  decay, failure.

suhen 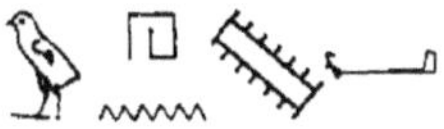 to overthrow: 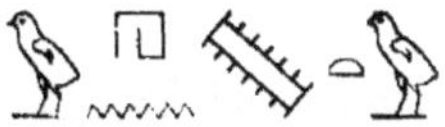 be overthrown.

uḥā 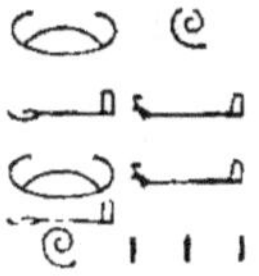 to unloose, be set free from, to return (in the evening).

uḥā 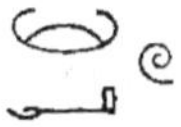 cord, rope.

uḥā  to catch fish, to snare game, fisherman, fowler.

uḥeset  to beat down, to slay.

uḥet  baked meats, stew (?).

ukha 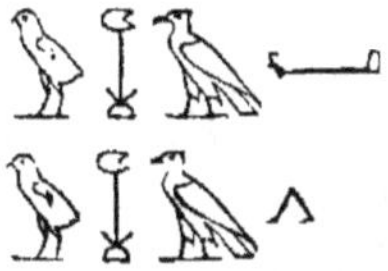 to lay down, set down, to seek after, search for.

ukha  darkness, night.

ukha  pillar.

ukhakh  to seek after.

ukheb  to shine.

ukhert  wooden implement.

ukheṭ to be angry, be pained, disgusted.

ukheṭet boat.

us to do away with.

usfau idle, lazy.

user to be strong, mighty, strength, might, power, strong; .

useru powers, mighty beings (human or divine).

usert strength.

usert skull, top of the head; plur. .

User-ȧb "Strong-heart"; a proper name.

User-ba "Strong-soul"; a proper name.

useru oars, rudders, steering poles.

useru to steer a boat.

Usert the name of a goddess.

useḥ 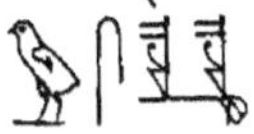 to advance.

usekh 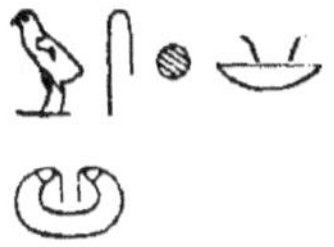 collar, neck ornament, pectoral.

usekh  to be in a wide space, to be wide or spacious, breadth, broad.

Usekh-nemmet  "He of the long stride", the name of one of the Forty-two Judges in the Hall of Osiris.

Usekh-ḥer  "Broad Face", a name of Rā.

usekht  the wide space of the sky, a large hall or room;   the great double hall.

Usekht Maāti 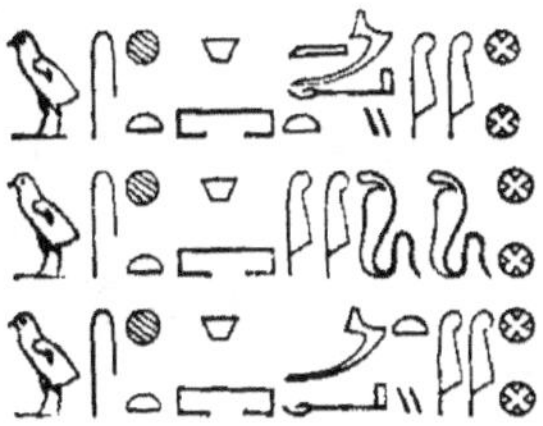 the name of the double Hall wherein Osiris judged the dead.

Usekt Shuu	the Hall of Shu, *i. e.*, heaven.
Usekht Ḳeb	the Hall of Ḳeb, *i. e.*, earth.
usekhu	plated (?).
usesht	urine.
usesh	to micturate.
usten, ***ustennu***	to walk, to follow.
Usṭ	a proper name.
ush	to cry out.
ush	~~misery~~.
ushau	night, darkness.
ushā	te eat, to gnaw, crunch bones.
usheb	to answer, to eat (?).
	to make an answer at the right time.
usheb	to beget, begotten.

ushen — to net, to snare.

ushenu — feathered fowl.

uḳ — to burn, be burned.

uḳa — name of a festival.

uḳaiu — wooden pegs or legs.

ut — the city of embalmment, the abode of Anubis.

utu — embalmment.

utu — the god of embalmment, *i. e.*, Anubis.

ut — coffin, mummy bier.

uta — to embalm, swathe a mummy.

Ut (*Uḥet*?) *meḥt* — the Northern Oasis (Baḥrîyah).

Ut (*Uḥet*) *res* — the Southern Oasis (Khârgah).

Utau — a class of divine beings.

utu — to set out on a journey, to make an expedition.

utu, *uṭeṭ* — to issue an order or command, to decree, to ordain.

utet, *uṭeṭt* — commands, behests, things ordered or decreed, records, documents, deeds, copies of deeds.

Utu-nesert — the name of one of the Forty-two Judges in the Hall of Osiris.

Utu-rekhit — The name of one of the Forty-two Judges in the Hall of Osiris.

utu =

utu — flowers.

utuit — oar rest.

Utent — the name of a country.

utet — to beget.

begetter.

Utet — "Begetter", a name of Osiris.

Utet-Ḥeḥ — "Begetter of millions of years"; a proper name.

uṭ, ***uṭet*** — to cast down or out, to shoot out, dart forth, to utter a cry.

to lay violent hands on some-one.

uṭaiu — strong ones.

uṭit — chamber.

uṭebu — mutable.

uṭeb — to go round, turn about.

uṭeb, ***uṭebu*** — furrow; plur.

uṭebtu — burned.

uṭen / ***uṭenu*** 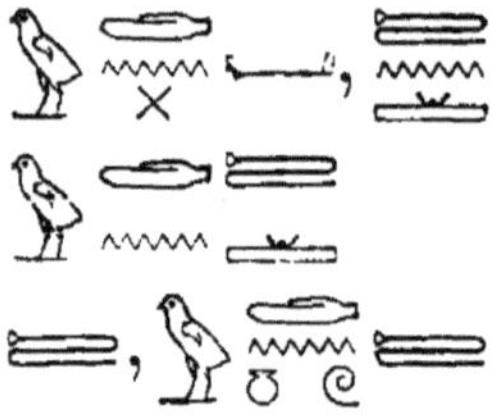 to bring something as a gift, to make an offering; 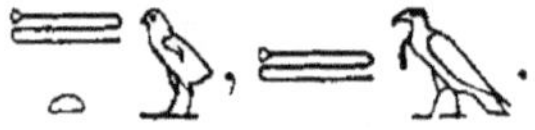.

uṭenu / ***uṭent***  offerings, things given as offerings.

uṭeḥ  altar, table of offerings; plur. .

uṭeṭ 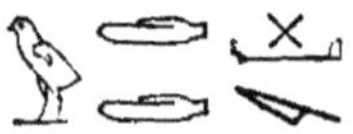 to void, shoot out.

uthes 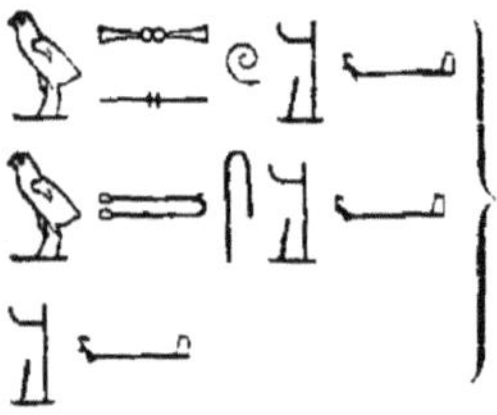 to raise up, to lift up, support.

utcha  to go out, set out, to begin a journey.

utchat  a journey, a going forth.

utcha  to be in a good state or condition, sound, healthy, well.

utchau  strength, power.

utchau  amulet, object of power.

 magical powers.

Utcha-re  "Strong-mouth"; a proper name.

utcha sep  strong with good fortune.

utchat  the "strong", *i. e.*, the Eye of Rā, whence came all power, strength, health, protection, etc.

utchat  the Utchat with legs and wings.

utchat  the Utchat of Sekhet, the great lady, the mistress of the gods.

utchati  "the two Utchats", *i. e.*, the two Eyes of the sky, or the Sun and Moon.

utchā to weigh, to estimate, to consider, to reckon up, to decide.

to consider or weigh deeds or words.

utchā senemm to weigh hair

utchā making the water to balance his throne, or making his throne to balance on the water.

utchāiu to estimate the fields; weighers, those who try something in a balance.

utchāt judges.

utchāti judgment, decision.

Utchā-aābet "computer of the offering", name of a god.

utchfau to delay, to tarry.

utcheṭ to walk.

I.

i, *iu* — to come, come, come!

i-tu, *iu-tu* — coming, a coming, advance.

it — a coming.

iu — comers; comers with glad tidings.

iu — to end (of a book) it has gone out in peace.

iu āq — going in and coming out, entrance and exit.

Iu pastu — a class of divine beings.

i, it — hail, O.

iu — O verily.

iumā — sea, lake, river, any large collection of water.

Ir-qai — a name of Ȧmen-Rā.

ikh to stretch out the heavens.

isu abodes, chambers.

B.

ba one of the two souls of man, the heart-soul, which was intimately connected with the *ka* and the heart, as opposed to the spirit-soul *khu*. Plur.

ba mentioned with and ; with , with , with and .

a perfect soul.

an equipped divine soul.

a living soul.

a living heart-soul and a perfect spirit-soul.

soul of souls.

my soul is the souls of the gods.

soul of eternity.

soul in the body.

soul of life.

a soul [made] of gold, an amulet.

thy soul is to heaven, thy body is under the ground.

ba the divine Soul, or soul of God.

ba soul of Osiris;

of Rā;

ba soul in Shu;

ba soul in Ḳeb;

ba soul in Tefnut;

Holy Soul, a name of Osiris.

Holy Soul, a name of Osiris.

the Soul which is in Nut.

the Soul of the gods who exist in the body of Osiris.

the Soul of the Great Body which is in Saïs, Neith.

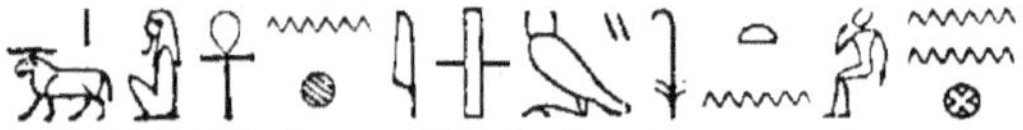
the Living Soul in Suten-ḥenen.

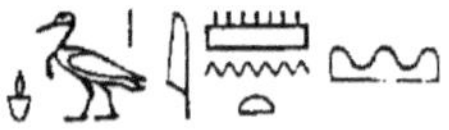
the Soul of Àmenti.

baiu 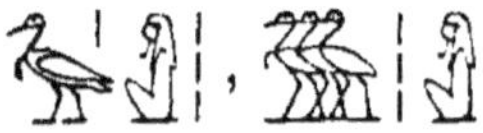 divine souls, souls of gods.

 the souls in the gods.

 the souls of the gods of the East.

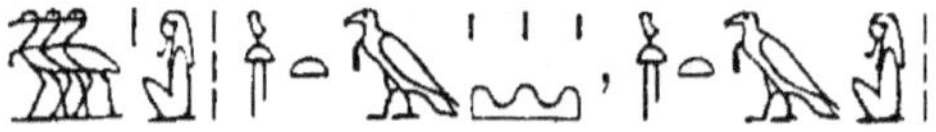 the souls of the gods of the West.

 the souls of Heliopolis.

 the souls of Pe-[Ṭep] (Buto).

 the souls of Nekhen.

 the souls of Hermopolis.

living souls.

souls who have appeared.

souls of the dead (*i. e.*, damned).

souls of his father (Osiris).

baui the double soul.

the double soul in the Tchafui, *i. e.*, the souls of Osiris and Rā.

Ꜣai the Soul-god, or the Divine Soul, or the Ram-god; the double-soul god.

Ꜣati a name of Osiris.

ꜣa divine soul with plumes.

ꜣa the metal-god; a proper name (?).

a to be endowed with a soul.

ba — to cleave, make a way through something.

Bau — a proper name.

baba — to work.

babau — cavern, cave, den or lair; plur.

Baba — the name of the first born son of Osiris.

Ba-neb-Ṭeṭṭeṭ — Soul-god, or Ram-god, lord of Ṭaṭṭu (Mendes), a title of Osiris

Barekathȧ tchaua — a proper name

baḥ , or , with  before, in front of.

Bakhau  the Mountain of sunrise.

Bast  the city of Bubastis in the Eastern Delta, the modern Zaḳâziḳ.

Bast  the goddess of Bubastis.

Bast  Bast dweller in Thebes.

Basti  the name of one of the Forty-two Judges in the Hall of Osiris.

bak  to work, to toil, to serve.

 works, labours.

baq  olive tree.

baḳ  to be weak, weary, feeble, helpless.

baḳ  weak one, the helpless one (*i. e.*, the mummy); plur. .

bat / ***bȧat***  plants, boughs, branches.

Bati  name of a fiend, or of a group of fiends.

bȧa 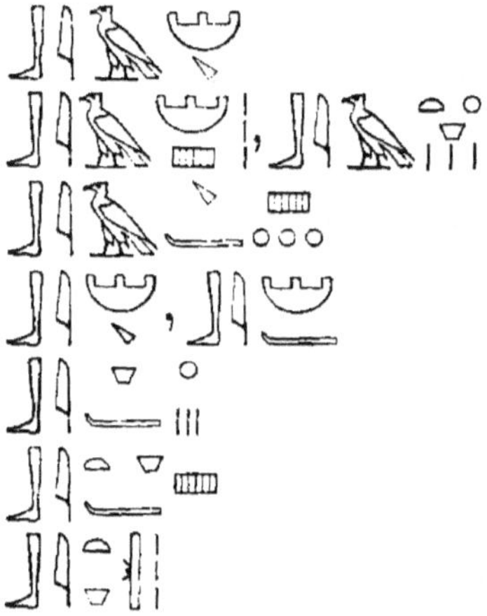 the ore of a metal, iron, copper, etc., a metal tool, a name of the sky or firmament.

bȧa en pet 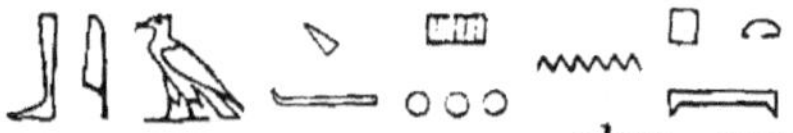 metal of the sky, meteoric iron (?).

 that iron in the sky.

bȧat shemāu  "the metal of the south", iron.

bȧat shemāu 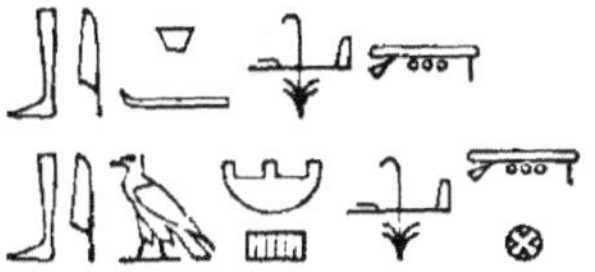 "the metal of the south", iron.

bȧau / ***bȧat***  wonders, wonderful things.

bȧaq  a kind of grain, or fruit.

Bȧbȧ  the name of a god, Baba (?).

bȧbȧ  a cry of joy.

bȧn  evil, wickedness.

bȧk  hawk; plur. .

 the double divine hawk.

Bȧket  the city of the divine hawk.

bȧt, bȧti  king of the north.

Bȧti  a proper name.

ābāt 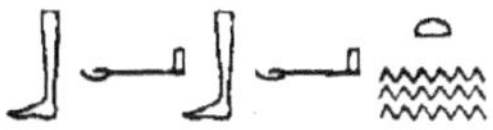 water-flood, stream.

9*

bāḥ 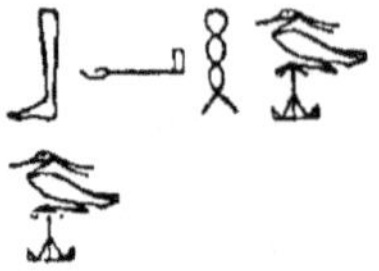 to be flooded, inundated.

Bāḥ  the god of the Inundation.

bi  name of a fiend.

biu  strength.

bu 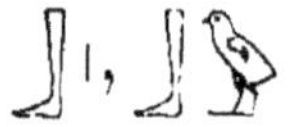  purity,  oneness (?), altogether,  lawfulness, legality, truth,  this place (?).

bu neb  everywhere, every place.

bu nebu  all men, all people, everyone, folk in general.

bu nefer  prosperity, happiness.

bu ṭu  evil thing, calamity.

bu  not, it is not; 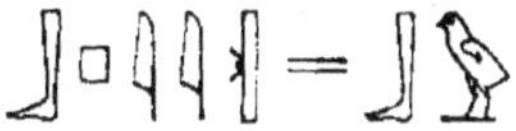

bu-pu   (?).

but  evil thing, abomination.

buṭ  offering.

bebait  the mantis.

bebuu  strong.

Bebi  the name of a god.

bebet  flowers.

bebet  fountain head.

bebet  hollow place, cavity.

ben  not.

benānā 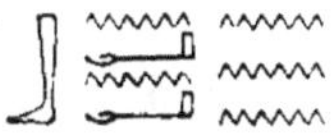 to bathe.

benben  a kind of wood.

benben  bier, funerary couch.

benbent 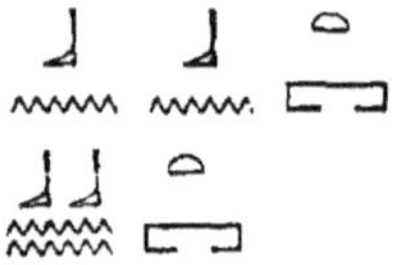 hall, pylon chamber.

ben  to pass away, to dissolve, to go on.

ben 
benen  to beget, to be united with, union.

benen 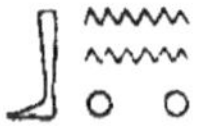 ring.

benen 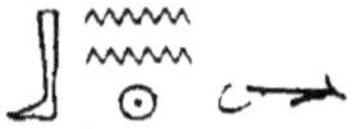 a kind of wood.

bennu  a bird commonly identified with the phoenix.

 the Bennu, the Soul of Rā.

bennut   matter, pus.

bennu 
bennut  cakes (?), bread.

Bener  the name of a city.

benrȧ  to be sweet, pleasant.

benrȧu 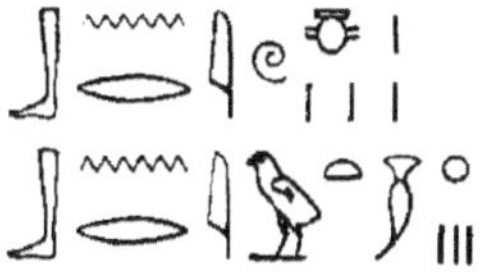 sweet things, dates, date wine, pleasant, nice.

benshu  bolts.

bent

benti  divine apes, incarnations of the spirits of morning.

beḥ 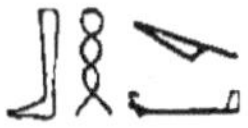 to cut, to split.

beḥen 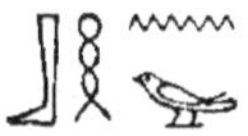 baleful one.

beḥen 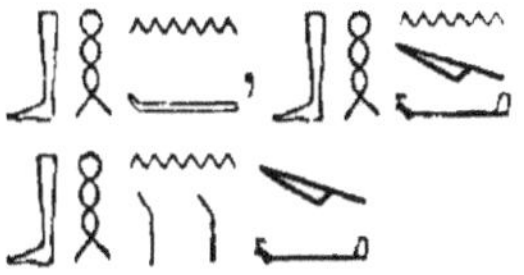 to cut, to pierce; 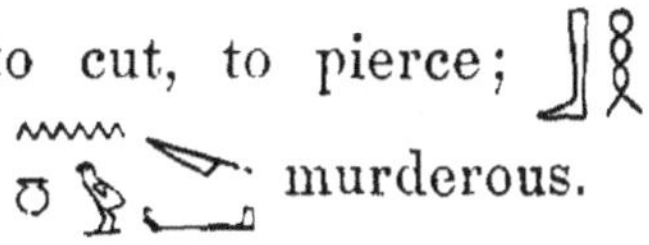 murderous.

beḥennu  animals of the wolf or dog species.

beḥes  calf.

Bekhennu  a proper name.

bekhekhu  fire.

bes 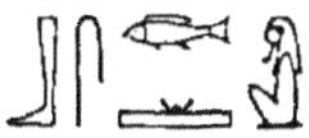 form (?).

bes  to enter, to pass in, to rise (of the river).

 increase.

bes 
besu  } flame, fire, blaze.

Besu-Aḥu  a proper name.

Besu Menu 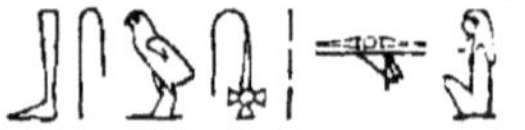 a proper name.

bessu  humours, excretions, filth.

Besek 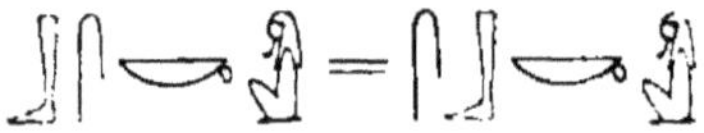 Sebek, the Crocodile-god.

besek 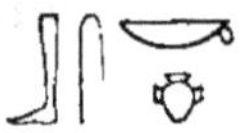 internal organ of the body; plur. 

besh 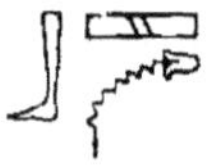 to vomit.

beshu (?)  metal plates, scales.

beka 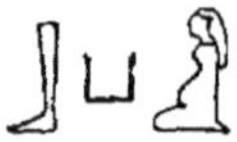 pregnant.

beka 
 } to shine, the dawn, to-morrow.

bekau  weakness.

beq olive tree, olives; the olive tree in Heliopolis.

beq a proper name.

beqsu ~~eyeball,~~ skin (?).

beqsu balance, scales.

Beqtui a proper name (?).

beḳ misery.

beḳi helpless one, sinner.

beḳa defect, sin, crime, evil, sinner; plur.

beḳa
beḳai } evil man, sinner.

beḳasu . . . .

beḳsu part of a boat.

beḳset . . . .

bet place, every place, everywhere.

bet 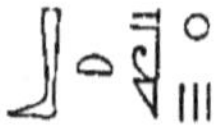 incense.

bet  grains, seed.

bet  flower.

beta  to sin, commit a fault, do wrong.

betau, ***betu***  sin, wrong, abominable thing; plur.  .

Betȧ  name of a city.

betennu, ***betnu***  swift.

beṭ  incense.

beṭ, ***beṭ-ti*** 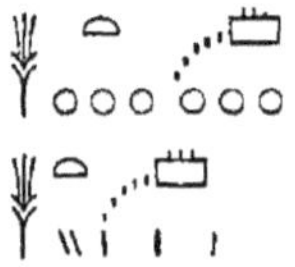 barley.

 white barley.

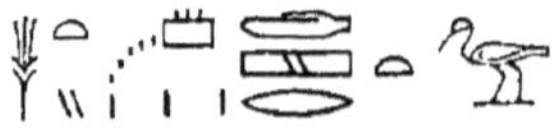 red barley.

beṭesh 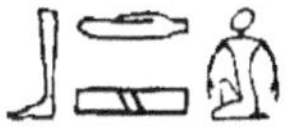 to be weak, powerless, but disposed to do evil.

beṭesh / ***beṭeshet*** 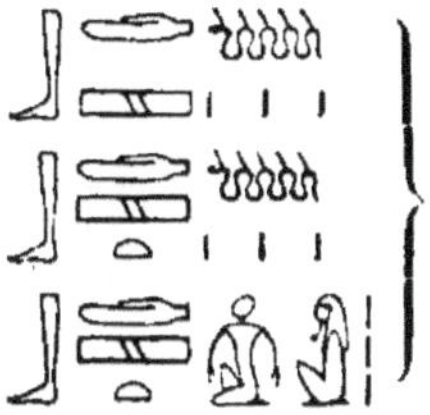 impotent fiends; fem. sing. .

Beṭshu  the name of a city.

Beṭ-ti 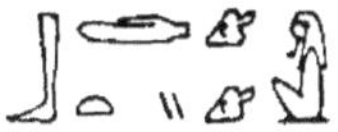 a proper name.

bethet (?)  brought.

betcha 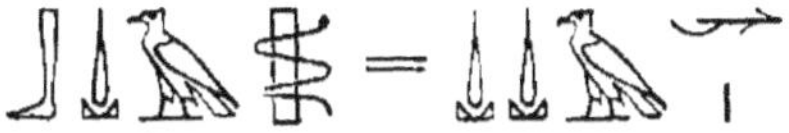 a tool or instrument.

 P.

Pe  One half of the city of Buto (Per-Uatchit).

Pe**.....**  the little Pe (?).

p  the.

pa  the;  the one who;   the one who is between.

pai-á  my.

pai-f 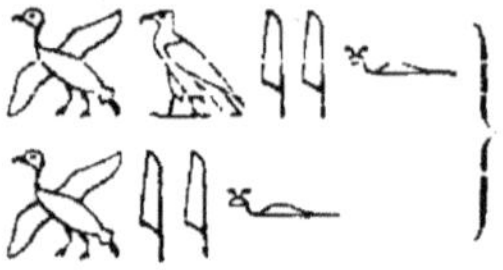 his.

pa, ***pai*** 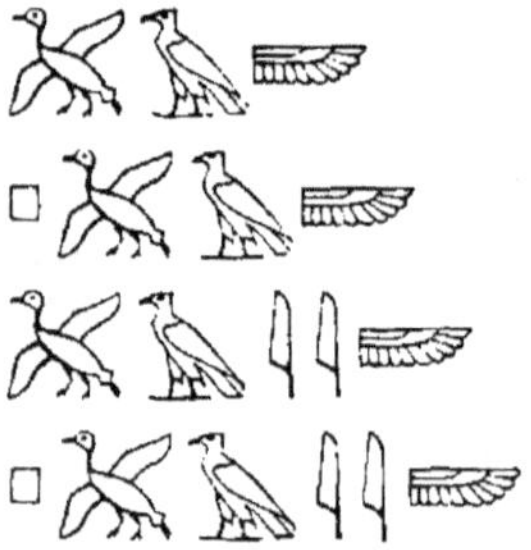 to fly, flight.

pait  bolt hole.

paut  stuff, substance, matter, cakes, offerings in general.

paut  primeval matter, the material out of which the gods and the universe were formed.

pauti 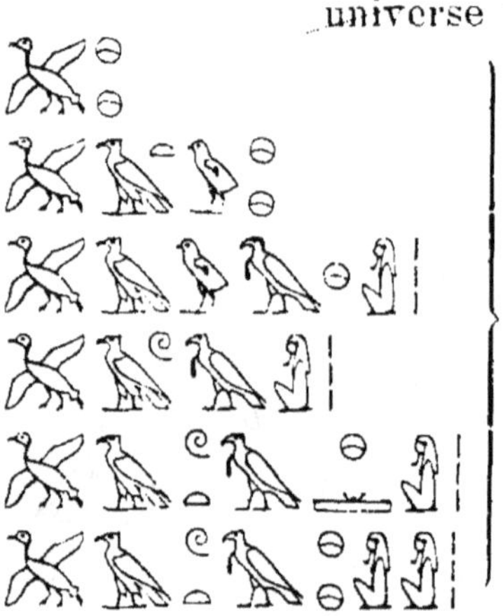 the god of primeval matter, the chief Egyptian god of the Predynastic Period.

paut ~~neteru~~ 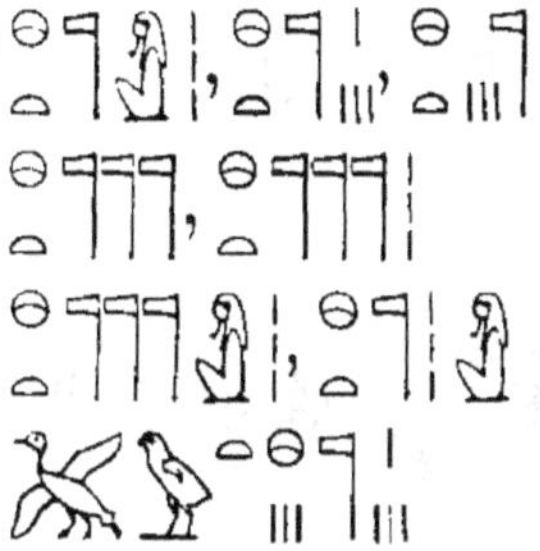 the whole company of the primeval gods, *i. e.,*  . The 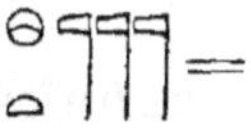 = the names  of Nu.

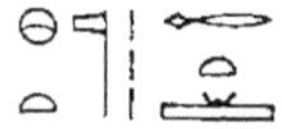 the Great Company of the gods.

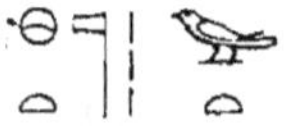 the Little Company of the gods.

 the complete Company of the gods.

paut-ti 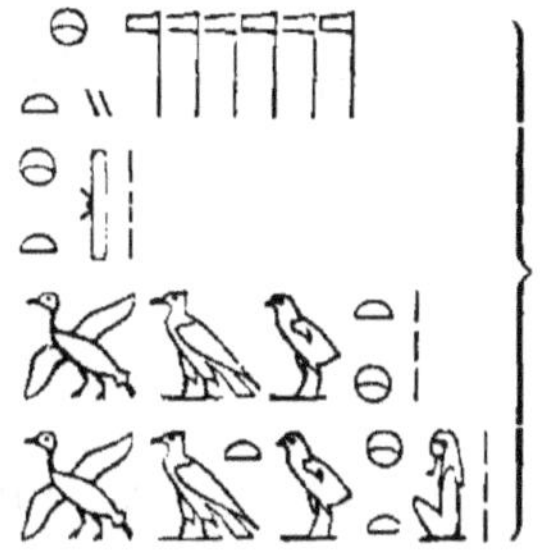 the Great and Little Companies of the gods.

pan 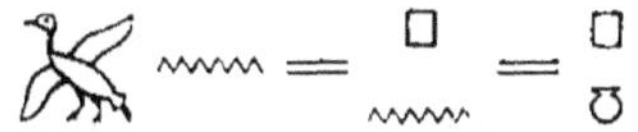 this.

Par, or ***Pal***  a proper name.

Parehaqakheperu  a proper name.

pas an ink jar.

pasekh

Pashakasa a proper name.

pat (?) light.

pā spark, flame, fire; plur.

pāt men and women, people, a class of people.

pāit ḥer-f human-faced.

pu a mark of emphasis:

puȧau cakes.

pui a demonstrative particle.

Punt

Punt the region whence came *ānti* (myrrh) and other aromatic gums and spices, a region in Africa near the southern end of the Red Sea. The district of Punt proper was probably situated some distance inland.

putrȧ (Nebseni Papyrus), an interrogative particle. What is this then? *i. e.*, what does this mean?

pef, ***pefa***, ***pefi***, ***pefat*** — a demonstrative particle.

pefes, ***pefses*** — to burn, be hot, fiery, a spark, to cook, bake.

pefsit — baked.

Pen, ***Pen-ḥeseb*** (?) — a proper name (?).

penā — to overturn, capsize (of a boat), to invert a matter.

peni — land (?).

penu — rat, mouse.

pens — . . . . . .

penq to beat to pieces ~~to macerate~~.

Penti the name of a god.

pert a season of the Egyptian year.

per house, abode, temple, habitation; plur. , celestial mansions.

perui double house

per āa "great house"

Per-ȧbu the temple of hearts, *i. e.*, the judgment hall.

per Ȧsȧr temple of Osiris.

Per-Ȧst the temple of Isis.

Per-Ȧsṭes the temple of Ȧsṭes.

Per-Unnut the temple of the Hour-goddess.

Per-ur the "great House", *i. e.*, the tomb.

Per-Ptaḥ 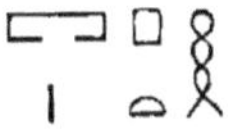 the temple of Ptaḥ at Memphis.

Per-Menȧ 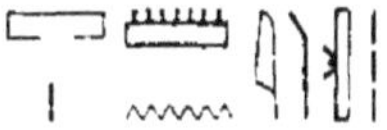 the house of coming into port, *i. e.*, the tomb.

Per-Menu  the temple of Menu.

Per-neḥeḥ  the house of eternity, *i. e.*, the tomb.

Per-neser 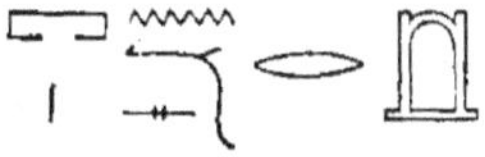 the house of fire.

Per-neter 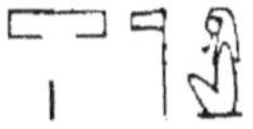
Per-neter-āa 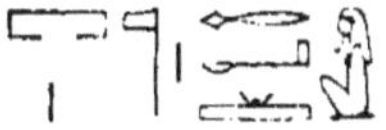 the temple of the god, *i. e.*, Osiris.

Per-Rertī (?)  the temple of Shu and Tefnut.

Per-Ḥapṭ-re 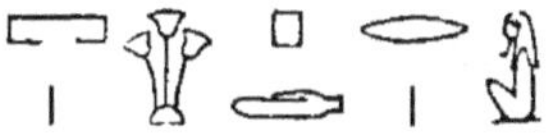 the temple of Ḥapṭ-re.

Per-ḥāt  the temple of hearts, *i. e*, the judgment hall.

Per-Ḥepṭ-ur  the temple of Ḥepṭ-ur.

Per-Ḥeru  the temple of Horus.

Per-Ḥetch 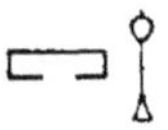 the "White House".

Per-Khenti-menȧtu-f 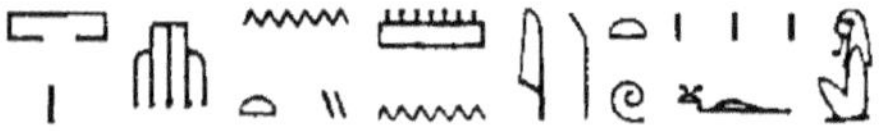 the temple of the "President of his dead".

Per-Sabut  the house of Sab (or Ḳeb), the earth (?).

Per-Sati 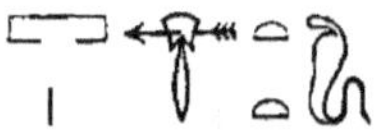 the temple of Sati.

Per-suten  the house of the king, *i. e.*, palace.

Per-seḥeptet 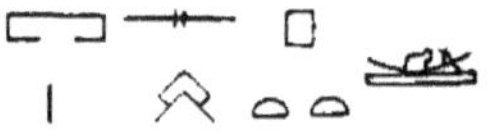 the temple of Seḥeptet.

per-shāt (?)  the house of books, *i. e.*, library.

Per-Kemkem  the temple of Kemkem.

Per-Keku  the temple of darkness.

per qebḥ 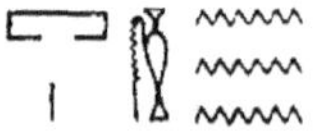 the house of coolness, *i. e.*, bath (?).

Per-tep-ṭu-f 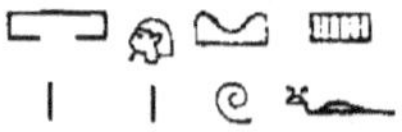 the temple of him that is on his hill, *i. e.*, Anubis.

Per-Tem 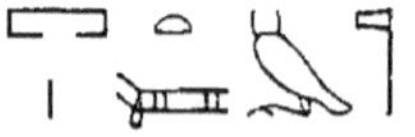 the temple of Tem.

Per-Ṭeḥuti 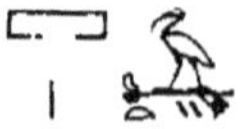 the temple of Thoth.

per, *peru*, *perr*, *perru* — to come forth, to rise up, to appear, to make oneself manifest; to come forth retreating; to appear in the presence.

comer forth; plur. things which appear, manifestations; to come forth; appearance, exit.

per-ā — to come forth boldly, brave.

per ḥer ta — to be born on the earth.

pert em hru — to come forth by, or in, the day; the title of several groups and Chapters of the Theban Recension of the Book of the Dead.

pert — offspring.

pert, *pertu* — things which appear, *i. e.*, offerings.

pert er kheru "things which appear at the words", *i. e.*, sepulchral offerings of bread, beer, oxen, geese, unguents, etc. Determinatives of these objects are usually added to thus:

perit temples.

peri strip of linen, bandage.

persen a kind of cake; plur.

pert [1] corn, grain in general.

white grain.

1. Perhaps "measures of grain" *ḥeqat*.

black grain.

red grain.

peḥ, *peḥu*, *peḥuut*, *peḥt* — to arrive at, attain to, to reach the end.

peḥu — the back part, the end.

peḥi, *peḥui*, *peḥti* — the lower part of the back, the buttocks, thighs.

peḥuit — stern of a boat.

peḥu — swamp, marsh.

peḥrer — to run.

peḥreru runners, a class of beings.

Peḥreri "Runner", a name of Rā.

peḥti strength of the thighs originally, then strength, might, power, in general.

pekha to separate.

Pekhat the name of a goddess.

pekhes to cover over, fall on.

pes ink-jar.

pesaḳes a mistake for to spit.

peseḥ to eat, to bite (of an insect or animal), to sting.

Peskheti a divine envoy.

pesesh to divide, to cleave, to allot.

divisions.

pesḳ to spit.

Pesḳ-re a proper name.

pesṭ (*pestch*) ||| ||| |||, nine, ninth.

pesṭ to shine, to illumine.

pesṭ
pesṭtu rays of light, radiance, brilliance.

Pesṭu the god of light.

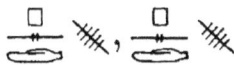

pesṭ to spread out like light.

pesṭ
pesṭu back, backbone;

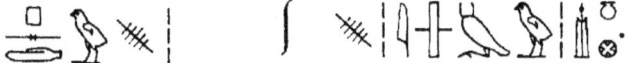

pesṭ tep to move the head.

pesh to spread out.

peshen	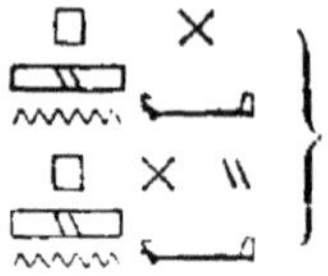	to divide, to cleave.
Peshennu		name of a city.
Peq		a region near Abydos.
pequ *peqt*	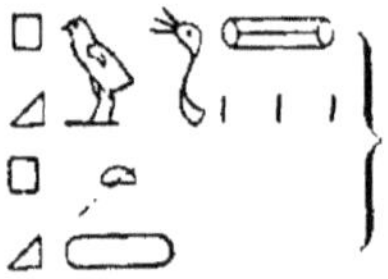	cakes, food.
peqt	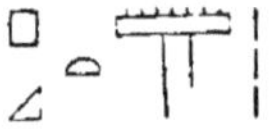	apparel of fine linen.
peḳ		to explain.
peḳ		byssus, very fine, semi-transparent linen.
Peḳa		name of a city.
peḳes *peḳas*		to spit upon.
Peḳes	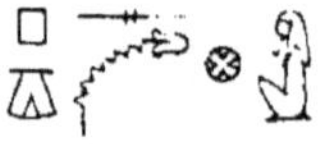	name of a city and a god.
pet		the sky, heaven; 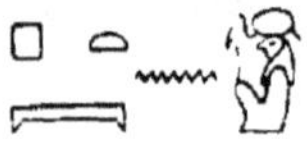 the heaven of Rā.

pet 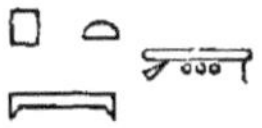 heaven and earth.

 heaven, earth and the Other World,

petti  heavenly beings, denizens of the sky.

pet  eastern heaven, or sky.

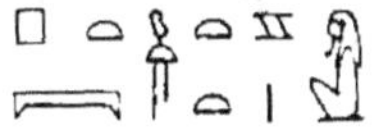 western heaven, or sky.

 northern heaven, or sky.

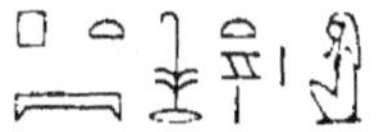 southern heaven, or sky.

petpet 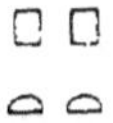 to crush, break.

Peti  a proper name.

pet  to see.

peti, ***peter***  who? what? an interrogative particle.

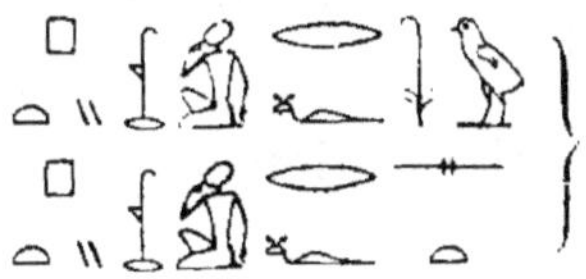 what then is it? *i. e.*, what does this mean?

peter / ***petrȧ*** 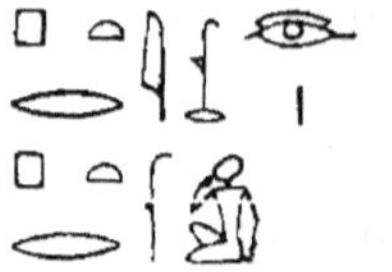 to see, look at, observe.

Petrȧ 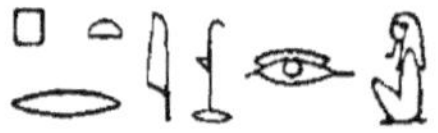 the name of a god.

Petrȧ-sen 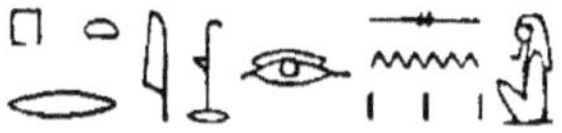 the name of a river.

Ptaḥ 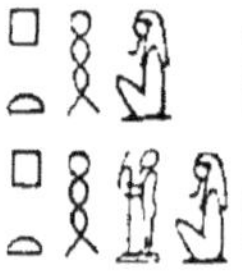 Ptaḥ, the blacksmith-god of Memphis. 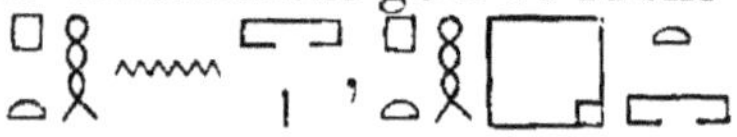 the temple of Ptaḥ.

Ptaḥ-ḥet-ka 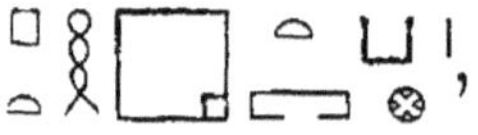, or Ḥet-ka-Ptaḥ, "House of the double of Ptaḥ", a name of Memphis. The common name of Egypt, Αἴγυπτος, appears to be derived from these words.

 Memphis of the Other World.

Ptaḥ res ȧneb-f  "Ptaḥ [to the] south [of] his Wall", Ptaḥ of Memphis.

Ptaḥ-Seker / ***Ptaḥ-Sekri*** 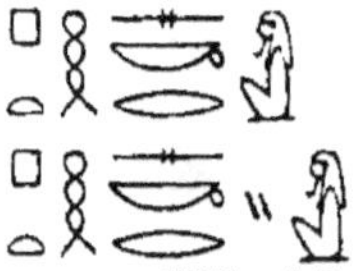 a dual god formed of Ptaḥ of Memphis and Seker, the old god of the Other World of the region of Memphis and Ṣakkârah.

Ptaḥ-Sekri-Tem  a triad formed of Ptaḥ of Memphis, Seker, and Temu, an old god of Ȧnu, or Heliopolis.

Ptaḥ-Tanen  a dual god formed of Ptaḥ of Memphis and Tanen, an old cosmic god of the region.

Ptaḥ-mes 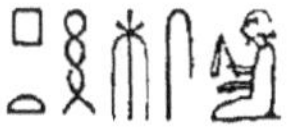 a proper name.

peṭ  to open out, to extend, to stretch out.

peṭ 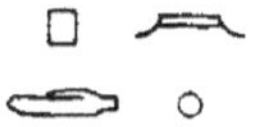 a kind of unguent.

Peṭeṭ 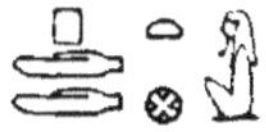 name of a god and city.

peṭsu  to break open, opener.

Peṭ-mer  "Broad Lake", the name of a shrine.

 F.

 he, him, it, its, his.

ʿa 

ʿat 

to bear, to carry, be carried, to lift up, to diminish through decay.

bearers, carriers.

Fa-ā — to raise the hand.
— the god of the lifted hand.

Fa-ākhu — a proper name.

Fa-pet — "Supporter of the sky"; the name of the god of the Seventh Āat.

Fa-Ḥeru — "bearer of Horus"; a name of Osiris.

Fat-Ḥeru — "the city of the bearer of Horus".

Fau-ḥeru-sen — "those who lift up their faces"; a class of divine beings.

fau — riches, wealth, abundance.

fenkhu — offerings.

Fenkhu — the name of certain dwellers in Syria.

fent — worm, serpent, reptile; plur.

fenṭ  nose; plur. 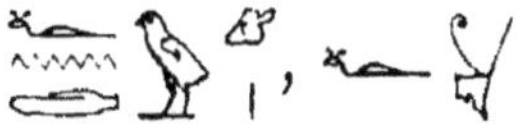 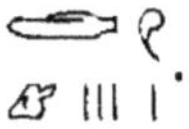

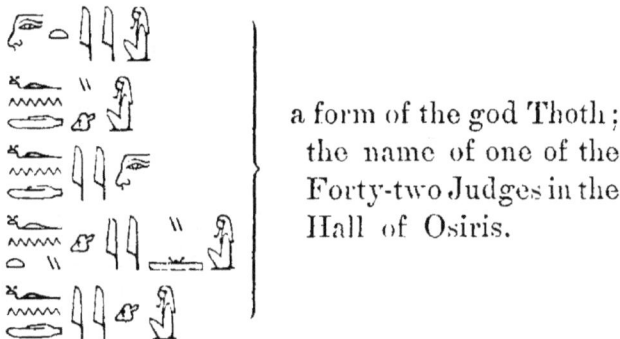

Fenṭi  a form of the god Thoth; the name of one of the Forty-two Judges in the Hall of Osiris.

fekh 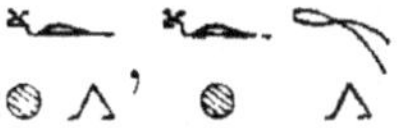 to untie, unloose, destroy.

fekhekh  to burst through.

feqat  a bread-cake, food in general.

feḳa  to make water.

fetu 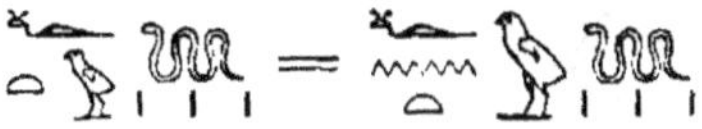 worms.

fettu  fish.

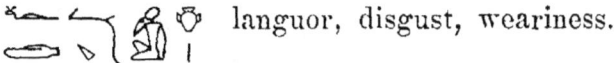

feṭ-ȧb 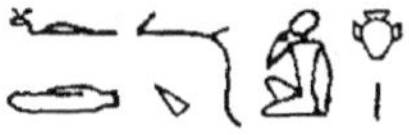 languor, disgust, weariness.

fṭu  four;  fourth.

feṭqu  destruction, damage.

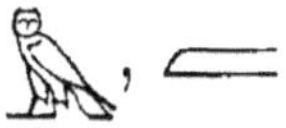 M.

em  sign of the present participle.

em  particle of negation, no, not; 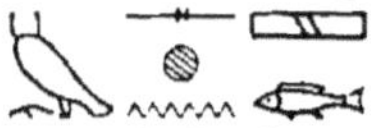 let not make to stink (my name).

em 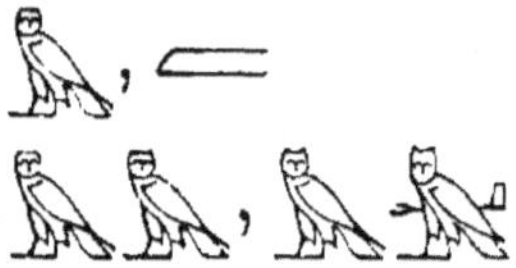 in, into, from, on, at, with, out from, of, upon, as, like, according to, in the manner of, among.

em āb 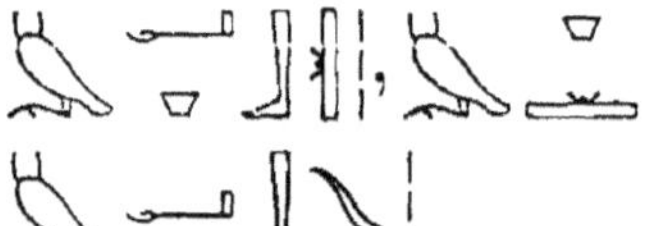

em ābu 

em āb sa  opposite, in front of, confronting.

em baḥ  before, in the presence of; the old form is .

em baḥ ā  before, in the presence of.

em paitu  before, when not yet.

em nem (uhem) 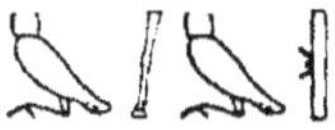
em nem (uhem) ā 
} a second time.

em ruti  outside.

em ḥāt 
em ḥāti ā 
} before.

em ḥer  upon.

em khen 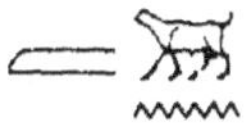
em khennu 

em khennu ā 
} inside, within.

em khert 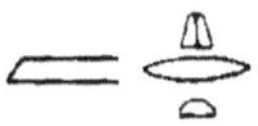 on behalf of.

em khet 
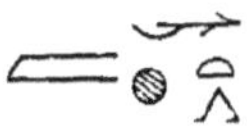
} behind, after, in the train of.

em sa  at the back of, behind, after.

em qeṭ round about, throughout.

ma part of a boat.

ma to be new, to renew, made new, new.

maui

mat

maa to see, to look upon, to behold, observe, perceive; seen, observed; plur. part.

maau

maat

maa sight, view, glance.

maat (or ***àrit***?) eye; eye t[o] eye; an eye

maati (or ***ȧriui***?) 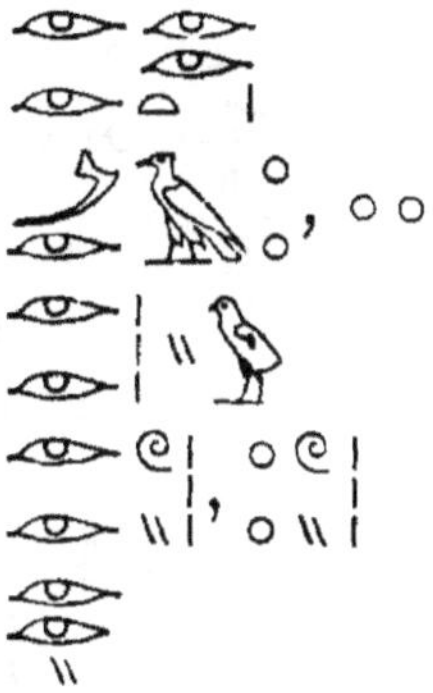 the two eyes.

maat  eyes.

maat nebt  every eye, *i. e.*, every body, all people, folk, mankind.

maat Rā 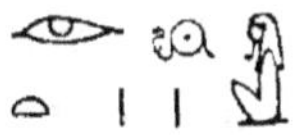 eye of Rā.

 right eye of Rā.

maat Ḥeru  eye of Horus, the name of offerings.

maat Shu  eye of Shu, *i. e.*, the sun.

maat Tem 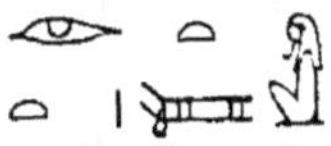 eye of Tem, *i. e.*, the sun.

maa-ȧnt-f  the name of a plank, or peg, in the magic boat (Chap. XCIX).

maa-ȧnuf  the name of one of the Forty-two Judges in the Hall of Osiris.

Maa-àtef-f-kheri-beq-f  the name of one of the spirits who guard the bier of Osiris.

Maati-f-em-khet  "he whose two eyes are of fire"; the name of one of the Forty-two Judges in the Hall of Osiris.

Maati-f-em-ṭes  "he whose two eyes are like knives"; the name of one of the Forty-two Judges in the Hall of Osiris.

Maa-em-ḳerḥ-ànnef-em-hru  "he who seeth in the night what is brought to him in the day"; a proper name.

Maa-ḥa-f, ***Maa-ḥa***  "seeing what is behind him"; a proper name.

Maa-ḥeḥ-en-renput  "seeing millions of years"; a proper name.

Maatuf-ḥer-ā  a proper name.

Maaiu-su (?)  a proper name.

Maa-thet-f 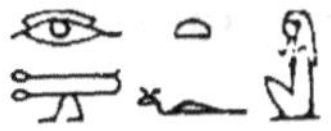 a proper name.

maar 
maȧr  } restraint, misery, affliction, wretched one, oppressed one.

maȧ  lion.

maȧuti  the lion-lioness god, *i. e.*, Shu and Tefnut.

maā
maāu 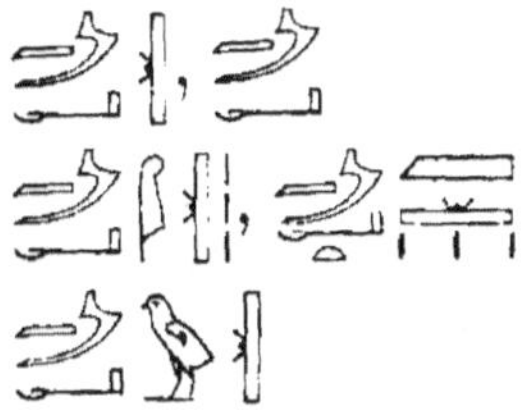 } to be right, straight, just, true, to pay which is legally due, or what it is right to pay, to give a statutory offering.

maā-kheru 
maāt-kheru 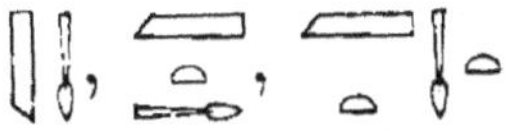 } "true word", or "true of word", or "true voice", or "true of voice", he whose word when spoken is followed unfailingly by the effect desired. These words are placed after the

names of the dead, and appear to mean something like "triumphant", a crown of triumph; to be right.

maāt truth, what is right, true, straightness, law, order; doubly true: the scales balance exactly. "[with] the cord of maāt", *i. e*, uniformly and regularly; beautiful truth.

a righteous judge.

true, right of heart.

real lapis-lazuli.

thy genuine friend.

real royal scribe.

in very truth.

really true.

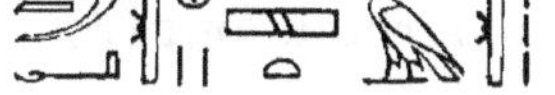 most truly a mystery.

Maāt 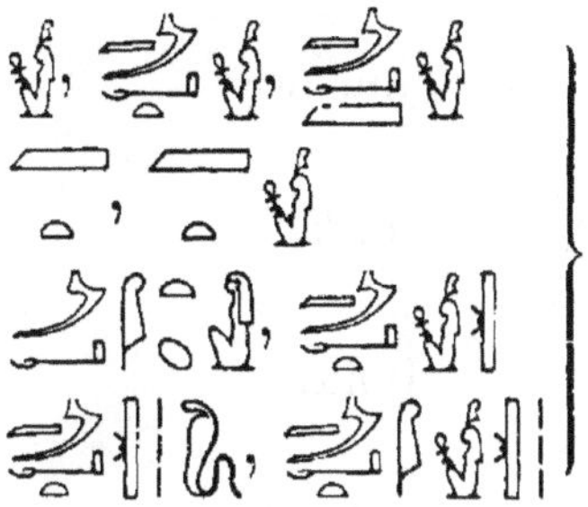 the goddess of truth, law, order, etc.

Maāti  the two goddesses of truth, law, order, etc.

maāti  truth, right.

Maātiu 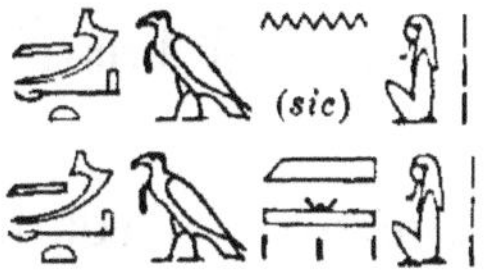 the gods of truth, law, order, etc.

maāt 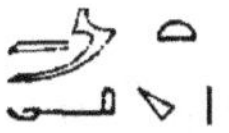 a district, or region.

Maāti 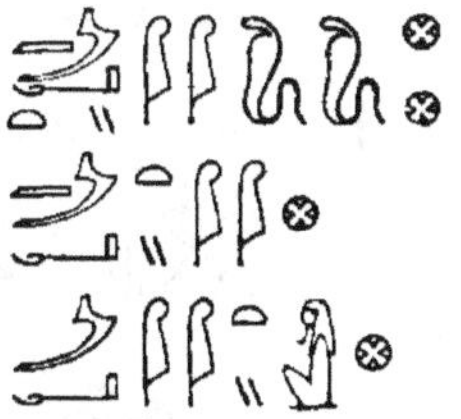 the cities or districts of the two Maāti goddesses.

maā  limb.

maā 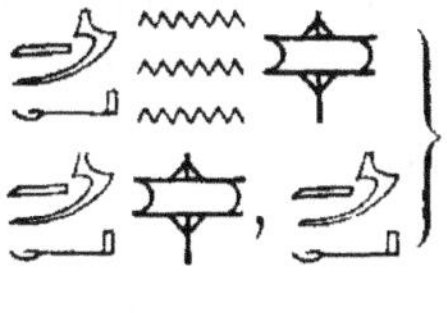 windsail, wind, breeze; plur. 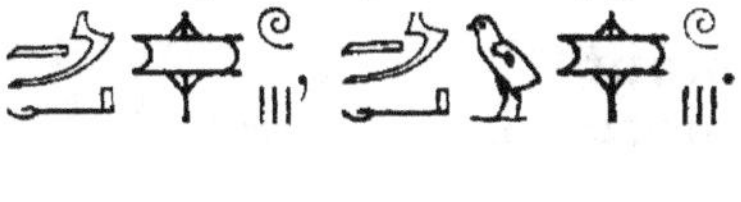

maā to stretch out (?).

maā to journey.

maautu stalk.

maftet lynx.

mama palm (?) tree.

Manu the Mountain of Sunset.

maḥa a part of the head.

maḥu part of a boat.

maḥu a crown, wreath.

mast leg; dual .

Mastiu a group of star-gods.

maqet ladder; plur. .

maḳ a precious stone.

maut / ***matu*** incense.

Matchat		the name of a city.
må		as, like, concerning, even as.
		like that same one.
		inasmuch as, even as.
		like that which.
		after the manner of.
måti		a person or thing resembling another person or thing, type, copy.
		divine image; his divine images.
måtet		picture, likeness, similitude, like unto, copy of; likewise.
mån		to-day.

mȧnt , , , with , daily.

mȧu to be like .

mȧu , cat, cat's skin.

mȧu lion; lions.

mȧu to knead, to mould, to fashion.

mā , give, grant, let there be! who? what? behold! behold thou! behold ye!

mā
māȧ
māȧi come! give! bring! .

Māau-taui name of a god.

māāt place.

māāat name of a place.

māb thirty.

mābiu the thirty great gods.

mābit 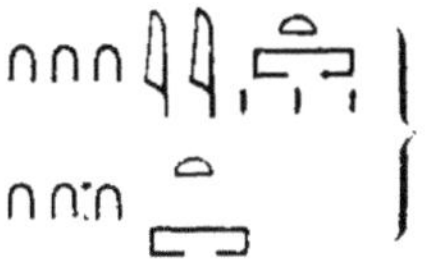 name of a place or building.

māfket 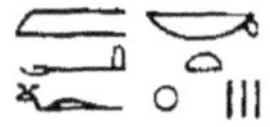 turquoise.

Mānāat 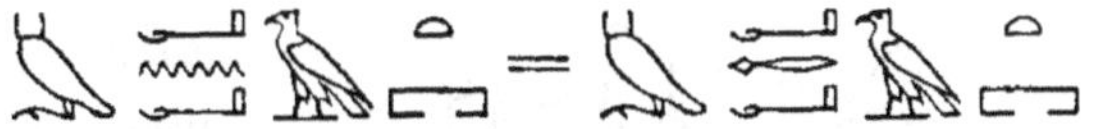 ?

Mārqathȧ  the name of a god.

māhaiu  people, tribe, generations (?).

māhaṭṭi  fire.

māhui  milk vessels, udders (?).

māhenȧ 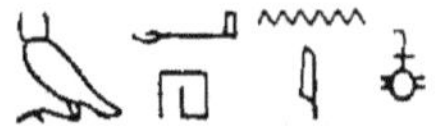 milk vessel.

māḥā  standard.

Māḥu 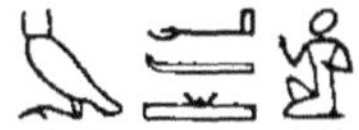 the name of a man.

mākha 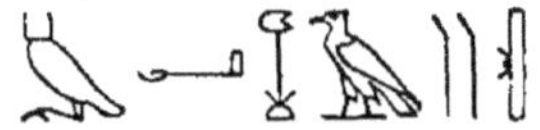 to weigh.

mākha 
mākhat 
mākhaȧt 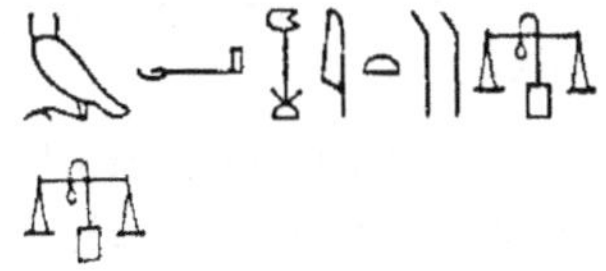
a pair of scales, a balance; 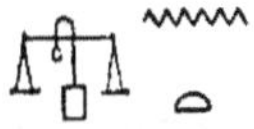  the balance of the earth.

mākhatu  intestines.

mākhait  sledge for a sacred boat or god.

mākhiu  altars with incense burning on them.

mākhent 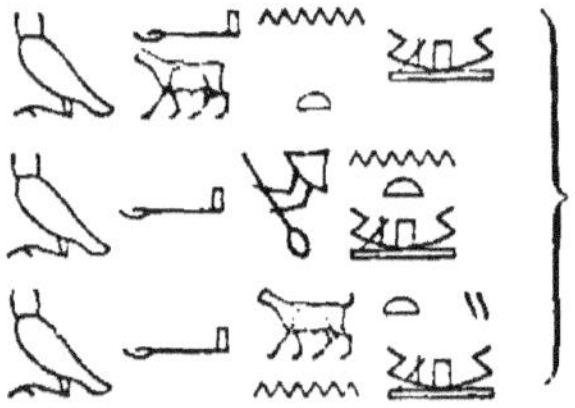 a boat.

māsheru  evening, eventide.

mākat  place.

māku  to protect, protection.

māki  protector.

māket  a thing which protects, amulet.

mākefitiu 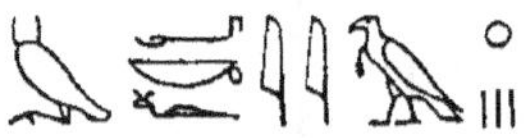 objects made of turquoise.

mākḥa 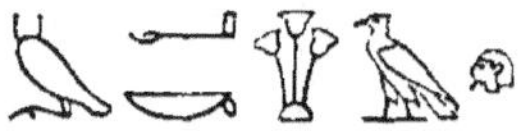 to turn round, or behind, back of the head.

māket  station, place.

māqet  ladder.

mātau  weapons, short spears, harpoons.

mātenu  ways, roads, paths.

Māṭes 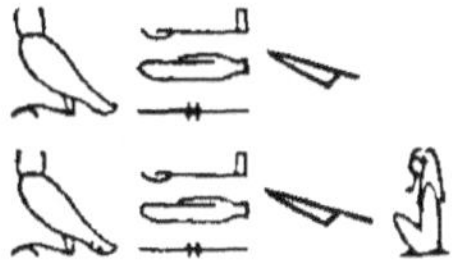 a proper name.

Māṭes-årui (?) 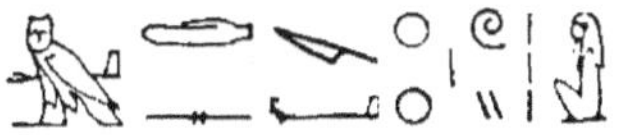 the gods with knife-like eyes.

māṭet (***māntchet***) 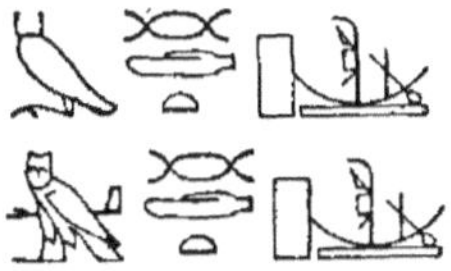 the boat in which the sun sailed from sunrise to noon.

māthennu  ways, roads, paths.

mātcha  phallus.

mātchabu 
mātchabet  chain, fetter.

mātchabet  part of a ship.

Mātcheṭ  a proper name.

mātcheṭ to use force, to compel, to constrain.

Mi-sheps a proper name.

mu water, essence.

pool; the pool of the well of Àmenti; the pool of Kher-āḥa.

the god of the water, or divine essence; essence of Rā.

brow (surface?) of the water.

what is in the water.

m[u]it water.

mu a decoction, as in:—

ānkham flower water.

myrrh water.

saltpetre water.

incense water.

incense water.

dirty water.

mut mother.

muti parents.

Mut the Mother-goddess *par excellence* of Egypt; "Mut in the horizon of heaven". mother-deities.

mut weights for scales.

Mut-restȧ a proper name.

Mut-ḥetepth a proper name.

mut to die, death, the dead, the damned; plur.

Menu name of a god of generation and fertility.

Menu-Ḥeru Menu + Horus.

Menu-suten-Ḥeru-nekht a name of Osiris.

Menu-qeṭ a proper name.

men, ***ment*** to be permanent, stable, firm, to be fixed, to remain; abiding, fixed.

menu possessions, things which abide.

menu chamber.

menu bases, pedestals.

Ment name of a god.

menti, ***mentiu*** the two thighs.

men to be in pain, sick.

ment, ***menut*** pain, sickness, disease.

men such and such an one.

Menȧ name of a god or city.

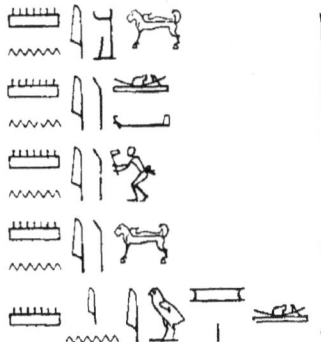

menȧ to tie up a boat to the mooring post, to come into port, to land, to die; arriving.

menȧ, ***menȧt*** post to which boats are tied up or moored.

menȧu mooring posts, stakes of death.

menȧ, ***menȧt*** end, ending a happy ending, or death.

menȧ, ***menȧ-tu*** the dead.

menȧt funerary bed, bier, death.

meni to slay, put to death.

menȧt 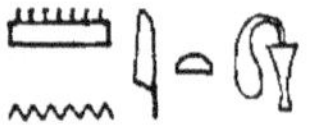 a musical instrument.

menāt 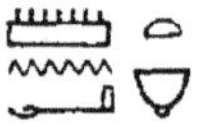 breast.

menu  ministrants.

menmen 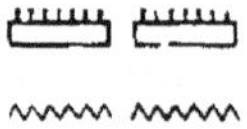 to go about.

menment 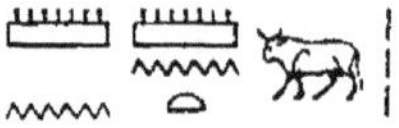 cattle, farm stock.

menḥ 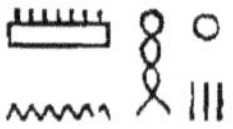 wax.

menḥu  to offer up.

Menḥu 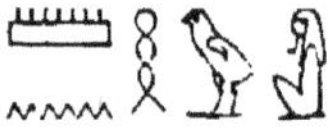 name of a god.

menkhu 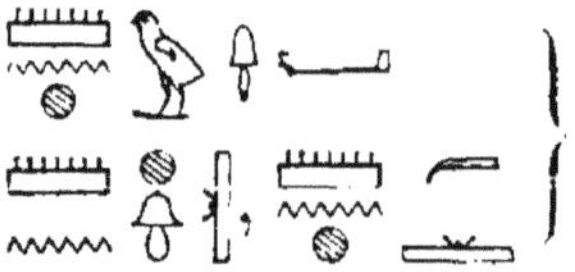 to work, wrought, well finished, excellent, worked or inlaid, perfect, well disposed, well-doing;  perfected;  valuable things.

Menkh 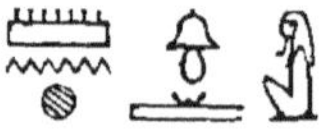 the beneficent god (?).

menkhet 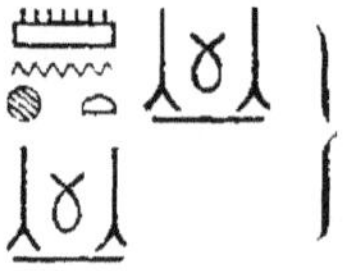 apparel, clothes, garments.

Menqet  the name of a goddess.

Ment  a proper name.

ment 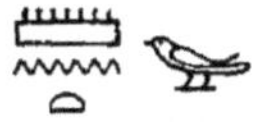 swallow.

menṭ-t 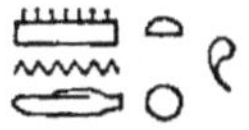 apple of the eye.

menṭi 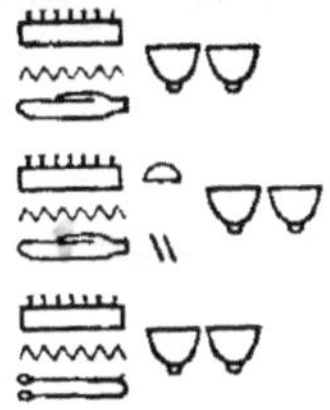 the two breasts.

Menthu 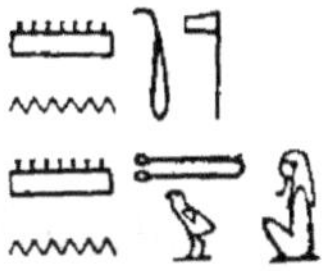 the War-god of Hermonthis, who was at a later period identified with Rā.

Mentchat  the name of a city.

ner  overseer, superintendent.

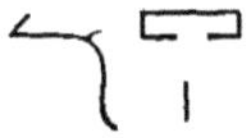 major-domo, steward.

 officer of soldiers.

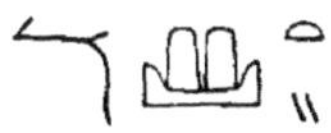 overseer of the granaries.

ner  a water-course, canal.

mer pool, tank, cistern; plur.

swamps, lakes.

Lake of Maāt.

Lake of the Maāti gods.

Lake of the geese.

Lake of the horizon-gods.

Lake of Fire.

name of a mythological Lake.

meru peasants, agricultural labourers

mer to be sick, ill; sick

diseased, or perhaps = the dead.

meru
meràu pain, sickness, disease, decay.

Mer a proper name.

mer	to love, to desire, to wish for, to will.
meru	loving, lover, beloved;
merr	lover, beloved;
merru	lovers.
mertu	love, desire, wish, will.
mert	
merit	
merrt	
Mer	a proper name.
Mert	name of a goddess.
Meritti	a group of gods.
Merti	two goddesses.
ner	to bind, to tie.

meru		swathing, bandage.
Mer-ur		the Mnevis Bull.
merāḥāt		tomb, sepulchre.
meruḥ		oar, paddle.
meriut	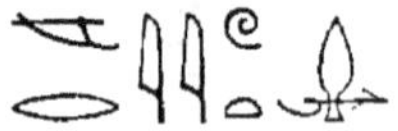	a kind of tree.
Meres		a proper name (?).
Meri-s	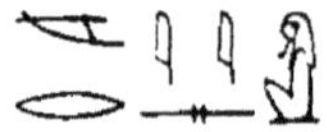	
merḥ	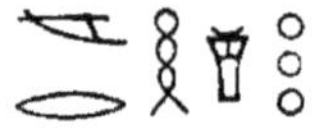	wax.
merḥet	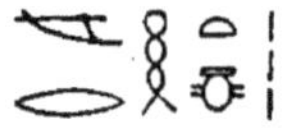	
mert	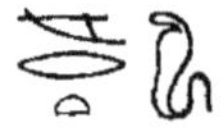	the name of a part of a boat.
Mert		name of a city.
Mert		a proper name.
mehait		roof.
meḥ		cubit, 

meḥ  to fill, be full; ,  full;  filling, filler;   the filling of the Ut-chat, *i. e.*, full moon;   the filling of the Eye of Horus;   a stream filled with flowers.

meḥ sa 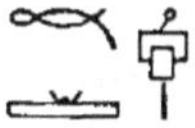 to be complete.

meḥ  to be inundated, submerged, drowned.

meḥit 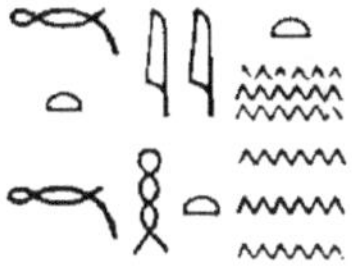 flood.

Meḥ-urt, *Meḥt-urt* 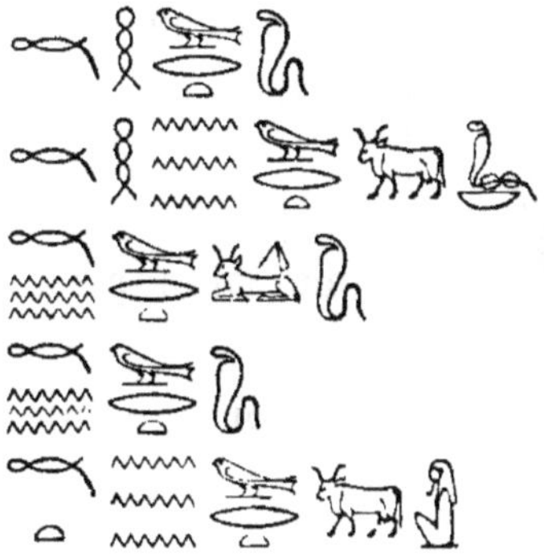 a very ancient sky goddess, afterwards identified with Nut.

neḥ 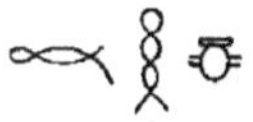 unguent (?).

meḥ 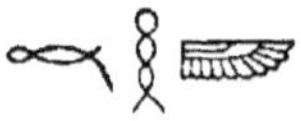 wing, pinion.

meḥ  garland.

Meḥānuti-Rā  a proper name (?).

meḥut  offerings.

meḥuti 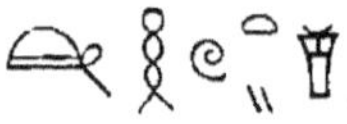 oil.

Meḥi  }
Meḥiu  } a proper name.

meḥit 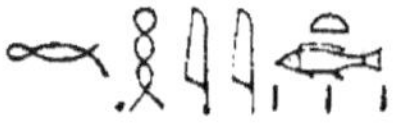 fish.

meḥef 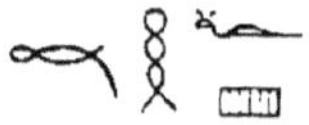 a kind of stone.

Meḥen  }
Meḥent 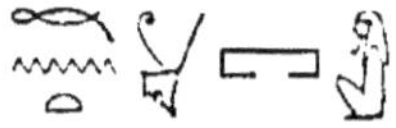 } name of a god and goddess.
Meḥenit 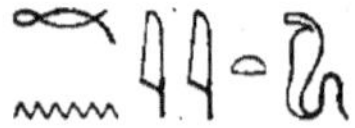 }

Meḥenet  name of a city.

meḥenet  the north wind.

meḥt  placed before numbers; 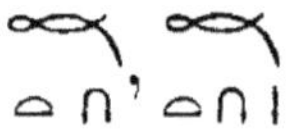 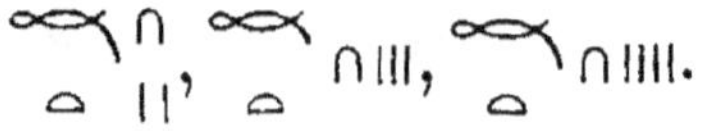

meḥt vessel, plaque (?).

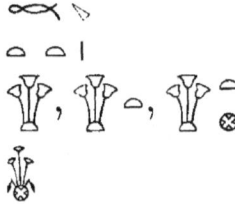

meḥt
meḥti the north in general, the north of Egypt, *i. e.*, the Delta; north-west.

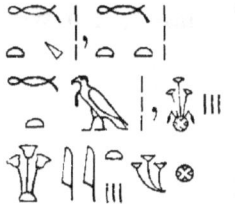

meḥtiu northern beings, men or gods, lords of the north, *i. e.*, in late times, the Greeks; nest of the northerners.

Meḥt the goddess of the North.

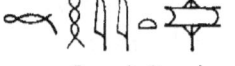

meḥt
meḥit
meḥuiu(?)
meḥu the north wind.

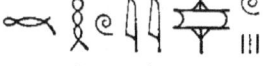

meḥti oil.

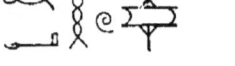

Meḥti* (?)*-sāḥ-neter the name of one of the Seven Cows.

meḥṭet to bathe.

Em-khent-maati (?) (?).

em khennu within.

mekhsef name of a wooden instrument.

mes, ***mesu*** to bring; bringer, bringing.

mest to walk, approach.

to give birth to, to bring forth, to produce, to fashion; , born of; born; giving birth a second time to mortals; ; .

mest , genetrix.

mest  birth; plur. 

mestu  birthday.

mes  child, offspring.

mesu
mesesiu  children.

mesu nebu  all who are born, *i. e.*, the human race.

mesu beṭesh  malicious but powerless fiends.

mesu ent Nu  children of the divine water, *i. e.*, plants.

mesu Nut children of the Sky-goddess.

mesu Ḥeru children of Horus (Kesthȧ, Ḥāpi, Ṭuamut-f, Qebḥsennuf).

mesu Serȧt beqet . . . .

mesit cakes eaten in the evening.

mesbeb (?) banded (?).

Mes-peḥ a proper name.

Mes-Ptaḥ a proper name.

Mes-em-neter a proper name.

mesmes to count (?).

mesmes Vol. II, p. 251, l. 2.

mesnekht birthplace.

emseḥ, ***emseḥu*** crocodile; plur. , eight crocodiles .

emseḥu  to slay.

meskhen

meskhent

the birth-place of a god or goddess; a region in the Sekhet-Àaru where the gods were produced:   the four birth-places of Abydos.

Meskhen-āat  the name of a goddess of birth, or of a birth-place.

Meskhen-ment 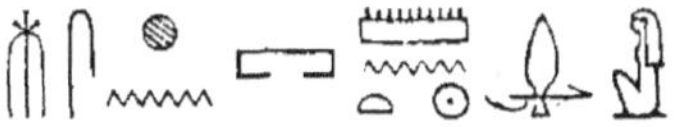 the name of a goddess of birth, or of a birth-place.

Meskhen-nefert 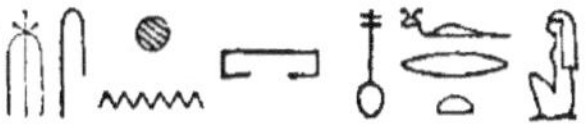 the name of a goddess of birth, or of a birth-place.

Meskhen-Seqebet 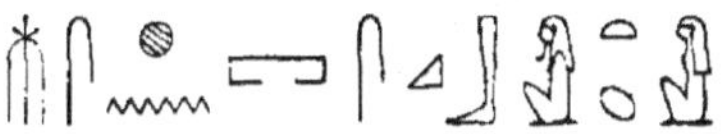 the name of a goddess of birth, or of a birth-place.

Mesespekh 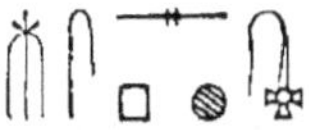 a proper name.

Messhenu 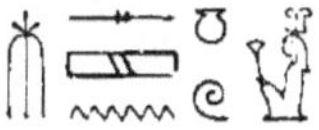 = Meskhenu.

meskȧ  skin.

Mesqen 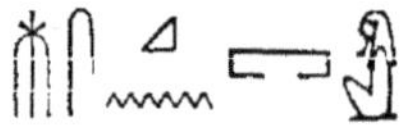
Mesqet 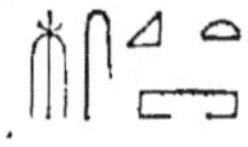 a region of the Other World through which the deceased must pass before he could reach the Sekhet-Ȧaru.

mesqet 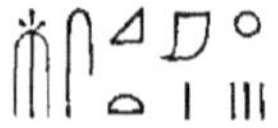 weapons.

mesṭemu  to paint the eyes with *koḥl.*

mesṭemet  eye-paint, stibium, *koḥl.*

mesṭet 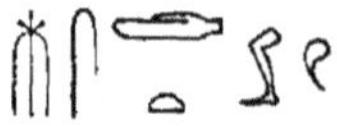 leg.

mesṭ 
mesṭeṭ 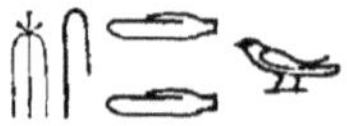 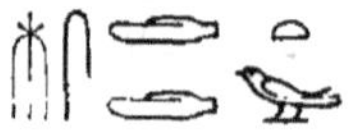 to dislike, to hate.

mesthȧ  palette. The true reading is Ḳesthȧ, *q. v.*

Mesthȧ 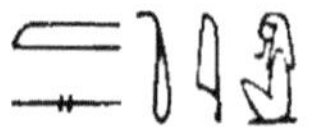 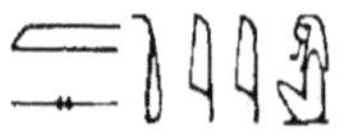 one of the four sons of Horus. The true reading is Ḳesthȧ, *q. v.*

mestcher  ear.

  the two ears.

mestchetch  to hate.

meshā  bowmen, soldiers.

meshen  Chap. CX. B. 16.

Em-qeṭqeṭ  the name of a spirit, or god.

met (***mut***)  the dead, the damned.

met ten.

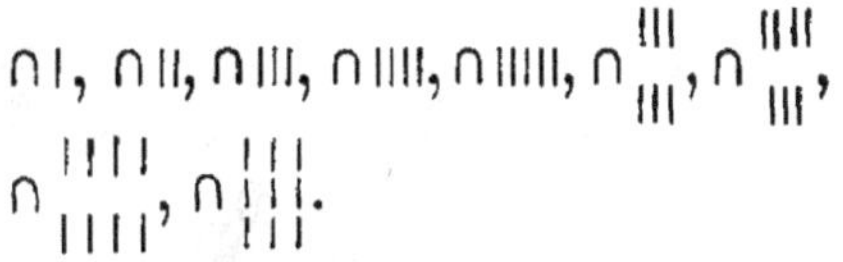

tenth.

metu  venom, poison.

metut  seed, progeny;

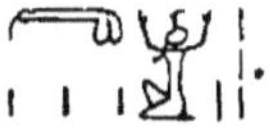

metmet 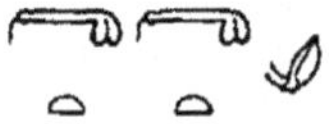 to eavesdrop (?).

met, ***meti*** 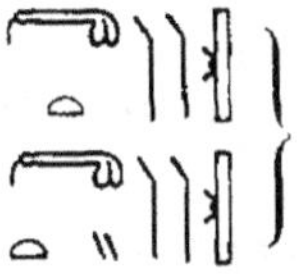 to be right, what is right, the mean; 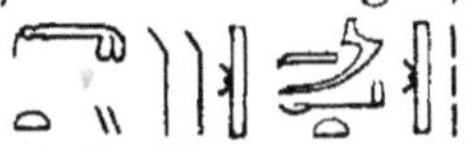 the exact truth (?).

meter, ***metru***  to bear witness, to testify, to give evidence.

meṭu  to speak, to talk, tell, declare.

meṭ, meṭu / ***meṭet***  word, speech, talk, declaration; pronouncement.

meṭut  words, speech, things (like the Hebrew דָּבָר);  word of wisdom; 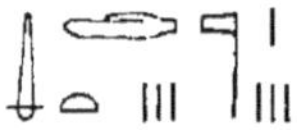 words of the gods;  words of truth:   words of evil, blasphemy.

Meṭu-ta-f  a proper name.

Meṭes-ḥer-àri-mer  "Knife-face, guardian of the Lake"; the name of the doorkeeper of the Sixth Ārit.

Meṭes-sen the name of the door-keeper of the Seventh Ārit.

metch to be deep; deep; very deep.

metchtu abyss.

deeps, depths.

metchaub to fetter.

metchet salve, ointment, oil.

N.

n a preposition, in, to, for, because. With additions:—

n of: with plural following,

n — we, us.

n — no, not = ; ; = ; invisible.

na — those, the; those who are after.

naiu — those of; those of thine; those belonging to.

na, *nai*, *nȧu* — air, wind.

Naȧrik — a proper name (?).

Naȧrruṭ, *Naȧrruṭf*, *Nanȧaruṭf*, *Nȧareruṭ* — "the place where nothing grows", a name for a region of the Other World. See Ȧn-ruṭ-f.

Nasaqbubu name of a god.

Nak (?) =en Aker (?).

Nathkerthi name of a god.

n-ȧ I, me, my.

nȧh injury.

nȧs to call, cry out, invoke;

nȧsu invoked.

Nȧk the name of a fiend and enemy of Rā.

fiends, enemies.

ā

āai to journey, to travel, to come, to arrive, to advance.

āt

āȧu name of a god or devil.

āu fiend, devil; plur.

nāā — a decree (?), a design, picture.

nār — a reed pen, painting reed.

Nārt — a proper name.

Nārtiānkhemsenf — name of a fiend.

nāsh — mighty one.

nāḳ — to break open, to split.

nāḳeḳa — to cackle.

ni (?) — in ... and ... .

nimā — who?

nini — to salute, to acclaim.

nu — of. ... .

Nu — name of a scribe.

ṇu		the watery abyss of the sky.
Nu		the Sky-god.
nu		these; these very ones; these; these who.
nu		season, period, time.
nu		to see, to watch, to observe
ɔu		to go away, go about.
ɔu		to be strong, to strengthen.
ɔu		hours.
ıu (?)		adorations, praise, worship.
ıuit		weapon, knife, short dagger.
ub		gold; fine gold; golden light.
ʼub-ḥeḥ		"Eternal gold"; a name of Osiris.

nub, ***nubȧu*** — to mould, to shape, to fashion, to form; , fashioned, inlaid.

nubḥeḥ — blossom, flower.

Nubti — name of the god of Ombos, *i. e.*, Set.

nun — to pay homage.

nur — a kind of bird.

nuḥ — to masturbate.

nuḥ — to bind, to tie, to fetter.

cords, cordage, rigging, tackle.

nuḥu — flower, blossom.

nuḥti — , pair of horns.

nukh — to be burnt.

nuk — I. ; I, even I.

nut  the sky, heaven.

Nut 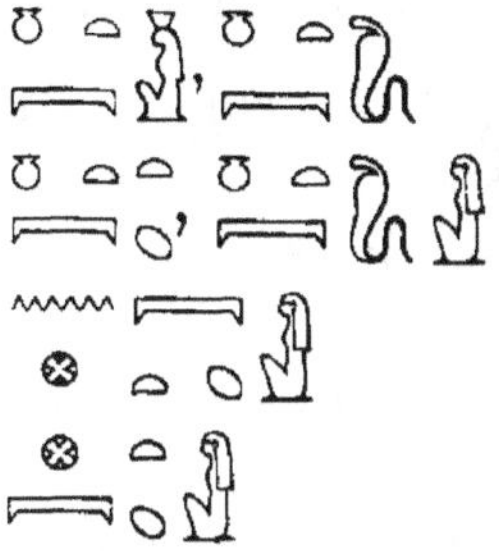 the Sky-goddess, the wife of Seb, or Ḳeb; the name of a sail in the magic boat.

Nut  the night sky.

nut  cords, ropes.

nut  city; plur. ; 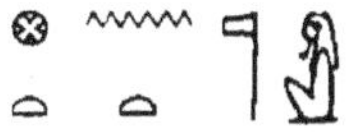 city of god.

nuti  citizens.

nui

nut 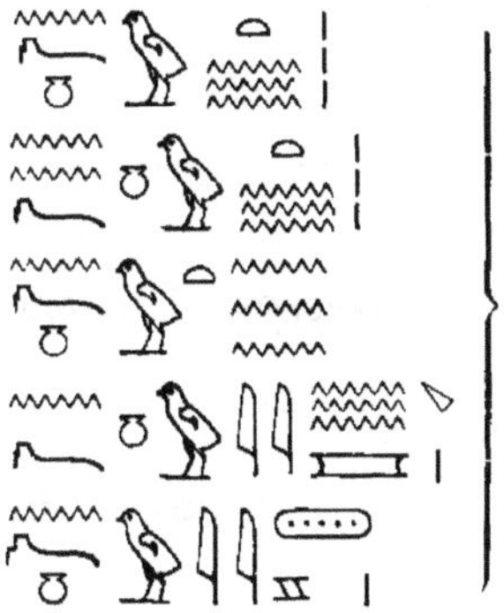 canal, stream, river, flood, any large collection of water.

Nut-urt "great city"; the name of a lake in Sekhet-Àaru.

Nutu-hru a proper name.

nuti sweet air (?).

nuṭ to bear, to carry, to journey.

Nuṭiu a class of divine beings.

neb, ***nebt*** (in late times or), each, every, any, all; plur. , ; ; every kind of evil thing.

neb with *bu*, , everywhere. See also under .

neb , , , lord, master, sovereign; plur. , , .

nebt lady, mistress; in late times "lord".

neb lord of, possessor of, owner of, *e. g.*, , , ; compare the use of בַּעַל.

neb ȧbu "lord of hearts"; a name of Ȧḥi.

neb Ȧbti "lord of the East"; a title of Ṛā.

neb ȧmakh "lord of veneration", *i.e.*, one to whom service is rendered and homage paid;

neb Ȧmenti "lord of Ȧmenti"; a name of Osiris; the lords of the Other World; "lady of Ȧmenti", a title of Hathor.

neb āāui "lord of the two hands".

neb ābui "lord of the two horns"; a title of Ȧmen; the name of one of the Forty-two Judges in the Hall of Osiris.

neb ānkh "lord of life"; a title of Osiris.

the title of the sarcophagus and the bier; late form

nebt ānkh "lady of life"; a title of Isis.

nebt unnut "lady of the hour"; a proper name.

neb urert "lord of the *urert* crown"; a title of Osiris and of Horus.

neb useru "lord of strength, or powers"; a title of the Sun-god.

neb baiu "lord of souls"; a title of several gods.

neb pāt "lord of mankind"; a title of Horus.

nebt per "lady of the house", *i. e.*, a married woman, house-wife. It is possible that is not intended to be read, and is only a determinative. The Egyptian to-day speaks of his "house", meaning his wife, or his wife and family.

neb mau possessor of many eyes, or good sight.

neb maāt possessor of truth or law, , .

neb Maāti lord of the double City of Truth.

nebt māket

nebu en meḥt "lords of the north"; the peoples of the Delta; in late times the Greeks.

Neb nebu "Lord of lords"; the name of one of the Forty-two Judges in the Hall of Osiris.

neb nefu "lord of winds"; a title of Osiris.

neb nemt "lord of steps", *i. e.*, one who has the power to walk.

neb neru "lord of victories"; a title of the heart of Osiris.

neb neter meṭut "lord of the words of the god", *i. e.*, one who understands the hieroglyphic language.

neb renput "lord of years", *i. e.*, aged one.

neb rekhit "lord of the *rekhit*", a class of men.

neb Re-stau "lord of Re-stau", *q. v.*, a title of Osiris.

neb henu "lord of praises", *i. e.*, he who is praised.

neb ḥeru "lord of faces"; the name of one of the Forty-two Judges in the Hall of Osiris.

neb ḥeḥ "lord of eternity"; a title of Osiris; plur.

Neb khat the goddess Nephthys (?)

nebu khaut "lords of altars", *i. e.*, gods to whom altars have been dedicated.

neb khāu "lord of crowns, or risings"; a title of Rā.

neb khut "lord of the horizon"; a title of Rā.

neb kheperu "lord of transformations", *i. e.*, he of many changes.

neb khet "lord of things", *i. e.*, lord of creation; plur.

nebu Kher-Āḥa "lords of Kher-āḥa", *i. e.*, Temu and his fellow deities.

nebt Sau the "lady of Saïs", *i. e.*, Neith.

neb setut "lord of light", *i. e.*, giver of light.

neb senṭ "lord of fear", *i. e.*, he who inspires fear.

neb sekhti 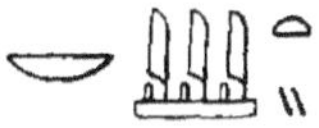 "lord of the field", *i. e.*, master of the field, a title of the Bull-god.

nebt Seker  "lady of silence"; a name of the Other World.

nebu kau  "lords of food", *i. e.*, gods to whom food offerings are given.

neb kesu  "lord of bowings", *i. e.*, he to whom homage is paid.

neb qerset  "lord of the bier"; a title of Osiris.

neb taui 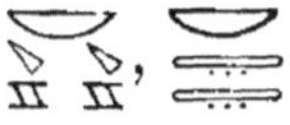 "lord of the Two Lands", *i. e.*, of Upper and Lower Egypt.

neb taiu 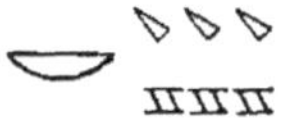 "lord of the lands", *i. e.*, of the world, a title of Osiris.

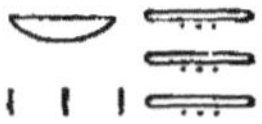 "lords of lands".

Nebt-taui 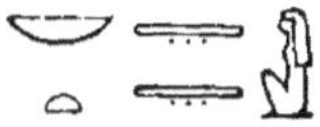 the name of a lake in the Sekhet Åaru.

Nebt-taui em karå  the name of the mooring post for the magic boat.

Neb ta ānkhtet  "lord of the Land of Life", *i. e.*, the Other World.

Neb ta tchesert  "lord of the Holy Land"; a title of Osiris.

neb tau "lord of cakes".

neb temu "lord of mankind".

nebu ṭuat "lords of the Other World".

neb ṭeshert "lord of the red things", red clouds, or desert (?).

neb tchefau "lord of divine food".

neb tchetta "lord of eternity", *i. e.*, Osiris.

Neb-peḥti-petpet-sebȧu "lord of might, crusher of fiends"; a proper name.

Neb-peḥti-thes-menment "lord of might, roper in of cattle"; a proper name.

Neb-maāt-ḥeri-reṭui-f a proper name.

Neb-er-tcher "lord to the boundary", *i. e.*, the Lord of the Universe, a title of Osiris.

Nebt-er-tchert fem. of preceding.

Nebt-ḥet 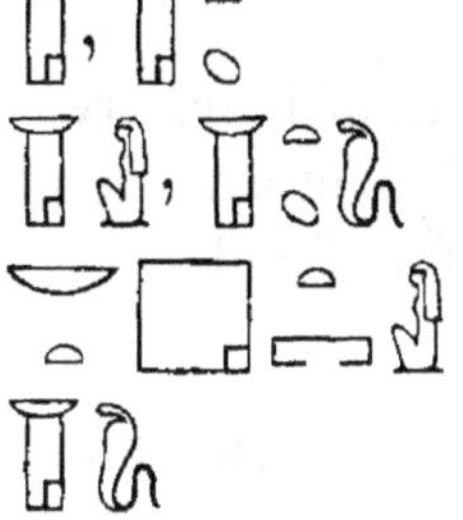 the goddess Nephthys, sister of Isis.

Neb-s 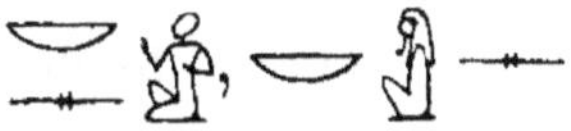 a proper name.

Neb-seni 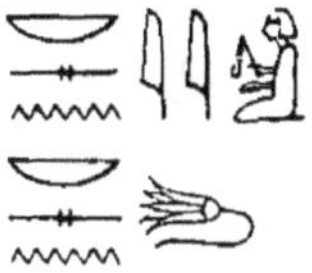 the name of a famous scribe.

Neb-qeṭ 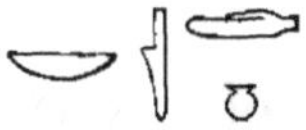 the name of a scribe.

neba  a weapon or tool, a pole.

Nebȧ  the name of one of the Forty-two Judges in the Hall of Osiris.

nebȧu 

nebȧnȧu  flame, fire, a burning.

nebȧt 

nebȧu 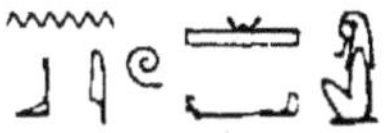 fashioner, moulder.

nebeḥ  a kind of bird.

nebti  (= 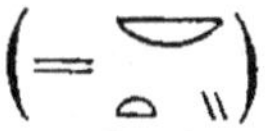), the two goddesses Nekhebit and Uatchit.

nebṭ, ***nebṭet*** lock of hair, tress; the name of a storm cloud; the name of a fiend.

nepu a part of the body.

neper grain, wheat, barley, dhura.

Neprȧ the Grain-god.

nepert corn-land.

Nepert the name of a city.

nef he, him.

nefa a sign of the demonstrative, this, that; plur.

nefu air, wind, breath; breath of life.

nefu sailor.

Nef-ur the name of a city or district.

nefer — to be good, to be happy, to be beautiful, good, pretty, gracious, well-doing; beautiful, good; twice good, very good; good one or thing; fine gold; gracious speech.

with , happiness, joy, gladness,

neferu / ***nefert*** — beauties, splendours, fair things, good things.

Nefer-ḥer — "fair face", a title of Rā and of Ptaḥ.

Nefer (?) — the name of a lake.

neferu — to be glad (?).

Nefert — girl, maiden; a proper name.

nefert name of a tree.

Nefer-uben-f , a proper name.

Nefer-sent name of a city.

Nefer-Tem , name of a god, the son of Ptaḥ and Sekhet.

nem to defraud = (?).

Nem a proper name.

nem ,

nemȧ

nemnem

nememti

to walk, to stride, go about, wander about.

nemt , step, stride; plur. , , ,

nemā who? who then? who then art thou?

nemm		to lie dead.
nemmȧt		bier.
nemmȧ		pygmy, dwarf.
nemeḥ		to understate the reading of the tongue of the balance, to be young, lowly, poor, humble.
nemes	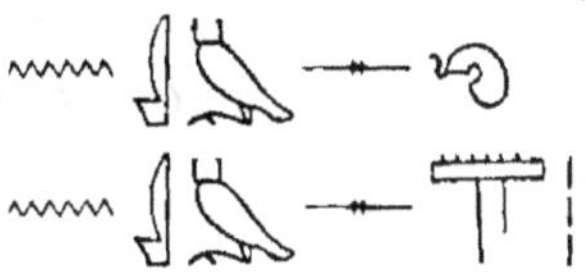	the name of a crown, tiara, or fillet for the head.
nemt		block for slaughter, the chamber in which the damned suffered decapitation and mutilation; plur. .
nemtchet		a place of slaughter.
en	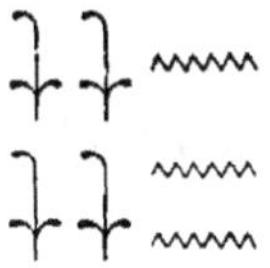	a sign of the demonstrative; 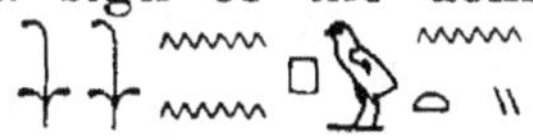 this is he who;  these who; 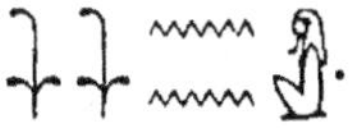.

nen 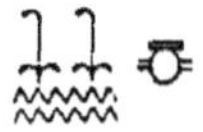 unguent.

nen 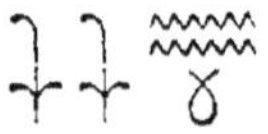 a kind of stuff, linen.

nen 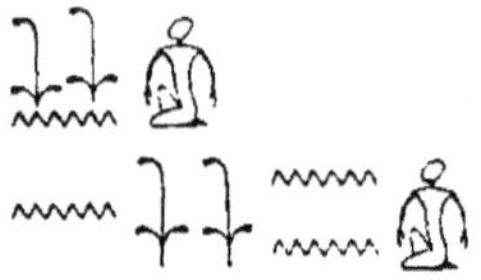 to be weak, helpless, exhausted.

neni, ***neniu***  weak or helpless folk, fiends, etc.

nenaiu  winds.

Nin-àrruṭ-f (?), ***Nen-aàrruṭ-f***  see Àn-ruṭ-f.

Nenunser  name of a Cow-goddess.

nenmet  (a late form) bier.

Nentchā 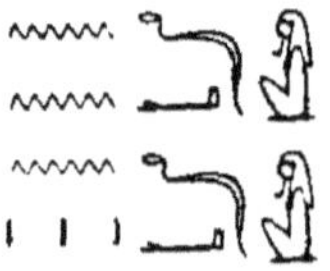 the name of a god.

Ner  name of the Herd-god a proper name.

Neráu — name of the Herd-god; a proper name.

ner, nert — men and women, mankind.

neru, *neráu*, *nerr* — to be strong, to strike fear into any one.

neráut, *nert* — victory, conquest; plur.

Neri — "mighty one"; name of a god.

Neráu-ta — a proper name.

neráut — vulture.

eh — to conquer.

eha — to alight.

eha — to advance.

nehaȧs to awake.

nehapu to shine, give light.

nehat sycamore, fig-tree; the two sycamores, fig-trees

Nehatu the name of a city.

nehep to copulate.

nehep to have power over.

nehpu strength.

nehpu light, fire, to shine.

nehem to rejoice.

rejoicings.

nehemnehem to destroy (?).

neheh fire.

nehhu needy one.

nehes — to wake up, rouse up.

Nehesu — a group of divine beings.

Nehes-ui — a proper name.

Neḥ — the name of a god.

neḥ — to beseech, pray, entreat.

neḥa — to be bad, stinking.

Neḥa-ḥāu — "stinking limbs"; a proper name.

Neḥa-ḥer — the name of one of the Forty-two Judges in the Hall of Osiris.

neḥait — flowers.

neḥit — time, eternity (?).

neḥeb — to coerce, put the yoke on some one.

neḥebet — neck; plur.

Neḥeb-nefert the name of or of the Forty-tw Judges in the Hall of Osiri

Neḥeb-ka

Neḥeb-kau "he who yoke together the Kau"; a prope name.

neḥep the divine potter's table.

neḥem to carry off, to plun der, to deliver, re lease; deliverers; delivered.

neḥeḥ eternity, for ever; witl time without be ginning or end.

neḥeḥ to invoke, entreat.

neḥes negro, a Sûdânî man in ge neral.

neḥṭ-t jaw teeth (?).

neḥṭ-ui the two jaws (?).

. . . .

nekh to cry out, complain.

nekha a sharp knife.

nekhakhat , humours (?), variant .

nekhȧu protector.

Nekhebet the goddess of the city of Nekheb (Al-Kâb).

nekhebet flowers.

Nekhen , a city of Upper Egypt, the god of Nekhen.

nekhen babe, child.

nekhenu , children.

Nekhenu the name of one of the Forty-two Judges in the Hall of Osiris.

nekhenit girls (?).

nekhekh old man.

nekhekh 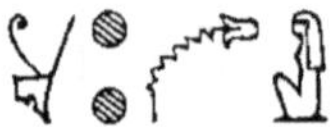 Vol. II, p. 251, l. 10.

nekhekh  whip, flail.

nekht 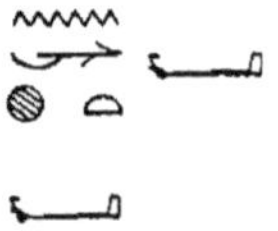 to be strong, strength, powerful.

nekhtu  valour, bravery, conquest.

Nekht  a proper name.

nekht  strong (in a bad sense).

Nekhtu-Åmen 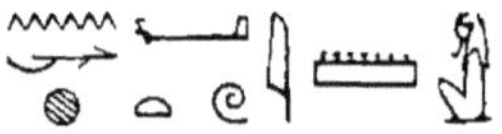 a proper name.

nes 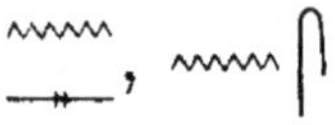 she, her, it.

nes 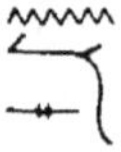 to belong to.

 belonging to him.

nesu 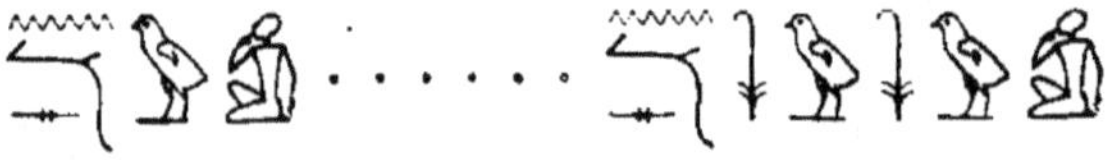

nes
nesau — tongue; ; plur. .

nes — to eat, devour, consume.

nes — to arrange (?), order (?).

nes
nesnes — flame.

nes — grain (?).

nesut — weapons of war.

nesb — to eat; .

nesbit — to eat, devour.

Nesbu — devouring gods.

nespu — slaughter, wound, knives.

nesert — flame, fire.

Nesert  a fire-goddess.

Nesersert  the Fire-city.

nest  throne; plur. 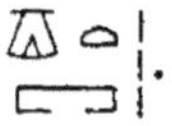.

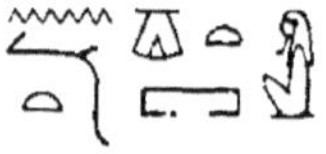 Throne.

nesti  a class of divine beings.

nest 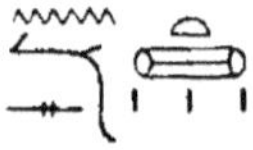 cakes (?).

nesh  to walk (?).

neshau  plates of metal.

neshu  a weapon (?).

neshi 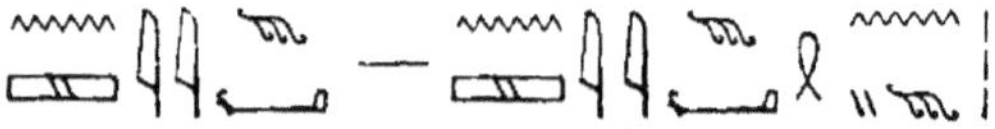 to make the hair bristle.

neshep  to snuff the air.

neshem 
neshmet  } a precious stone.

neshmet 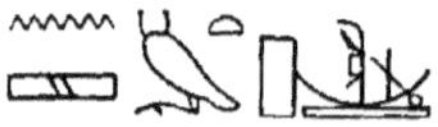 the name of a sacred boat.

neshni
neshen
neshenu — to be stormy, to revolt, a thunder-storm, destructive winds, whirlwind, tempest in general, revolt;

nek — thou, thy.

nek — to copulate; to have union with himself.

nekek — to commit sodomy.

nek nekek — to have union with a sodomite.

nekau — . . . . . .

nekai — injury.

ill-doing fiends.

Nekȧ
Nekȧu — the name of a fiend.

neken 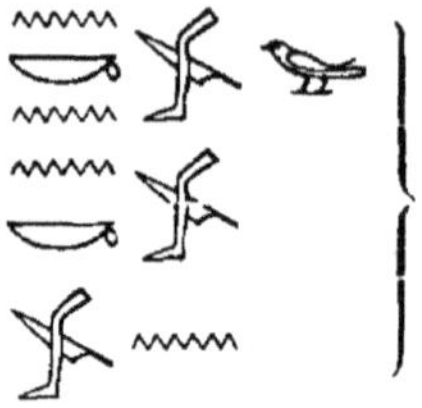 to do harm or injury to anyone.

nekent  injury; plur.  .

nekenu  injury, evil, harm.

neqāut  shackles.

neqāiut  those who steal away.

neḳa  to chew.

Neḳau  a Bull-god.

neḳeḳ  to cackle.

Neḳeḳ-ur  "Great Cackler"; name of the Goose-god.

Net  Neith, the great goddess of Saïs.

ent  of.

net 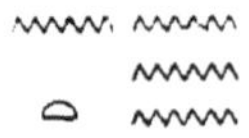 water, stream.

ent-ā 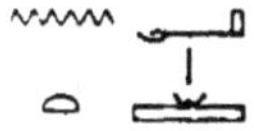 to ordain, order, ordinance, decree, customary rite; 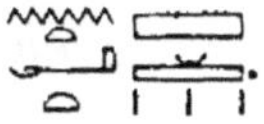.

enti  who, which, that which; plur. 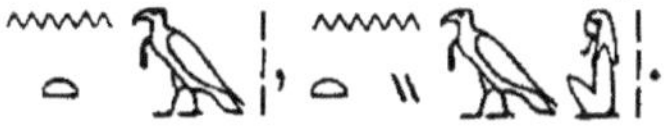.

entiu / *entet*  things which exist, persons or beings who are.

enti  sign of the negative, no, not, without.

neti  to vanquish, conquer.

Enti-mer-f 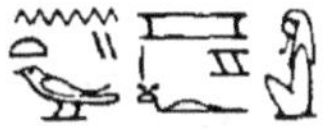 a proper name.

Enti-ḥer-f-emm-mast-f  a proper name.

entu 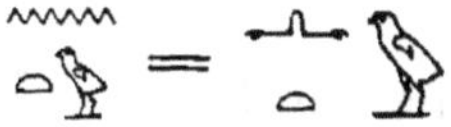

netu  fastenings, cords.

entuten  ye, you.

entef  he.

netnet  that which flows.

neter god, Copt. ⲛⲟⲩⲧⲉ great god; self-created, great god; god One; the City-god; god with a dog's face.

neteru gods, all the gods of the Three Companies, *i.e.*, Heaven, Earth, and the Ṭuat; all the gods.

the father-gods.

the mother-goddesses.

the Four gods.

the Forty-two gods.

gods celestial and gods terrestrial.

gods of heaven and gods of earth.

gods of the Ṭuat.

gods of the Qerti.

gods guides of the Ṭuat.

gods of the East.

gods of the North.

gods of the West.

gods of the South.

neter-ui the two gods Horus and Set; ; the two divine eyes, *i. e.*, Sun and Moon.

netert goddess, late form ; plur. , , .

netri to be a god or like unto a god, divine , , , divine.

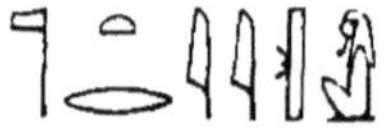 he who is divine ; 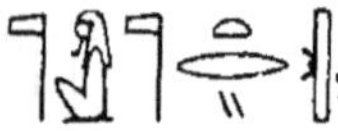,  "divine god".

neter àtfui  the two divine fathers.

neter meṭu 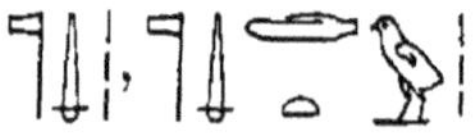 "the words of the god", *i.e.*, hieroglyphic writing.

neter nemt  the block or execution chamber of the god (Osiris).

neter ḥāu 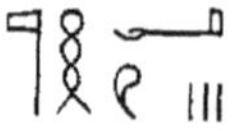 the body, or limbs, of the god.

neter ḥet  "god-house", *i. e.*, temple.

neter ḥetepu  "god-offerings", holy offerings, sepulchral meals.

neter khert 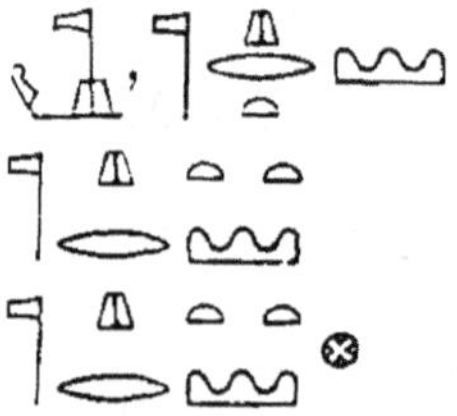 "underworld of the god"; a name for the grave and for the place of departed spirits.

neter khet  "god-property", *i. e.*, things dedicated to the service of the god.

neter shems 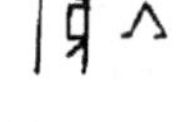 "god-follower", a member of the god's "body-guard".

neter ṭuai  "god-star", the morning star, Venus.

neter ṭuau "god-adoration", to give thanks to God.

neter ṭept "god-boat", divine barque.

neter tcheṭ "god-word", sacred speech.

Neter name of a lake in the Other World.

Neteru
Netri name of a town or city.

Netert-utchat name of a place.

entes she.

ent-sen them, they.

entek thou (masc.).

Netqa-ḥer-khesef-àtu the name of the herald of the Fourth Ārit.

ent thou (fem.).

netet cattle for sacrifice.

entet which, that which is.

neṭ to bandage, to tie.

Neṭit a proper name.

Neṭbit name of a town or city.

Neṭet name of a town or city.

netch, ***netchet*** to protect, guard, avenge.

netch ḥer "homage to thee", a form of salutation to gods.

netchti protector, advocate, avenger.

netch meṭu, ***netchtu re*** to discuss a matter with someone, to converse, to take counsel.

netchnetch to take counsel with someone, to discuss a matter.

Netcheb-àb-f a proper name.

Netchfet name of a town and its god.

netchem, ***netchemu***, ***netchemet*** — to be sweet, pleasant, to rejoice, be glad; very pleasant; pleasant things.

netchemmit — love-making, the delights of sexual love.

Netchem — the god of love.

netcher — to grasp, hold fast.

netcheriu, ***netcherit*** — clinchers, grapplers.

netcherȧ — to hew, to carve.

netchḥet — to strengthen.

Netcheḥ-netcheḥ, ***Netcheḥ-tcheḥ*** — the name of one of the Seven Spirits who guard Osiris and his bier.

netches  to be little, little, weak.

netcheset  lesser gods, perhaps "false gods".

Netchesti 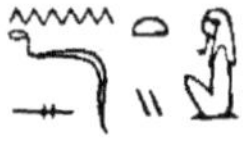 a name of Osiris.

Netchses 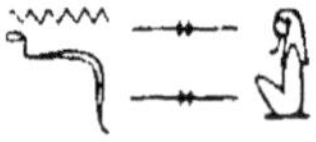 a name of a god.

Netchet 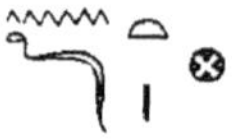 a name of a town or city.

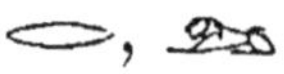 R or L.

er  at, to, with, into, among, against, from, according to, near, by, towards, upon, concerning. With compounds :—

er àmi  among.

er àmi tu 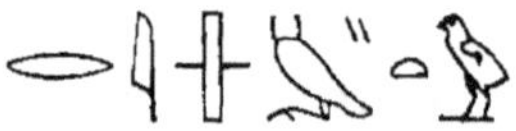
er àmi thu 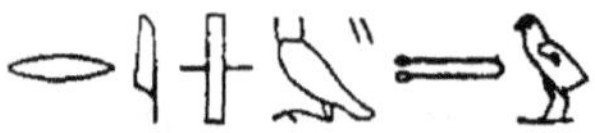 among, between.

er àsu  in return for, as reward or recompense for.

er mā  with, near.

er men 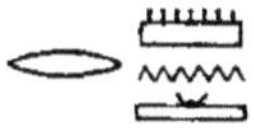 as far as.

er entet 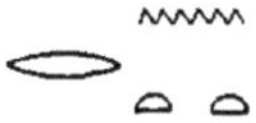 because.

er ruti  outside.

er ḥāt  before.

er ḥenā 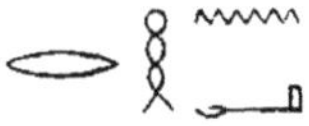 with.

er ḥer  away from.

er ḥeru  above.

er kheft ḥer  in the face of.

er kher  under.

er kherth 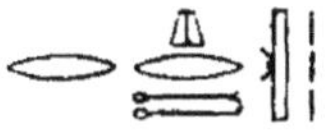 on behalf of.

er sa  by the back of.

er ḳes 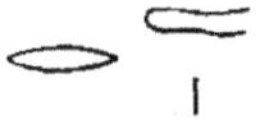 near, by the side of, in the track of.

er  sign of the comparative: more than, *e. g.*,

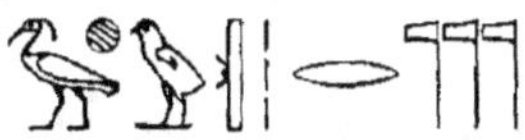 glorious more than the gods.

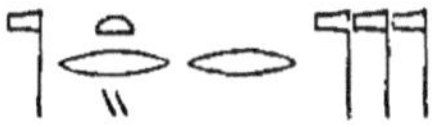 divine more than the gods.

 swift more than greyhounds.

 swift more than the shadow.

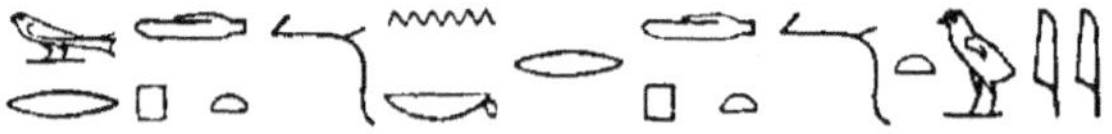
great is the taste to thee more than that taste.

Horus is bolder than all the gods.

 provided more than the gods.

 a name greater than yours.

 stronger than the gods.

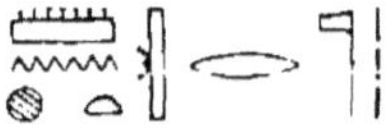 more gracious than the gods.

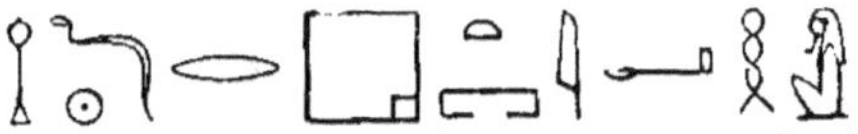 brighter than the House of the Moon.

thy speech is more piercing than the [cry of] the *tcheru* bird.

er 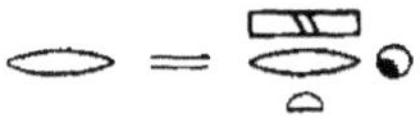 cake, offering.

re  goose.

re worms (?),

re door, opening, entrance, mouth, speech, chapter; plur. ; opening of the mouth, appearance; strong of mouth; doors of the Ṭuat; chapters of commemorations; a single chapter; a chapter of words; a chapter of mysteries; to set the mouth in motion against any one, *i. e.*, to slander.

re ȧpt (?) brow.

Re-āā-urt "opening of the great door"; the name of a town.

e-uat entrance to the roads.

e Ḥāp mouth of the Nile.

e Khemenu the entrance to the city of Hermopolis.

re Sekhait 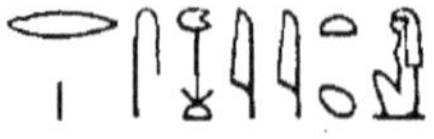 mouth of the goddess Sekhait.

Re-stau 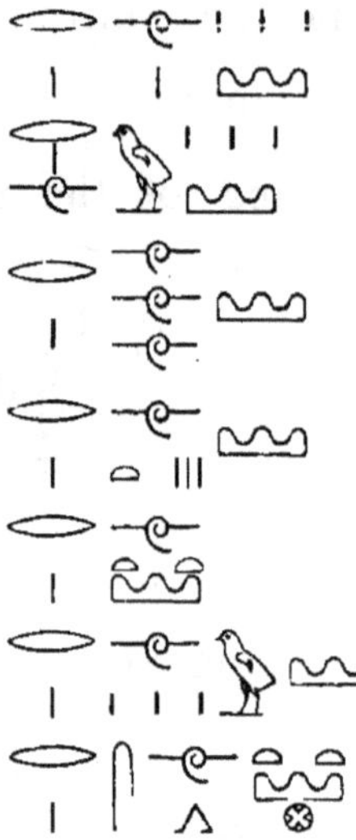 the "entrance to the corridors" in the Other World of Seker at Ṣaḳḳârah.

re-pu  or.

re-per 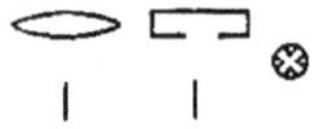 temple.

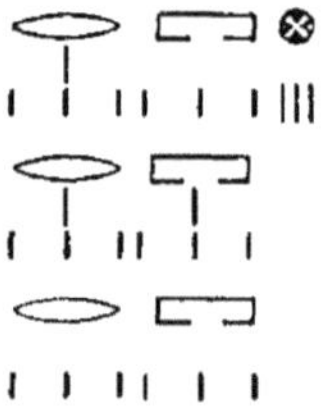 temples; 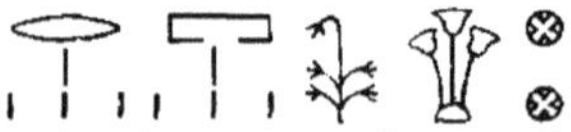 temples of the South and North.

Re (***Maȧu*** ?)  the Lion-god.

Re (?)-***Iukasa***  the name of a god.

Re (?)-***Rā***  the Lion-god Rā.

rā  work.

Rā  the Sun-god *par excellence*;  like Rā.

rā  day. 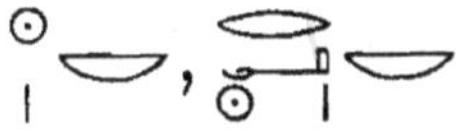 daily, every day.

Rā-Åsår  Rā-Osiris, the Sun-god of day and night.

Rā-Ḥeru-khuti  "Rā-Horus of the two horizons", Rā-Harmachis.

Rā-Tem 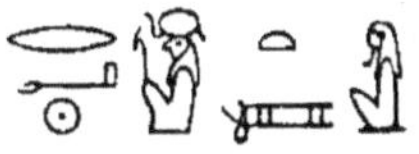 Rā-Tem, the Sun-god of day and night.

Rā-Maāt-men  the prenomen of Seti I.

Rā-men-kau 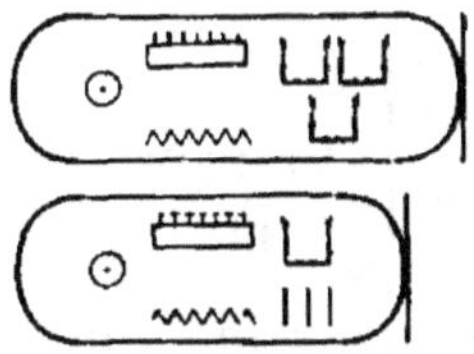 the Mykerinos of the Greeks.

Rā-mes-meri-Åmen-meri-Maāti  Rameses IV.

Rā-er-neḥeḥ  a proper name.

ri	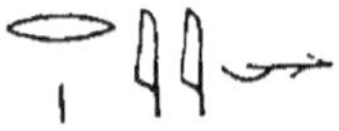	door.
ri		bandage, swathing.
riu		emanations.
ru		. . . . . .
ru		. . . . . .
ru		to fall, drop (of the wind).
ruȧ	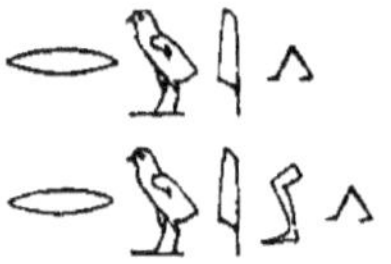	to separate from, move away from, depart.
ruȧa		
rui		journey, departure.
ruti		the two leaves of a door.
ruṭ	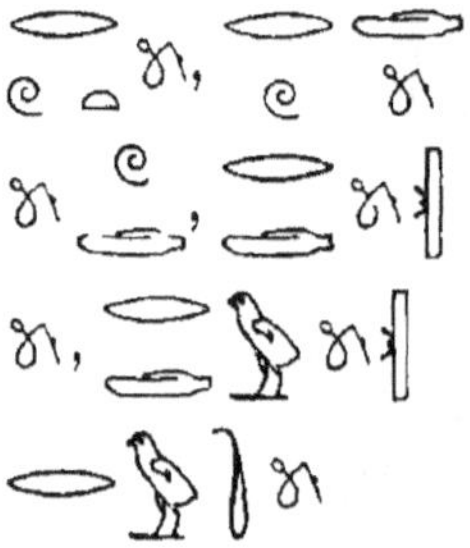	to grow, flourish, to be firm and healthy, to be taut (of ropes and sails);  .
ruṭi		strong, vigorous.

ruṭ, ***ruṭu*** — plants, things which grow.

Ruṭ-en-Ȧst — a proper name.

Ruṭu-nu-Tem — a proper name.

Ruṭu-neb-rekhit — a proper name.

·uṭu — superintendent, overseer.

·uṭ — staircase.

·ref — an intensive particle, then, therefore.

·rpā, ***·rpāt*** — hereditary tribal chief.

·rpit — image, statue, august person.

rpti — the two august goddesses, *i. e.*, Isis and Nephthys.

·emu — fish.

·emu — the "town of fish"; a proper name.

Remi  the Fish-god.

rem 
remu  } to weep.

remt  tear; plur. , .

rem-tȧ  studded (?).

ermen 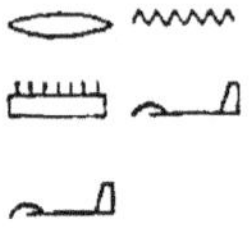 } arm, shoulder, one side of the body.

ermenui  } the two arms, shoulders.

 the two sides of a ladder.

ermenu 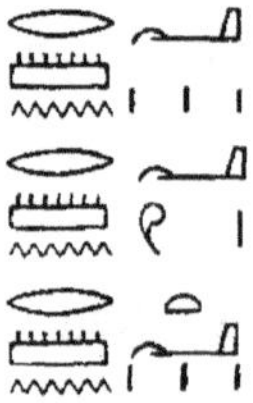 } shoulders, arms, supporters, the branches of a tree.

ermen to carry away, to bear, to remove something, to shoulder.

Remrem the name of a god.

·en name; plur.

·en to nurse (see *renen*).

'enp to be young or youthful, renewal of youth, to become young; youthful one.

enp-tȧ youthful, made young; very young.

:npit year; plur. *renput*.

:npit plants, vegetables, fruits.

Renen the name of a god.

renen to nurse, to suckle.

Renenet
Renutet } the goddess of grain crops and the harvest.

***rer* (*peḥer*?)** territory, a place for walking about.

rer
reru } to walk about, to go round about, to revolve, to encircle ; *thes rer* again, repetition, conversely.

rertå encircled.

reri those who revolve, or go about.

rer khet going about retreating.

rert circle.

rert drugs, medicine.

rer pig.

reru  . . . .

reru  . . . .

rert  mistake for  or  men.

Rertu-nefu 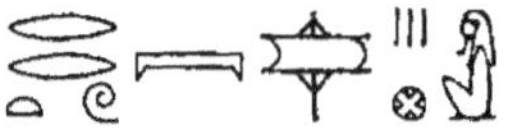 a proper name.

Rerek  name of a serpent fiend in the city of Åses.

Rerti (?) / *Maȧuti*?) 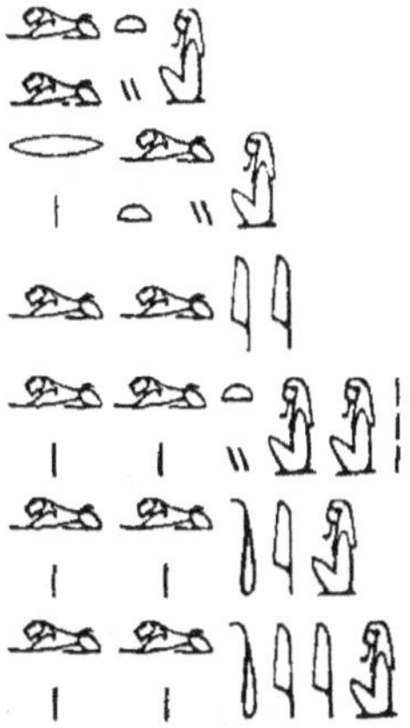 the Lion-god and Lion-goddess, *i. e.*, Shu and Tefnut (?). The name of one of the Forty-two Judges in the Hall of Osiris.

ehebu  flame, fire. Compare Heb. לַהַב.

ehen 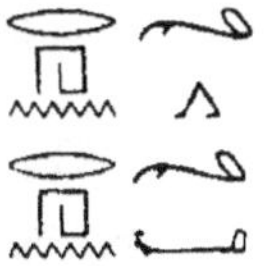 to rest upon, to support.

ɜḥ 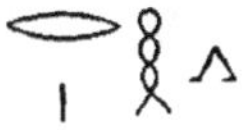 to enter.

ɜḥu  a man deified, later a god.

reḥui 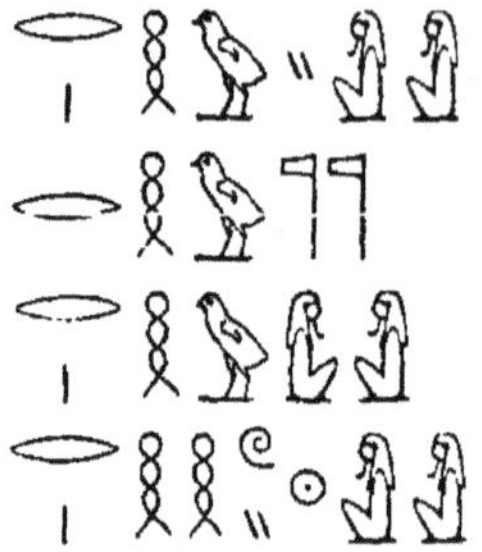 the two combatant gods, Horus and Set.

reḥti 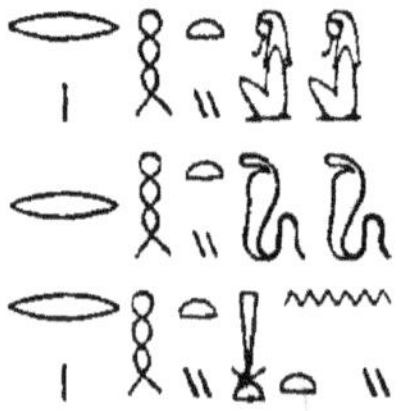 the two combatant sister goddesses, Isis and Nephthys.

Reḥui 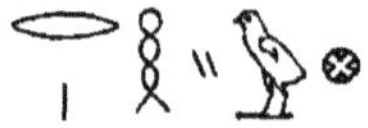 the town of the two combatant gods.

Re-ḥent  a proper name.

Re-ḥenent  name of a lake or canal.

Re-ḥenent  the name of a town or its god.

rekh  to be wise, to have knowledge; 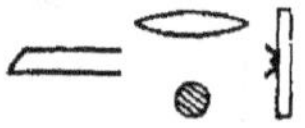 knowingly, with intent; 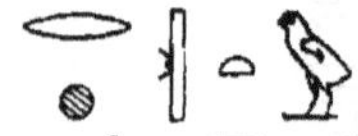,  known; 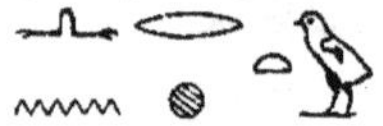 unknown.

rekht  knowledge, a list, inventory, total.

rekh àb to understand.

rekhu khet "knowers of things", *i. e.*, the wise gods.

rekhit beings of knowledge, rational beings, men and women, people, mankind.

rekhes to sacrifice, to slaughter.

Rekhti the two goddesses Isis and Nephthys.

Rekhti-Merti-neb[ti]-Maāti the two goddesses who were the ladies of the city of Maāt.

es to watch, be awake; awake; rouse up! wake up!

esu

esit the nine watchers.

estu night watchers.

Res-àb	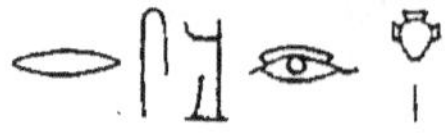	the warder of the Fourth Ārit.
Res-ḥer	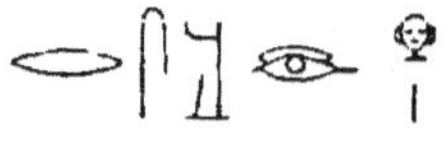	the warder of the Third Ārit.
res	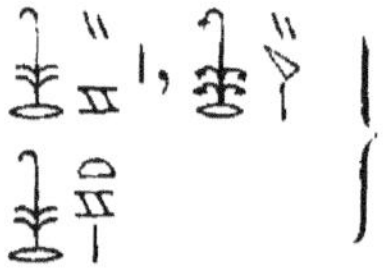	south, southern;  South and North, all Egypt.
resiu	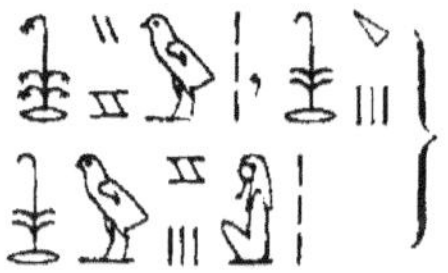	southerners, southern gods.
Resu		a proper name; fem. 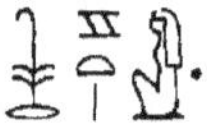.
resu	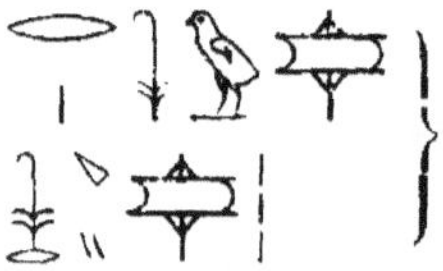	south wind.
Resenet (?)	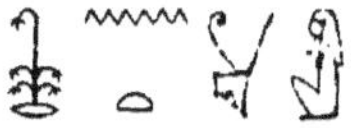	a proper name.
resh	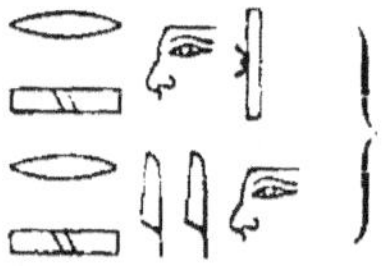	to breathe with joy, to rejoice.
resht	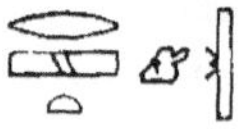	gladness, joy, to snuff, to inhale.
reshui		the two nostrils.
rek		then, an emphatic particle

rek  time.

rekḥ 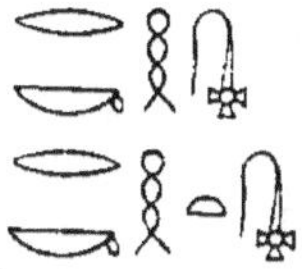 to burn, to be hot.

rekḥu 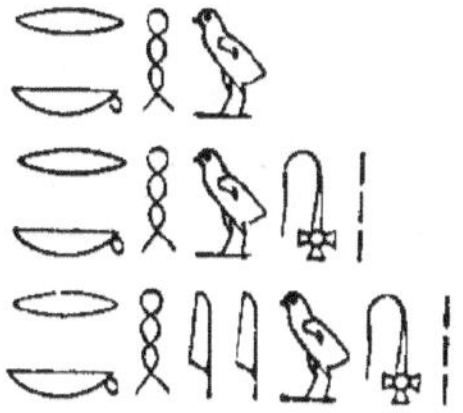 fire, flames.

Rekes 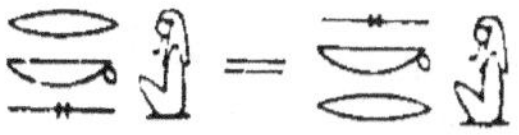

req, ***reqa***  to incline away, fall away from ; .

reqi 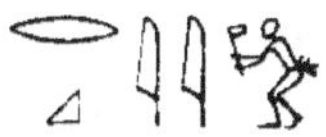 fiend, enemy.

reqau  (or ) fiends, enemies.

ret  *i. e.*, *reret*, or *peḥrert*.

***ret* (*remt*)**  men and women, people, mankind.

 everybody.

Retasashaka  a name of Ȧmen.

16*

reti — the two leaves of a door.

reṭ — leg, foot.

reṭui, *reṭi* — the two feet.

reṭȧu — feet.

reṭ (*remt*) — men and women, people, folk, mankind.

reṭ — steps, staircase.

erṭā, *erṭāt* — to give, to set, to place, to put, to cause or make to happen;

As an auxiliary verb:

and see *passim*.

Erṭā-nefu  a proper name.

Erṭā-ḥen-er-reqa 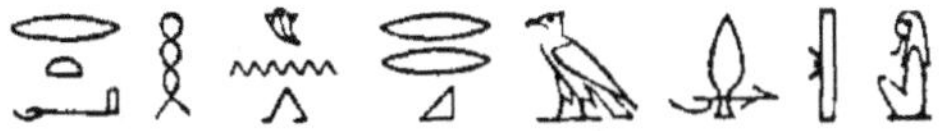 a proper name.

reṭut  places, abodes.

reṭu 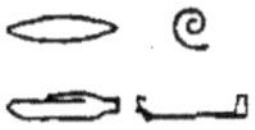 . . . .

reṭu 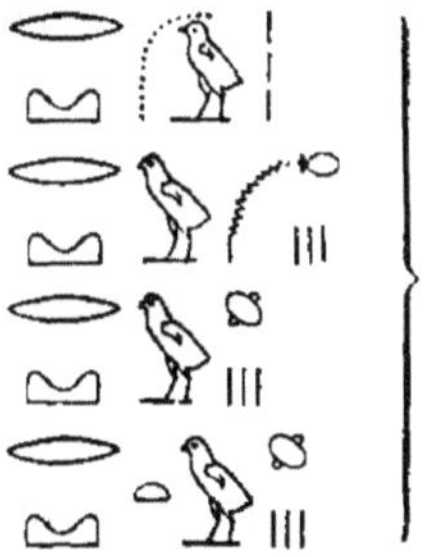 emanations, effluxes, droppings.

reth 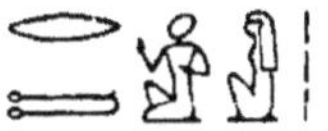 men and women, people, folk, mankind.

 everybody.

 H.

ha  interjection, O! Hail!

ha  to be strong;  strength.

ha 

hai 

hait 

to descend, to go down into a place, to embark on a ship, to fall, to go in, enter, advance into  those who enter.

hau  time, period, reign.

Haȧker  name of a festival.

Hai  "phallus"; the name of one of the Forty-two Judges in the Hall of Osiris.

hai  interjection, O! Hail!

hai  to shout with joy, rejoice.

haiu  the gods who rejoice.

hait  a large chamber, heaven (?).

hab  to send, to send forth, to go forward.

habu  those who fall down.

Hab-em-atu  "advancing at the moment"; a proper name.

habeq  to fail.

hamu  blemish, defect, sin.

Hart-âb  to please.

Hahuti-âm- . . . . . 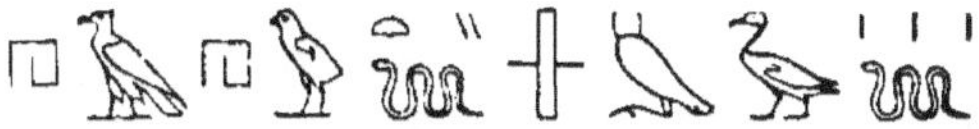 the name of a fiend.

Haḥetep  a proper name.

Hakheru 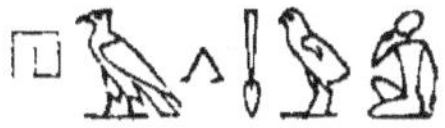 a proper name.

Hasert  a city in the Seventh Âat.

haker 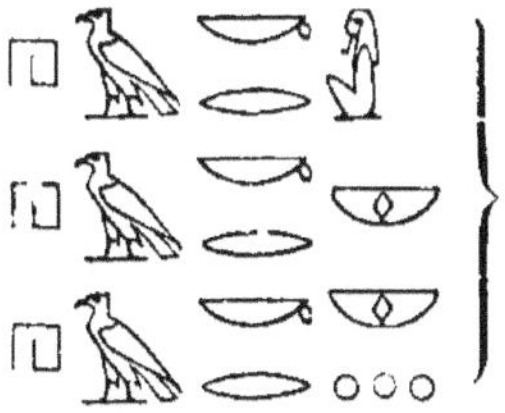 the name of a god and of a festival.

haq 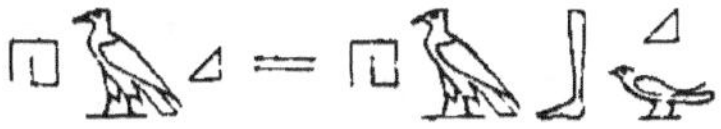

Haqahakaḥer  a proper name.

hat		interjection, O!
hat		descent, entrance, embarcation.
hatu		brow (?).
haṭ		to suppress, to beat down, subdue.
hi		to rejoice.
hu	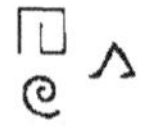	to enter, descend, fall.
Hunefer		the name of a scribe.
Hu-kheru		the name of the herald of the first Àat.
heb		ibis, the bird sacred to Thoth.
heb / ***hebt***		to send out, to go forward.
hepu		laws, ordinances, regulations.
hem		fire.

hemu		men and women, folk, people: see also ***ḥenmemet.***
hemhem		to roar, cry out, bellow (of a bull).
hemhemet	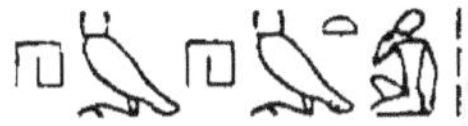	outcries, roarings.
Hemti		runner.
hen	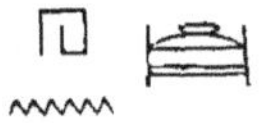	funeral chest, coffin.
Henȧ		the name of a city.
henȧnȧu	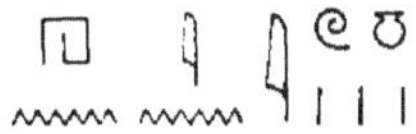	pleasant things.
henu		to sing songs of joy, to praise.
henu		praises, shouts of joy, singers.
henhenu / ***henhenit***	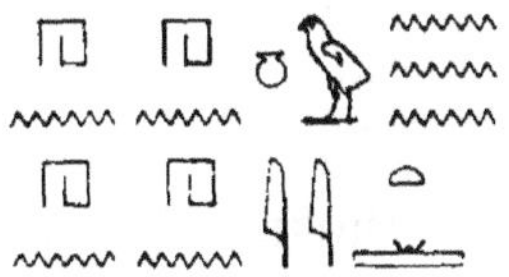	the watery abyss of heaven, flood.
hensheses	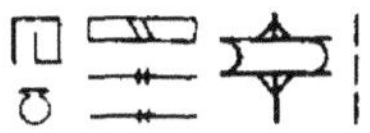	the east wind.
her		to be content, pleased.

her-àb / ***hert-àb***	pleased in heart, content, pleasure.
herà	a vessel.
heru	day; plur.
	this day, to-day.
	judgment day.
	birthday.
	birthday of Osiris.
	day of the funeral.
	every day, daily.
	a happy day.
	daily, course of each day.
heriu	those who are content (?).
herret	things which please.
heh	flame.

heker | hekeru — name of a festival.

heq

hetu — to be addressed.

hethet — to go round about.

het — to subdue. sub-dued.

H.

. . . . . with . . . . . .

a — behind, get back! back thou! (in addresses to fiends).

a — back of the head and neck.

a — a cry, a precative particle.

Iaás — a proper name.

ḥaȧu  the dwellers in the Delta and in the marshes near the sea-coast.

ḥai  to be bright, to shine.

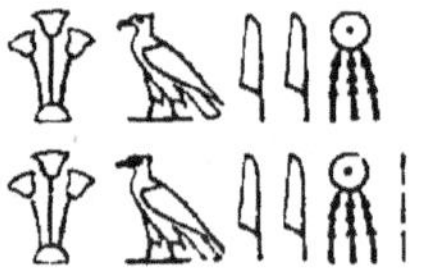 light.

Ḥai 

Ḥait  a proper name.

ḥait  to grasp.

ḥau 

ḥauu 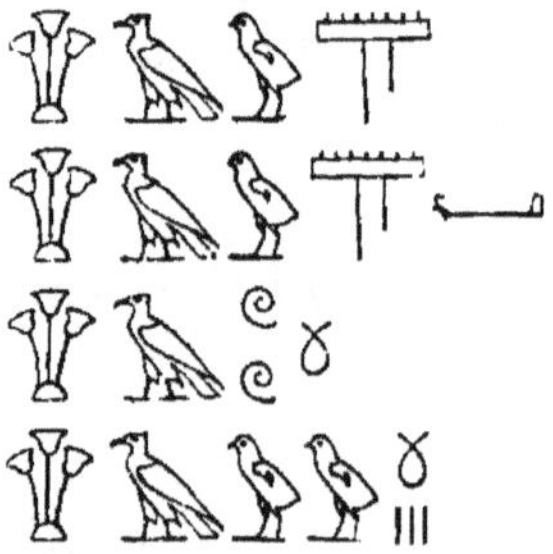 to be unclothed, to strip off apparel.

ḥaui  naked man.

ḥau  addition, increase, things added.

ḥauatu 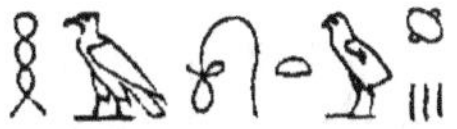 filth, dung.

ḥan-re  to have a care for, assuredly.

Ḥa-ḥer  a proper name.

ḥap 
ḥapu 
ḥapt 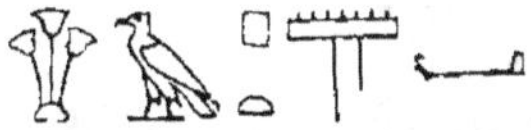
} to enshroud, to hide, to cover over.

ḥap  to advance, move forward.

ḥaputi  runner (?).

Ḥap  the Bull Apis;  .

Ḥap 
Ḥapi 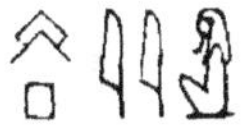
} one of the four sons of Horus who protected one quarter of the body of the deceased.

ḥapu  oar, steering pole, rudder.

ḥaptu 
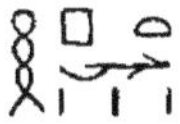

} oars, paddles.

Ḥapu-en-neb-sett 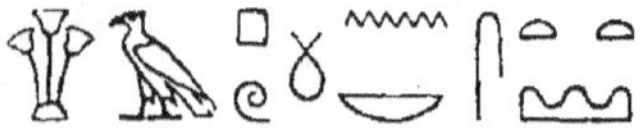 a name for the cemetery.

Ḥapṭ-re  a proper name.

ḥam  to net birds and fish.

ḥamt  to net birds and fish.

ḥamiu 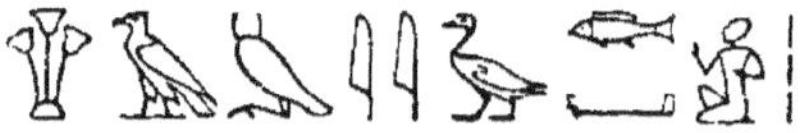 fishermen, fowlers.

Ḥarpuḳakashareshabaiu  a proper name.

Ḥareti  a proper name.

ḥaqet  to capture, make prisoners, captives.

ḥaqet  fetters.

ḥaqu  name of a plank or peg in the magic boat.

ḥat  pit.

ḥaṭ  tomb.

ḥaṭ  net.

ḥaṭu 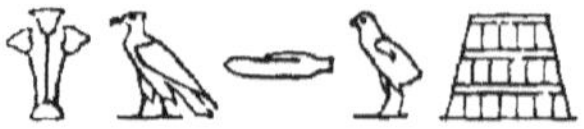 net.

ḥatȧ, ḥatȧtu, ḥattui 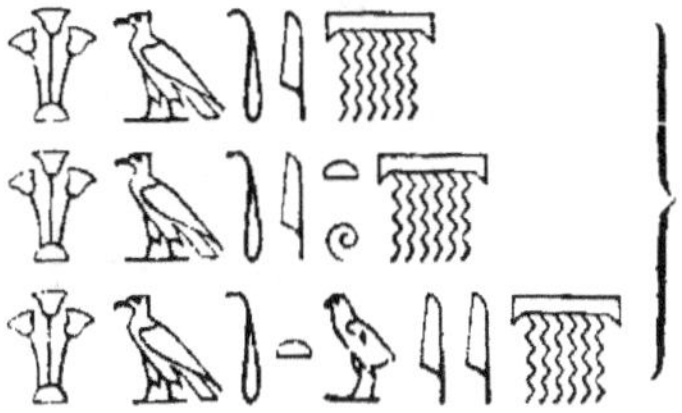 storm, whirlwind.

ḥā, ḥāa  to rejoice, be glad ; , , rejoicing ;  glad.

ḥāiu 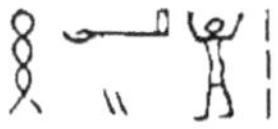 rejoicings.

ḥāā  to rejoice.

ḥāāiu, ḥāātu 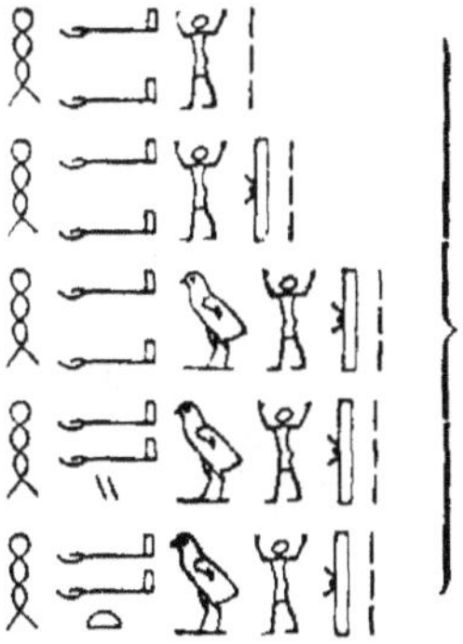 rejoicings, those who rejoice.

ḥā 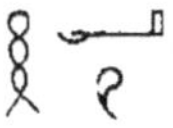 limb, member of the body, the body itself.]

ḥāu, ***ḥāt*** limbs, members of the body; one body; thy own self.

Ḥāp, ***Ḥāpi*** the Nile.

Ḥāp-ur the Great Nile.

ḥā[t]-ā the beginning or front of anything; the opening words of a book.

ḥāt the beginning or front of anything, bows of a boat, the breast; before.

[***ḥāt-ā*** prince, chief] the two divine princes.

ḥāti the heart; plur.

ḥātet a rope in the bows of a boat.

ḥāti 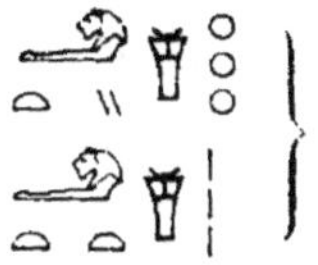 unguent of the best kind.

Ḥi-mu (?)  the name of one of the Forty-two Judges in the Hall of Osiris.

Ḥit  a proper name.

:u  a mistake for .

u  hair, tresses.

Ṭu 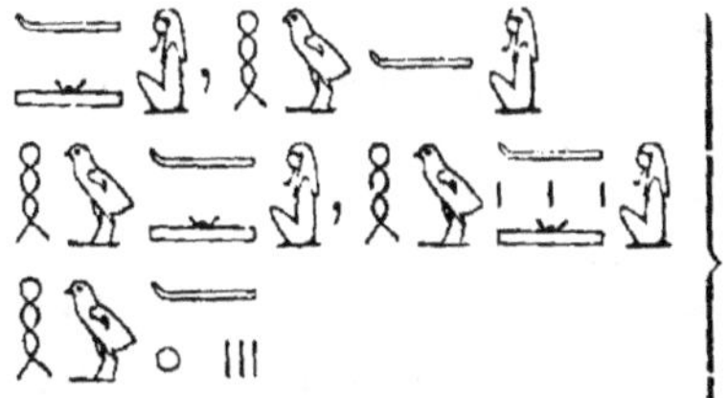 the god of food, divine food.

ui 

t  to smite, to strike;  smiting (*i.e.*, clapping) their hands;  smiting.

t  a smiting.

it-Rā  smiters of Rā.

Ḥu-tepa a proper name.

ḥua to be filthy, in a stinking, corrupt, or rotten state.

ḥuaat filth, dung, offal; "filthy cat".

ḥui, ***ḥuia*** to decree, issue a command.

ḥun, ***ḥunu***, ***ḥunen*** to be in the state of a child; boy, child, young man; plur.

ḥunt maiden, girl.

Ḥunt-Pe-... . . . .

ḥuḥu waterflood, a large mass water.

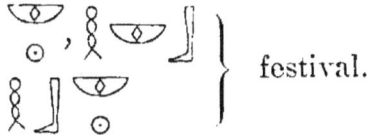

ḥeb — festival.

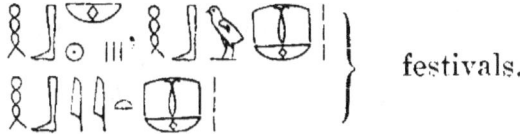

ḥebu, **ḥebit** — festivals.

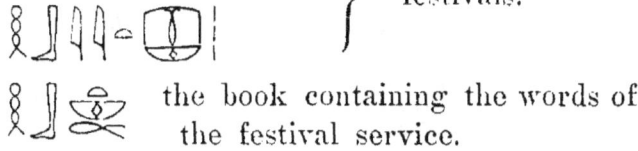

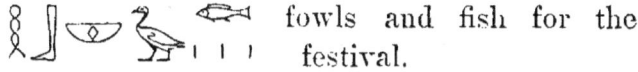

ḥebt — the book containing the words of the festival service.

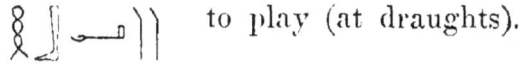

ḥeb — fowls and fish for the festival.

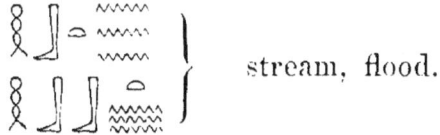

ḥebā — to play (at draughts).

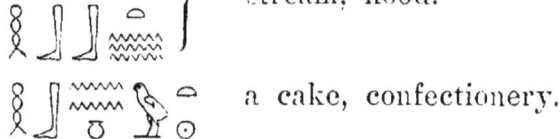

ḥebt, **ḥebbet** — stream, flood.

ḥebenut — a cake, confectionery.

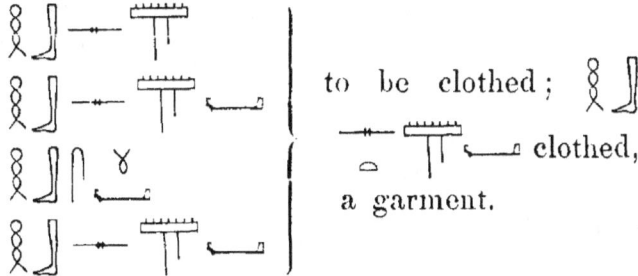

ḥebs — to be clothed; clothed, a garment.

ḥebs — garment, clothing, a swathing; plur.

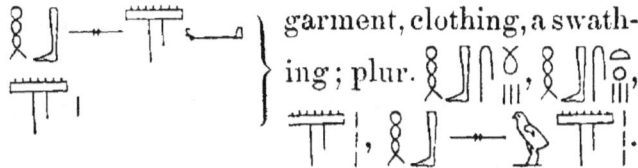

Ḥebṭ-re-f 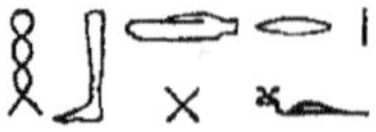 a proper name.

ḥept 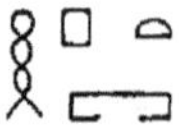 for  *q. v.*

ḥept 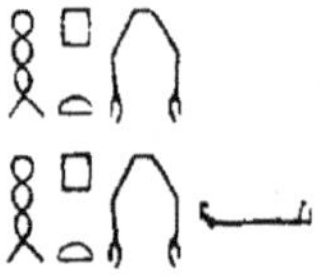 to embrace, embrace; , 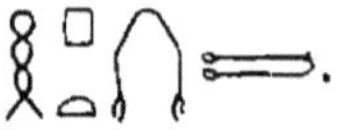.

ḥept  breast (?), embrace.

Ḥept-ur 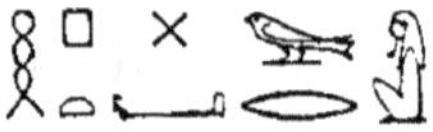 a proper name.

Ḥept-shet  the name of one of the Forty-two Judges in the Hall of Osiris.

ḥeptu  oars of a boat, doorposts.

ḥept 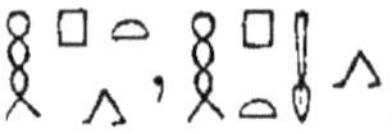 to move forward, advance; see  advancing.

ḥeptet  a course, a place for walking.

Ḥepṭ-ur  a proper name.

Ḥepṭ-re  a proper name.

ḥepṭ-re  to shut the mouth, to gnaw (?).

ḥefau  serpent, snake.

ḥefi  a serpent with two legs.

ḥefait 
ḥefiu 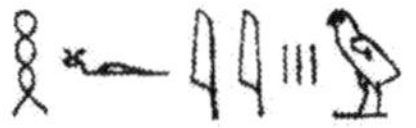 . . . .

ḥefen 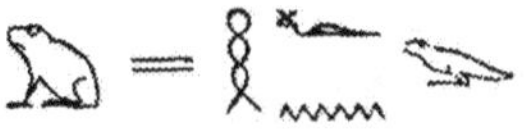 one hundred thousand.

ḥefṭ  to sit down, to rest.

ḥem  a particle.

ḥem 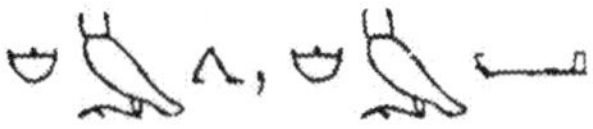  to retreat, make to go back.

ḥem  to steer, or paddle a boat.

ḥemu 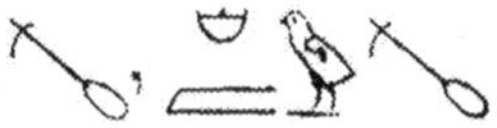
ḥemi  paddle, oar, rudder, steering pole.

ḥemu 
ḥemit 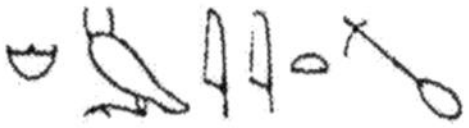 paddles.

ḥemaḳa  to grasp.

Ḥemaḳa   the name of a town and of a god.

ḥematet 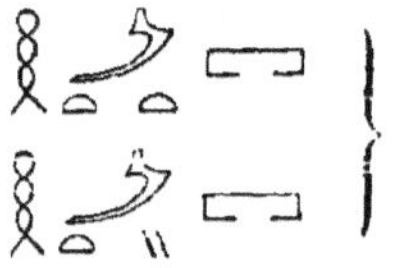 name of a chamber.

ḥemu  artificer, workman.

ḥemt  work, handicraft.

ḥemt  a mineral.

ḥemt  copper, bronze.

ḥemen 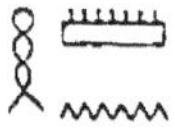 slaughter.

Ḥemen 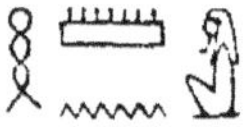 the name of a god.

ḥement  forty.

ḥems 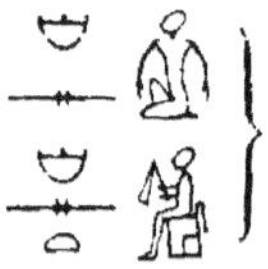 to sit, be seated, to dwell; 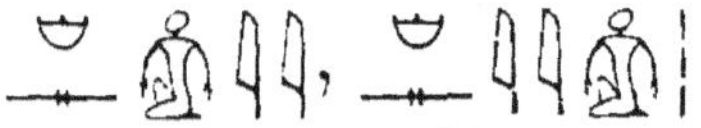 sitting sitting ones;  seated

ḥemset 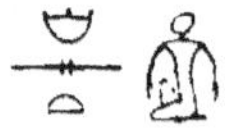 a sitting, seat.

ḥemt  woman, wife; plur. 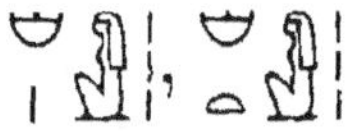

 woman belonging to man, wife.

 king's woman, *i. e.*, queen.

god's woman, *i. e.*, priestess.

Asiatic woman.

women goddesses.

a proper name (?).

ḥemt cow, cow-goddess: plur.

ḥen servant, slave; plur.

ḥent servant (fem.), slave.

ḥen neter god's servant, *i. e.*, priest.

ḥen ka priest of the *Ka*, or double.

ḥen majesty;

ḥen, ***ḥenen***, ***ḥenḥen*** to go forward, to run.

ḥen, ***ḥenu*** to bestow, to be given or provided with, ordered, arranged.

ḥen, ḥeni flowers, plants, blossoms.

ḥen to praise;

ḥenā with, along with, and; with; triumphant with you; god spake with god.

ḥenu, **ḥeniu** offerings, gifts.

ḥenu pillars.

ḥenu to draw to oneself.

ḥenbet corn-land.

ḥeneb offerings of grain produce.

Ḥenbi the god of the cultivated lands.

ḥenmemet also men and women, folk, people, mankind.

ḥenemnemu devourers (?).

ḥenen to labour, toil.

enen phallus; phallus of Rā.

enu (or ***ḥennu***)

enu name of a sacred boat which was drawn round the sanctuary at dawn at Memphis.

ennu

ennui to go about, to wander, move forward.

nnui the beginning and end of time or of eternity.

nnuti crocodiles.

nnuit fraud, deceit.

nnut

nnuti two horns, a pair of horns.

s to block the way.

ḥenseki, ***ḥensekit***, ***ḥensekt***, ***ḥensekti***, ***ḥenkesti*** (*sic*) — hair, lock of hair, tress.

Ḥensek — a god with much hair.

Ḥensektiu — the gods with much hair, *i. e.*, the gods with long hair and beards.

Ḥenseket-menȧt-Ȧnpu-em-kat-en-utu — name of a rope.

ḥenk — to give, present, offer; offered, given.

ḥenket — offerings.

Ḥenku-en-Ȧrp — a proper name

Ḥenku-en-fat-Maāt — a proper name.

ḥenku		balance.
ḥenket		the funerary bed, or chamber.
ḥenkit	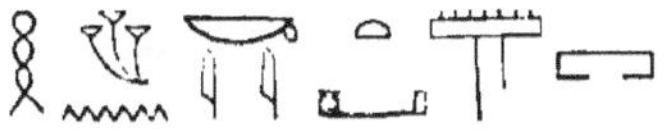	
Ḥenket	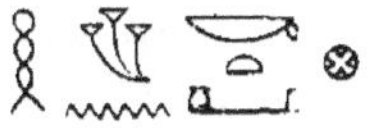	the name of a town.
ḥent	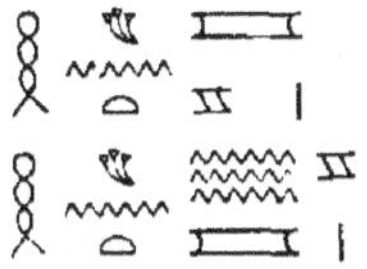	lake, canal, stream, pool.
ḥent	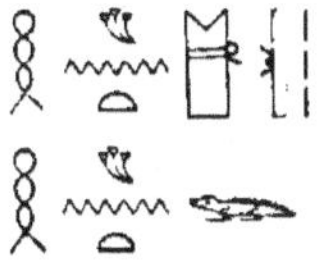	to be hostile.
ḥent	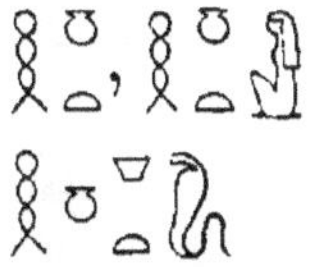	mistress, lady, sovereign, queen.
	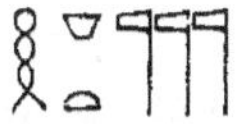	queen of the gods.
		lady of the crowns of the South and North.
	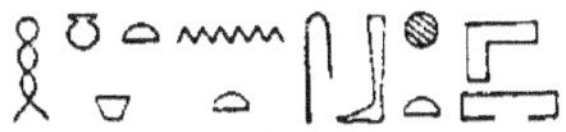	mistress of the pylons.
	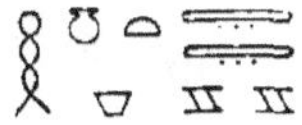	queen of the Two Lands.
Ḥent	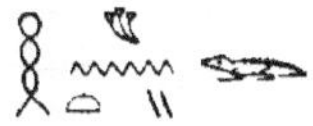	crocodile.
ḥenta		to fall into oblivion, or decay.

Ḥenti  god of the two crocodiles, a name of Osiris.

ḥenti  crocodile.

ḥenti  a pair of horns.

 the two-horned gods, or the two two-horned gods.

ḥenti 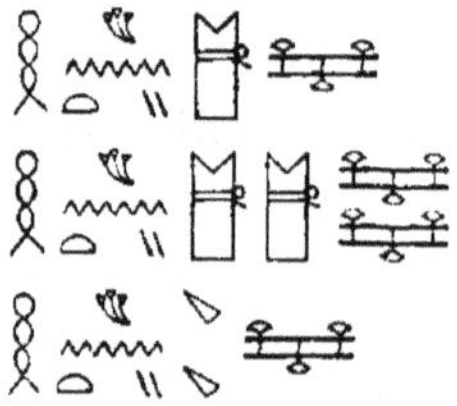 the beginning and end of time, or of eternity.

ḥenti pet 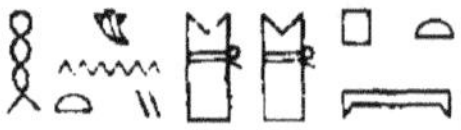 the two ends of heaven.

Ḥenti-requ  a proper name.

Ḥent-khent-ta-meru  a proper name.

ḥer  in, at, upon, on, by, etc.; 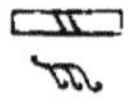 *en ḥer* upon.

ḥer-ā 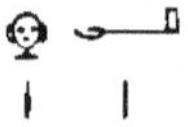 on the hand, *i. e.*, straightway, immediately.

ḥer-àb  in the middle of, dweller in; plur. 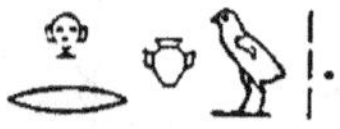.

ḥer-àbt 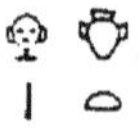

Ḥer-àb-uàa-f "within his boat"; a proper name.

Ḥer-àb-àrit-f "within his eye; a proper name.

Ḥer-àb-karà-f "within his shrine"; a proper name.

ıer mā straightway, forthwith.

ıer entet
ıer enti sa } because.

ıer sa besides, in addition to.

eri , , } he who is above, or over, chief of, principal of.

chief scribe; chief of the writings; chief of the altar; chief of the altars.

eriu , , } those who are over, those who are above, celestial beings; chiefs.

ḥeriu, ***ḥertu*** — those who are over, those who are above, celestial beings; chiefs.

ḥeru — the upper regions, what is above; heaven.

ḥeri tchatcha — chief, governor, president.

chieftainess, goddess.

ḥert — the upper regions, the sky, heaven.

the heaven of eternity, *i. e.*, the everlasting heaven.

Ḥeri-aḳebȧ-f — "chief of his ocean"; a proper name.

Ḥeri-uatch-f — "chief of his sceptre"; a name of Horus.

Ḥeri-uru — "chief of the great ones"; the name of one of the Forty-two Judges in the Hall of Osiris.

Ḥeri-sesh "chief of the writings"; a proper name.

Ḥeri-sep-f "chief of his time"; a proper name.

Ḥeri-sesh[eta] "he who is over the secrets"; *i. e.*, secretary.

Ḥeri-shā-f "he who is on his sand"; a title of Osiris.

"those who are on [their] sand"; a name of the dwellers in the desert.

Ḥeri-ta "governor of the land".

Ḥeri-tchatcha-taui "governor of the Two Lands"; *i. e.*, Egypt.

ḥer and.

ḥer face; plur. , ; two faces; the divine face.

ḥer em ḥer face to face.

ḥer neb every one.

ḥeru nebu , folk, all men, mankind, all the people.

Ḥerui  the god of the two faces.

Ḥerui-f  he of the two faces.

Ḥer-uā 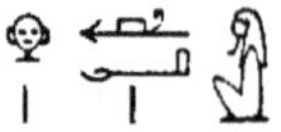 a proper name.

Ḥer-f-em-qeb 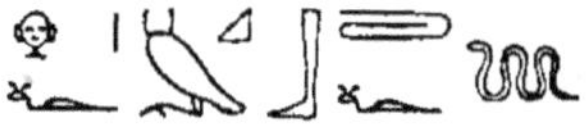 the name of a fiend.

Ḥer-nefer 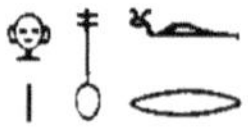 "beautiful Face"; a name of Rā and Ptaḥ; 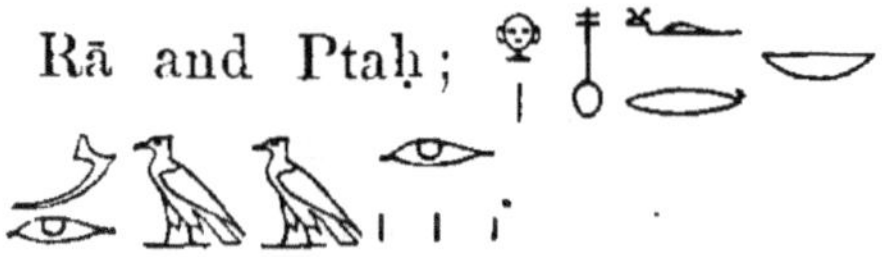

Ḥer-f-ḥa-f  "he with his face behind him"; the name of one of the Forty-two Judges in the Hall of Osiris.

Ḥer-k-en-Maāt 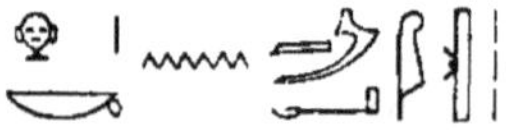 a proper name.

ḥer 
ḥeru 

} to terrify, be frightened.

ḥerit  terror, fright.

ḥeri 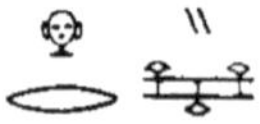
ḥeru 
} to go away, depart, be away, be afar off; .

Ḥer  the ancient name of the Sun-god; applied to the king as the representative of the Sun-god on earth.

Ḥerui  the pair of Horus gods, *i. e.*, Horus and Set.

Ḥerui-senui  the two Horus brethren.

Ḥeru-āa-ȧbu  "Horus, great one of hearts".

Ḥeru-ȧmi-ȧbu-ḥer-ȧb-ȧmi-khat 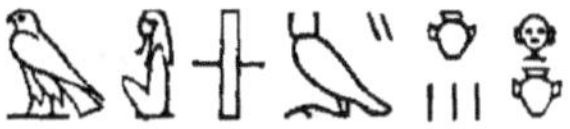 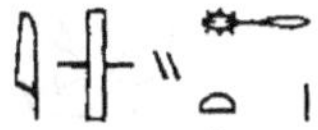 "Horus, dweller in hearts, he who is in the intestines".

Ḥeru-ȧmi-ȧthen  "Horus, dweller in the Disk".

Ḥeru-ȧrit (?) 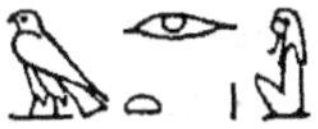 the "Eye of Horus".

Ḥeru-āḥāi 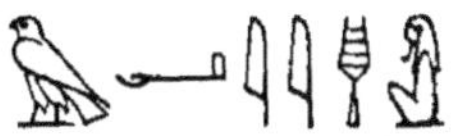 Horus the Fighter (?).

Ḥeru-Un-nefer  "King of the South and North, Horus Un-nefer".

Ḥeru-ur  The elder Horus as opposed to Horus the son of Isis.

Ḥeru-merti  Horus of the two Eyes, *i. e.*, Sun and Moon.

Ḥeru-em-khebit  Horus of the North.

Ḥeru-em-khent-en-merti 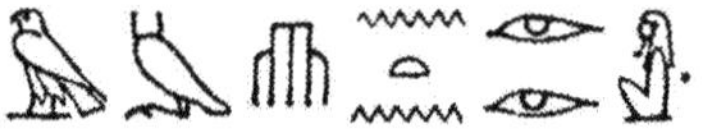.

Ḥeru-neb-urert  "Horus, lorc of the Urert crown".

Ḥeru-netch-ḥer-àtef-f  "Horus, the advocate of his father"

Ḥeru-ḥer-neferu  "Horus oı the pilot' place [in the Boat of Rā]"

Ḥeru-khuti  Horus of the horizon of sunrise and sunse

Ḥeru-Khuti-Kheperȧ 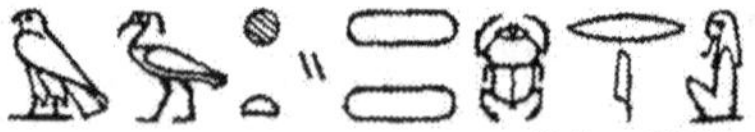 Haı machis Kheperı

Ḥeru-khenti-ȧn-Merti (?) 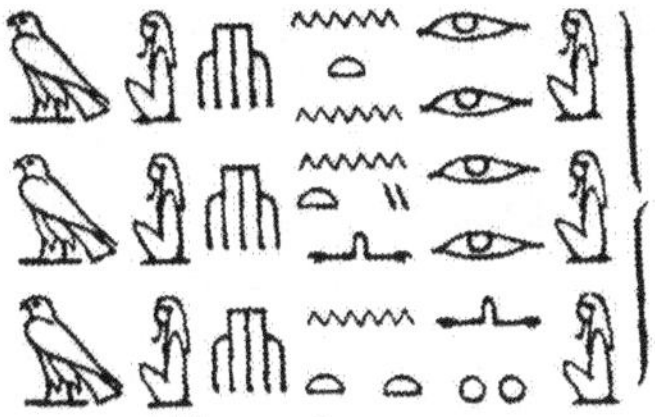 "Horus dwelling in blindness", *i. e.*, Horus (the sky) when neither the sun nor moon is visible.

Ḥeru-khent-Ḳhaṭti 

Ḥeru-khenti-ḥeḥ 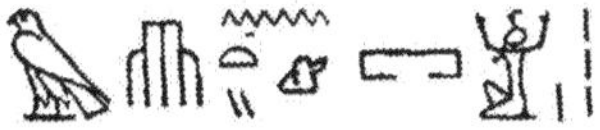 "Horus, governor of eternity".

Ḥeru-khenṭ-ḥeḥ  "Horus, traveller of eternity".

Ḥeru-khenti-Sekhem 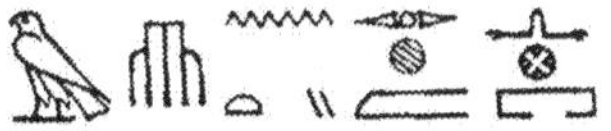 "Horus, governor of Sekhem" (Letopolis).

Ḥeru-khesbeṭ-merti  "Horus with eyes of lapis-lazuli", *i. e.*, blue-eyed Horus.

Ḥeru-sa-Ȧst  "Horus, son of Isis".

Ḥeru-sa-Ȧsȧr  "Horus, son of Osiris'.

Ḥeru-sa-Ḥet-Ḥeru  "Horus, son of Hathor".

Heru-sekhai 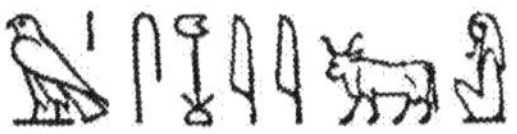

Ḥeru-sheṭ-ḥer  an obscure form of Horus.

Ḥeru-Ṭeḥuti  "Horus-Thoth".

Ḥeru-ṭesher-merti  "Red-eyed Horus".

Ḥeru-shemsu  "followers of Horus", or "body-guard of Horus"; a class of mythical beings.

Ḥeru ṭāṭāf 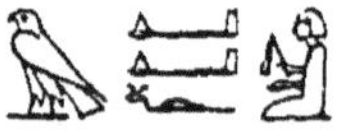 a son of King Khufu who "found" certain Chapters of the Book of the Dead.

ḥerset  crystal.

ḥeḥ  million, a number past counting; plur. . Two millions (?) .

ḥeḥui  . . . .

ḥeḥ en sep 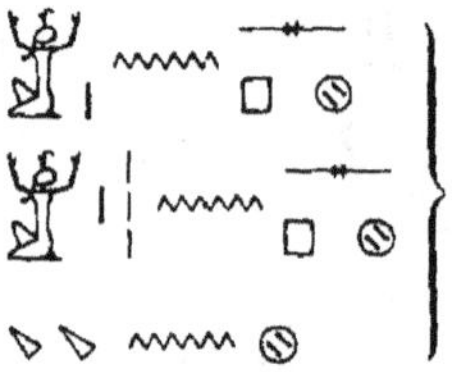 a million times, millions of times.

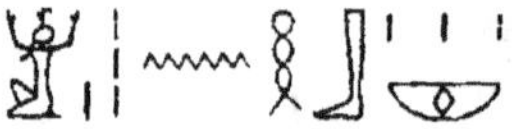 millions of festivals.

ḥeḥ . . . . the land of millions of years.

ḥeḥ eternity, everlastingness.

for ever and ever.

Ḥeḥi the name of a god.

ḥeḥi to hasten after, search for:

ḥes

ḥes to praise, be praised, to give a reward as a sign of praise; praised.

ḥesu

ḥeset favour, act of grace, the gift of praise.

favours, praises.

ḥesi he to whom favour has been shewn by the king or god.

ḥesiu — plur. of preceding.

ḥesuiu

ḥesu — a hymn of praise; the 70 hymns of praise of Rā.

Ḥest — name of a very ancient goddess.

Ḥes-ḥer, **Ḥesi-ḥer** — "savage face"; a proper name.

Ḥes-tchefetch — "savage eye"; a proper name.

ḥesu — dirt, filth.

ḥeseb — faïence (?).

. . . .

ḥeseb 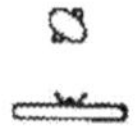 to count up, reckon, estimate, calculate;  reckoned up.

ḥesbet  a reckoning, an account.

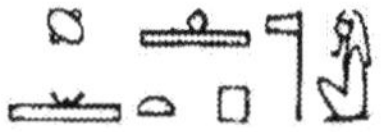 computer of holy offerings.

ḥeseb qeṭu 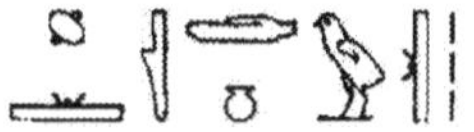 he who estimates characters or dispositions.

ḥeseb ..... 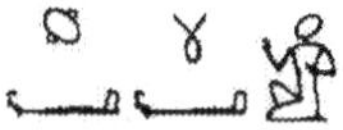 accountant of the linen cloths.

ḥesbet  knife (in the passage 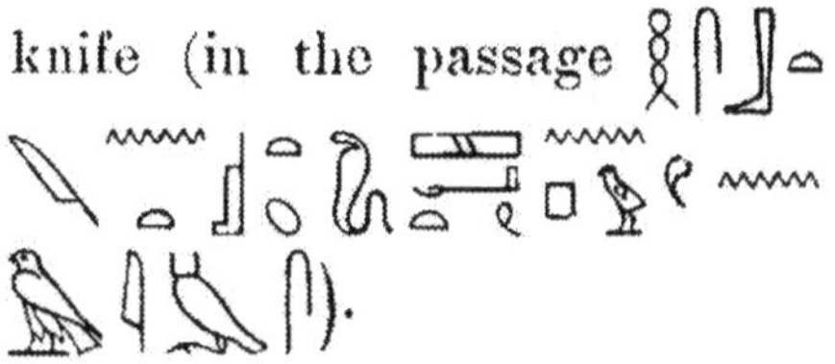).

ḥesepu, ***ḥespu*** 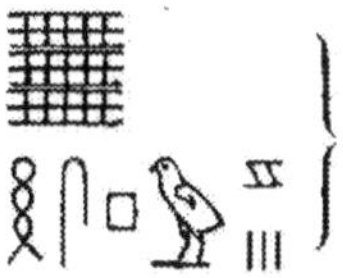 nomes.

ḥespet  gardens.

Ḥesepti 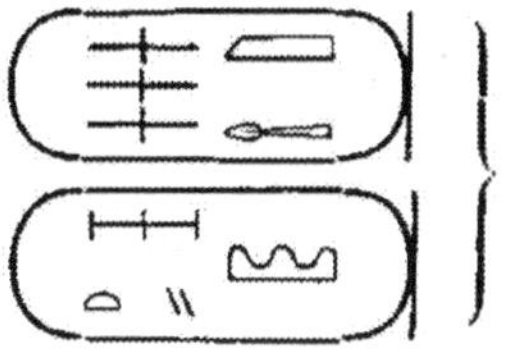 a king of the 1st dynasty. The true reading of this name is Semti, *q. v.*

ḥesmen	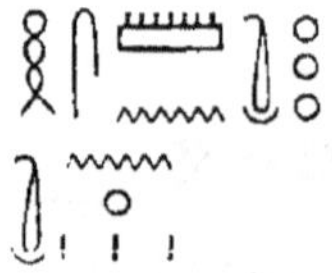	natron.
Ḥesert		the name of a town sacred to Thoth.
ḥesq		to cut, be cut, cut off, to wound, to mow.  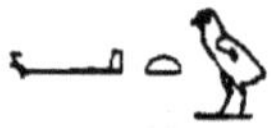 cut.
ḥesqet	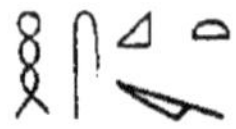	knife.
Ḥest		the name of a city.
ḥest	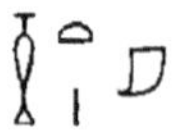	libation vase.
ḥekau		incantations, enchantments, magical formulae, charms, amulets.
ḥekat		
[*ḥeken*		to praise.
ḥekennu		a hymn of praise, praise.
		praises, songs of praise.

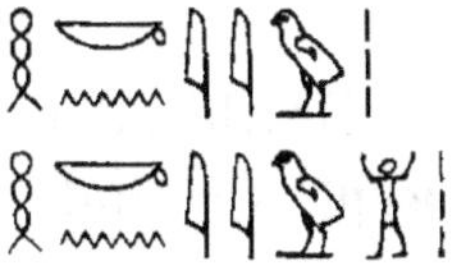 those who praise, singers.

ḥekennu  an unguent or salve.

Ḥekennut  the name of a city.

ḥeq 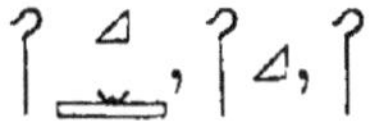 to rule, give commands.

ḥeq  ruler, governor; plur. .

ḥeqet 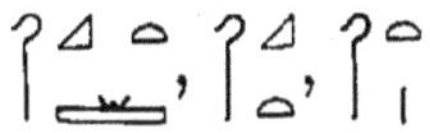 rule, sovereignty, dominion.

ḥeq 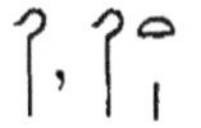 sceptre, emblem of rule.

 ruler of Àmenti.

 governor of towns.

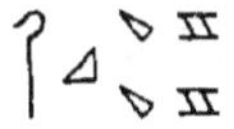 governor of the Two Lands.

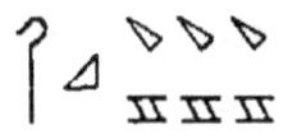 governor of the world.

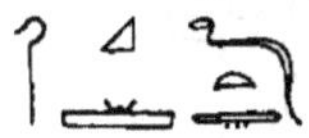 governor of eternity.

Ḥeq-ānṭ the XIIIth nome of Lower Egypt (capital Heliopolis).

Ḥeq-Maāt-Rā setep-en-Ȧmen prenomen of Rameses IV.

ḥeq, ***ḥeqt*** ale, beer.

ḥeqr to be hungry.

ḥeqr hunger.

ḥeqr, ***ḥeqrȧu*** hungry man.

Ḥeqtit a goddess.

ḥet to rejoice.

ḥet house, section of a book, chapter. Compare the Arabic بيت *bêt*, couplet, stanza, portion of a poem. first section, , etc.

ḥet  house, temple; plur. 

Ḥet-āāḥ 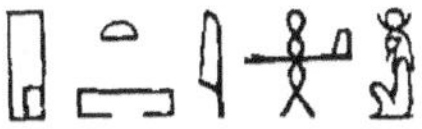 House of the Moon-god.

Ḥet-Ȧsȧr 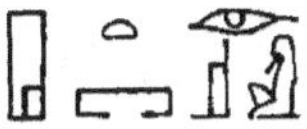 House of Osiris.

Ḥet-Ȧmen 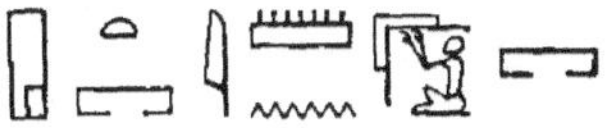 the Hidden House.

Ḥet-Ȧnes 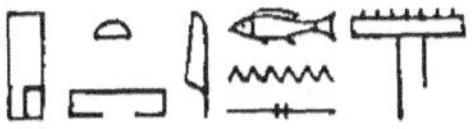 House of the Ȧnes garment.

Ḥet-āshemu 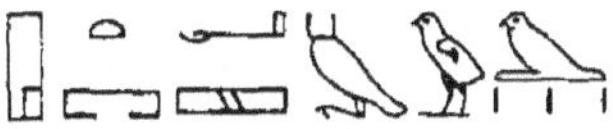 House of the statues of the gods.

Ḥet-ur 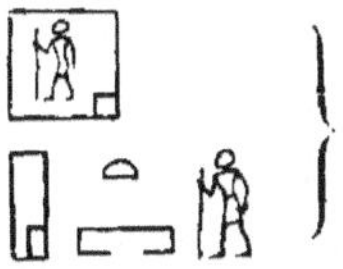 House of the Prince.

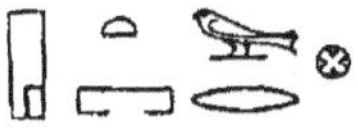 city of the Prince.

Ḥet-uhem-ḥer  House of the Face Renewer.

Ḥet-Usekh-ḥer 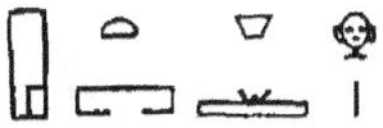 House of Broad-face, *i. e.*, Rā.

Ḥet-Ba  House of the Soul.

Ḥet-Bȧti  House of the king of the North.

Ḥet-Benbent 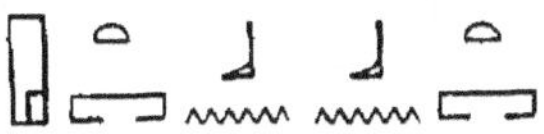 House of the Obelisk.

Ḥet-ka-Ptaḥ House of the Ka of Ptaḥ, *i. e.*, Memphis.

Ḥet-nemt House of the . . . . .

Ḥet ent Ȧnpu House of Ȧnpu.

Ḥet ent ḳem-ḥeru House of the gods who have . . . . their faces.

Ḥet-nub House of gold, *i. e.*, sarcophagus.

Ḥet-nemes House of the Nemes tiara, or headcloth.

Ḥet-Ḥeru House of Horus, *i. e.*, the goddess Hathor.

Ḥet-Kheperȧ House of Kheperȧ.

Ḥet-seru House of the Ram-gods.

Ḥet-kau-Nebt-er-tcher House of the Kau of the Universal Lady.

Ḥet-ṭesheru House of the red-gods.

ḥeti smoke.

ḥeti a wooden pole.

ḥeti heart.

ḥeti = strength.

ḥeti, **ḥetit** throat, gorge.

ḥetep to be at peace, to rest, be satisfied or content, to be at peace with anyone, to remain in one place, to set (of the sun); , satisfied, content; setting in life, *i. e.*, alive when setting; "I make Rā to set like Osiris, and Osiris to set as Rā sets".

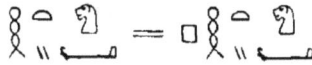

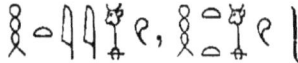

ḥetep, **ḥetepu** peace, content; peace of heart; at peace on truth, or resting on truth.

 in peace; 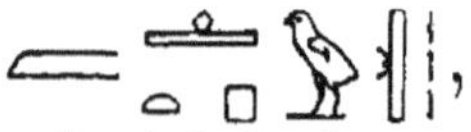,  .

ḥetep  a table of offerings.

ḥetep 
ḥetepet 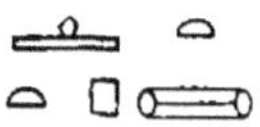 food which is offered to the gods and the dead.

ḥetep neter 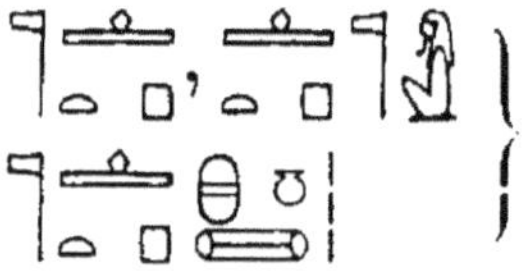 offerings, sacrifices, temple property in general.

ḥetep
ḥetepet  offerings of cakes, ale, oxen, fowl, etc., offerings of propitiation.

Ḥetep  the god of offerings; plur. .

Ḥeteptiu  gods who are regularly provided with offerings.

Ḥetep  the town of the god Ḥetep.

ḥetepu  geese.

Ḥetep-mes  a proper name.

Ḥetep-Ḥeru-ḥems-uāu  a proper name.

Ḥetep-sekhus 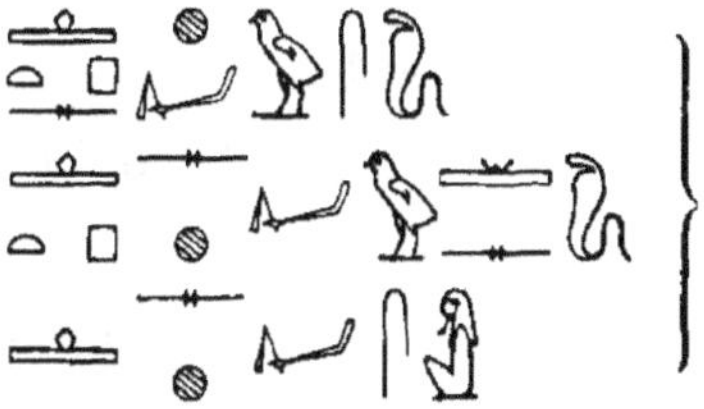 the name of a goddess.

Ḥetep-ka 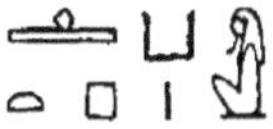 a proper name.

Ḥetep-taui  a proper name.

ḥetem  to destroy, be destroyed.

ḥetemu  destroyers.

ḥetem — to be filled with, provided with; provided.

Ḥetem-ur — "great destroyer"; name of a god.

Ḥetemt-ḥer — "destroying face"; name of a god.

ḥeter — to pay something which is obligatory, legal due, something like tithe.

ḥetru — impost, tax.

ḥetes — to be lord of.

ḥeṭeṭ — scorpion.

Ḥeṭeṭ-t — Scorpion-god.

ḥetch — to do evil, to plunder, steal, waste, destroy, filch away.

ḥetchet — theft, wickedness.

ḥetch — white metal, silver.

ḥetch — to be bright, to shine.

ḥetch ta 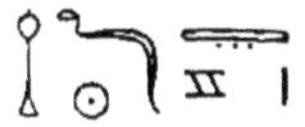 dawn, daybreak.

ḥetchu  light.

Ḥetch-àbeḥu 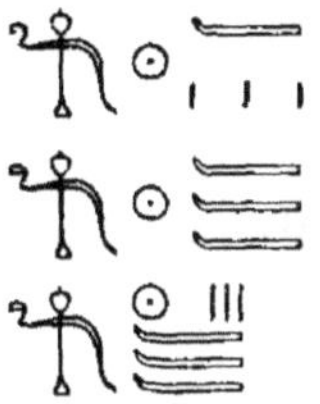 "White teeth"; the name of one of the Forty-two Judges in the Hall of Osiris.

Ḥetch-re 

Ḥetch-re-pesṭ-tchatcha 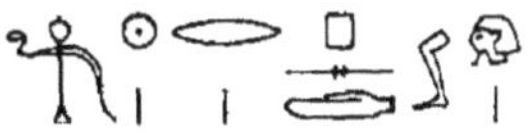 a proper name.

ḥetch-ḥetch  light.

ḥetchet  white.

ḥetchet  the White Crown, or Crown of the South.

ḥetchti  white sandals.

ḥeṭṭ 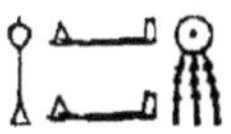 light.

ḥetchu  loaves.

ḥetchas  . . . .

KH.

kha one thousand; two thousand; plur.

kha chamber.

kha
khat the material body, dead body; divine corpse; plur.

khaā to set aside, cast away, to throw.

khāā emissions.

khaām to hasten.

khaāmt throat.

khaibit shade, shadow; plur.

khaitiu slaughterers.

khau  fire.

khaut  fire-altar, altars for burnt offerings.

khaut  festival of burnt offerings.

khau  evil, sin.

khau  basins, bowls.

khau  to be plentiful, abundant.

khaui  darkness, night.

khaut  fiends, the dead.

Khau-tchet-f  a proper name.

khabesu 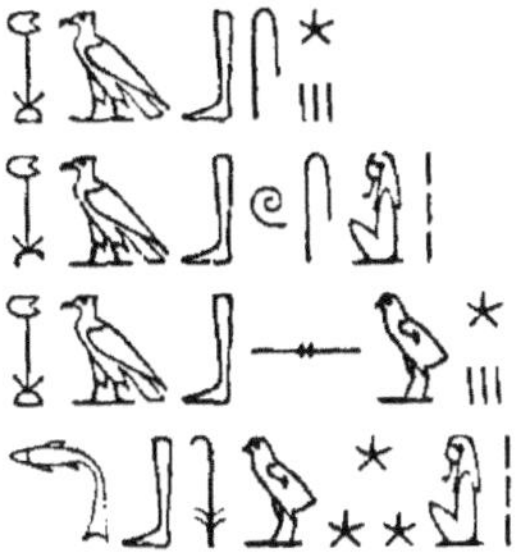 the stars, the thirty-six dekans; the sing. is .

khabet  fraud, deceit.

khapa  a portion of the body, the navel; plur.   buttocks (?) *pudenda muliebris* (?) thighs (?).

Khap-khap  a part of the sky, the god of the Ecliptic (?).

kham  to subdue, be submissive.

khamesu 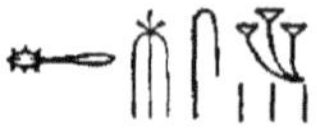 ears of corn.

khart 

kharu 
} a kind of bird with a piercing cry.

Kharsatȧ 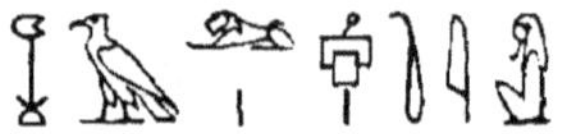 a proper name.

khakh  } to seek, run after.

 } swift.

khasu  the lower eyelids.

khasi bad, evil, wicked, cowardly.

khast territory, country. Perhaps the reading of .

khak-åbu the timid-hearted, enemies.

khaker to be decorated, pretty.

ornaments, decorations.

Khatiu a class of divine beings.

khat fire altar.

khat body, belly, womb; core of the sycamore; plur. , , .

khat the XVIth nome of Lower Egypt (?).

khat a kind of ground.

khatu dead body.

dead bodies.

khatememti nostrils.

khā, ***khāu*** — to rise like the sun, to ascend the throne, to be crowned, to appear (of the king or god). , he who rises ; , one who rises ; , rising ; , , , , risen, crowned ; , beautiful appearance.

khāu — risings, splendours, coronations.

khāu — crowns, diadems.

khāi — crown.

khi — babe, child.

Khiu — the name of a god.

khiuaut — perfume.

khu — to dress.

khu, ***khui***, ***khaui***  to protect, strengthen, to do good to.

khu, ***khut***  protection.

khū  the spirit soul of man which was immortal, as opposed to the  or heart soul which fed upon offerings and lived with the Ka.

 the equipped soul.

 the perfect soul.

khu 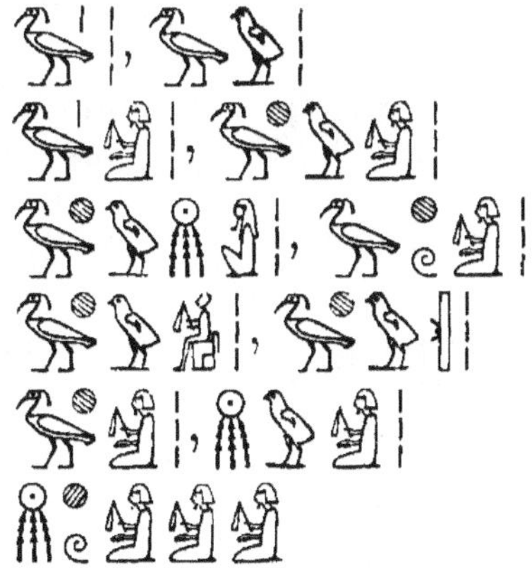 plur. of preceding. Four Khu and Seven Khu are mentioned, and certain of the Khu were nine cubits high.

khu  the spirit soul of Osiris, or Rā.   is a title of Osiris.

khu  to shine, be glorious.

khu 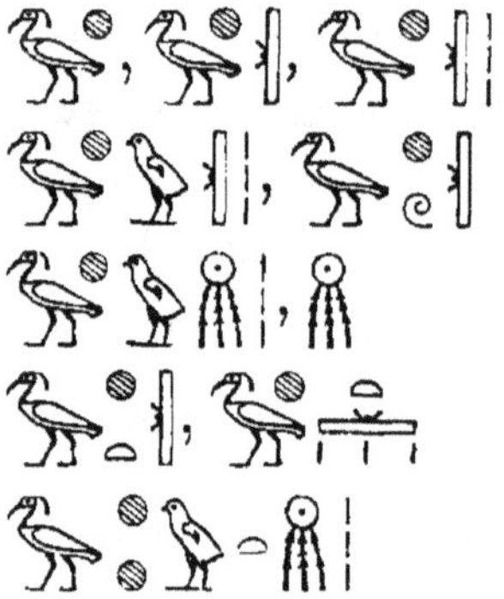 glory, splendour, radiance, brilliant things, light.

khut

khu  words of power.

khut  the name of a light-goddess.

Khu-kheper-ur  a proper name.

Khu-tchet-f  a proper name.

khunt 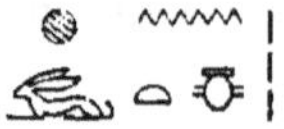 drink offerings.

khus 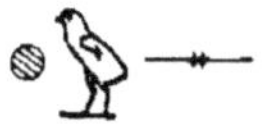 to construct a building, make a cistern.

khut  fire.

khut  the place in the sky where the sun appears on the horizon in rising or setting, the horizon.

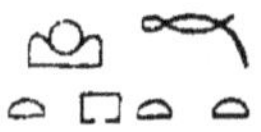 northern horizon.

 western horizon.

 eastern horizon.

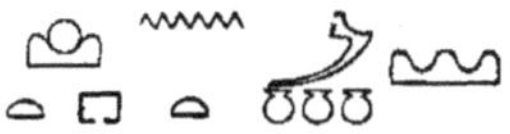 the horizon of the mountain of sunset.

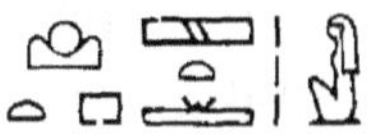 the hidden horizon.

khuti  the gods or beings of the horizon.

khui  words of power.

kheb 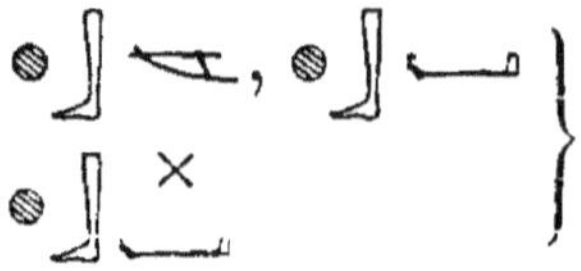 to defraud, pilfer, steal.

kheb  slaughter.

kheb 
khebȧ  to be defeated, overthrown.

khebu 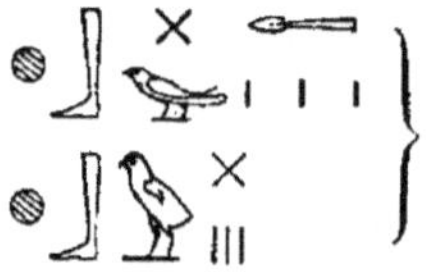 defeat, defeated ones.

kheba  to destroy.

khebu  to be dipped into some liquid, steeped.

Khebent  a proper name.

khebent  evil, wickedness.

khebenti  evil doers.

khebkheb  to destroy.

khebkhebt  destruction.

khebkheb  torture chamber.

khebs  to plough ;  plougher.

khebs ta 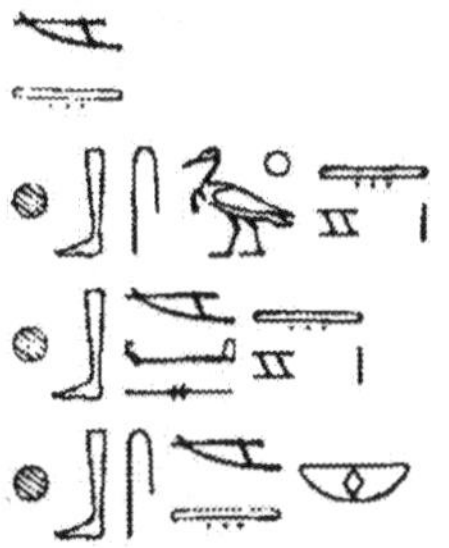 the ceremony or festival of ploughing the earth.

khebsu  devourer (?).

khebs  star, lamp.

 stars, the Thirty-six dekans.

khebt 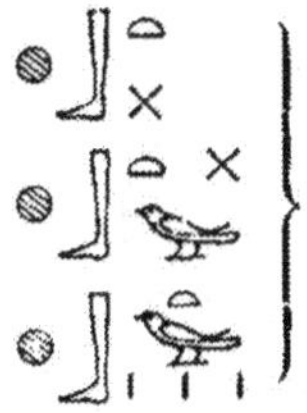 loss, injury, damage ;  destroyer.

khebt 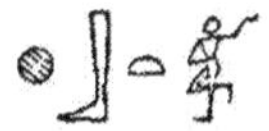 dance.

khebt 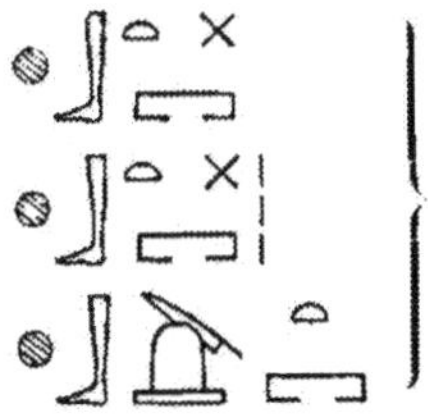 torture chamber, slaughter house.

khep  to travel, journey.

khept  journey.

khep  a part of the body, navel (?).

khepu 

Khepiu 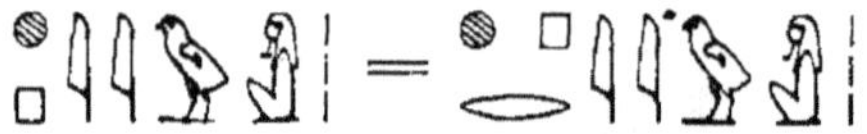 the gods who are.

kheper, *kheperu* 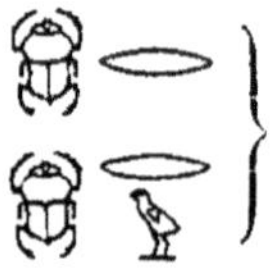 to come into being, become, exist, subsist, to turn into something, to create, to form, fashion; 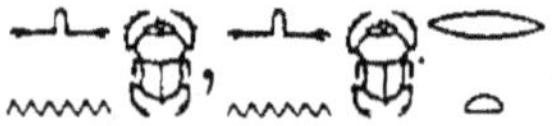 non-existent; 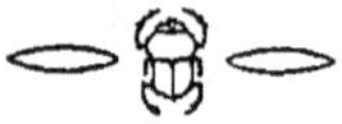 when takes place, when it happens;  to be or become satisfied;   is thy name what?  those who become.

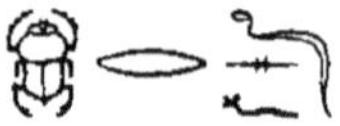 self-created.

khepert  that which is, what exists, thing.

kheperu 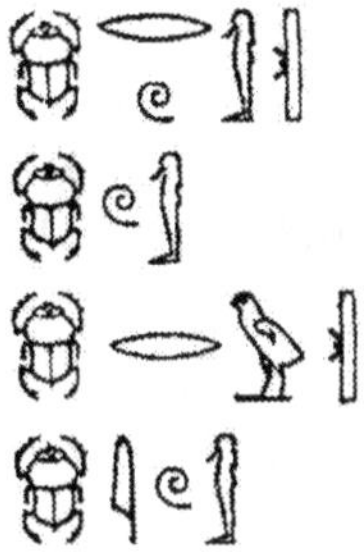 form, phase of being, something evolved, transformation, change.

kheperu 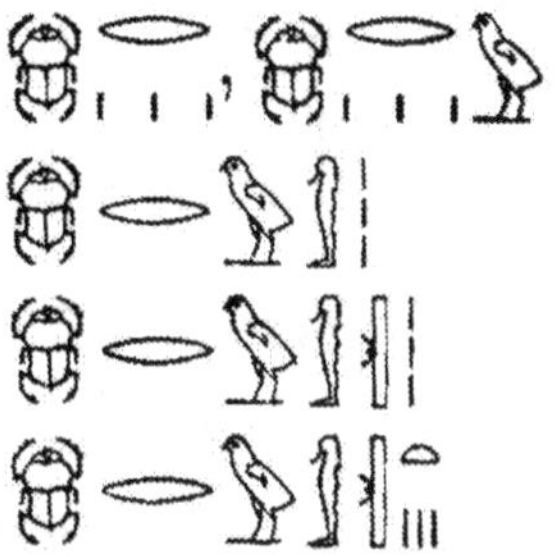 forms, transformations.

kheperut

kheper 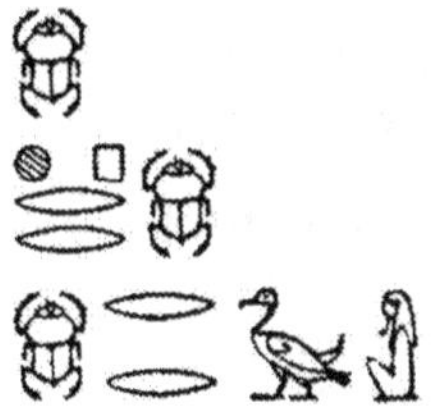 scarab, beetle.

khepprer

Kheperȧ / ***Kheperrȧ*** (?)  the Beetle-god, a form of the Sun-god. 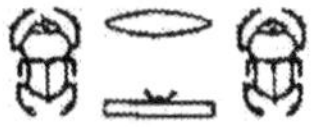 .

khepesh 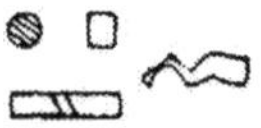 thigh; plur. 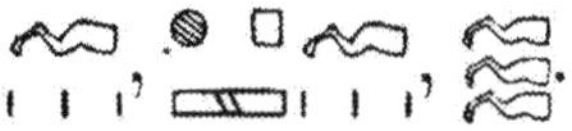.

Khepesh 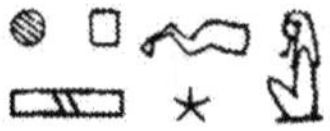 the constellation of the Thigh.

khept

kheptet } buttock; plur.

khept }

khefa food.

khefā to grasp, to seize with the hand;

khefā } fist, grasp.

khefāt }

khefit quay, river bank.

kheft in front of, according to, conformably to, when.

kheft ḥer opposite to, before the face of.

khefti , } enemy, fiend.

kheftiu , } enemies.

khem — to burn.

khem — shrine.

khem — to be ignorant, to put an end to (?); ignorant, helpless; unknown is his name.

khem — an ignorant man.

khem — to overthrow, destroy.

khemiu, ***khemit*** — overthrower, those who overthrow, destructions.

Khemi — the name of one of the Forty-two Judges in the Hall of Osiris.

khemā — to lay hold of, to seize and carry off.

khemāu — snatchers, seizers.

khemu — wind, air.

khemenu  eight;  eighth.

Khemenu  the eight gods of the Company of Thoth who dwelt at Hermopolis.

Khemenu  the city of the Eight gods, Hermopolis.

khemt 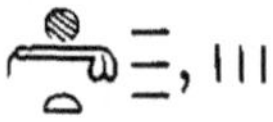 three;  third.

khemt 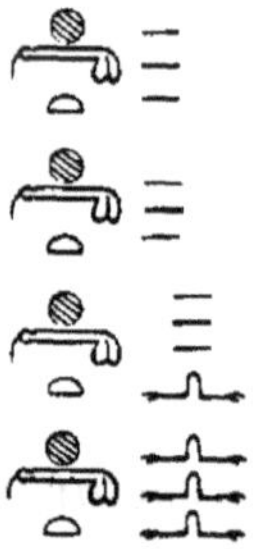 to think, to know, to intend.  is sometimes written by mistake for .

khemt 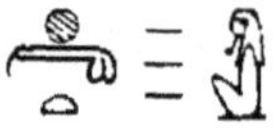 the god of thought.

khen, ***khenn***, ***khennu***  to hover over, to flutter like a bird when alighting on a tree, to perch on something.

Khenit  the goddesses who fly or dance.

khen 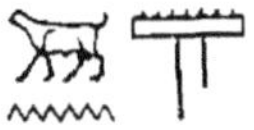 to be dressed, garment.

khen 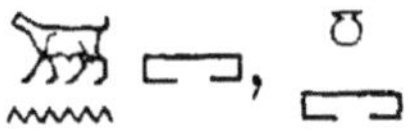 the inner part of a house, house.

 within.

Khennu  the name of a city in the Sekhet-ḥetep.

khen 

khenn  to decay, to rot, to wither.

khen  to break, smash, destroy, stir up strife, disturb, trouble.

khennu 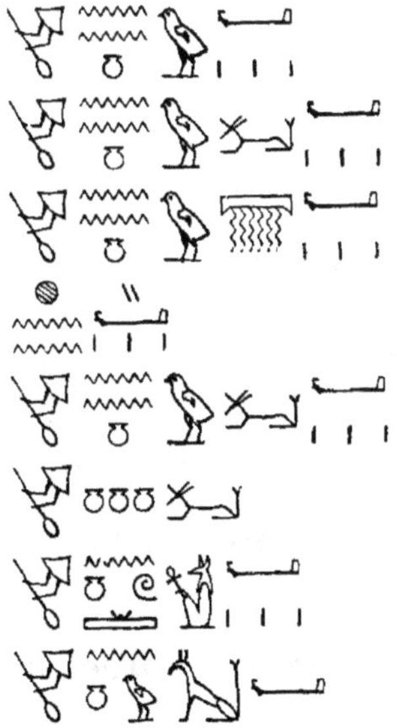 trouble, revolt, destruction, storm, opposition.

khenui 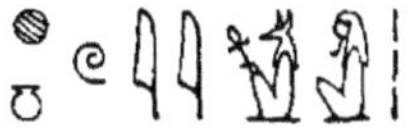 rebels.

khen
khenen

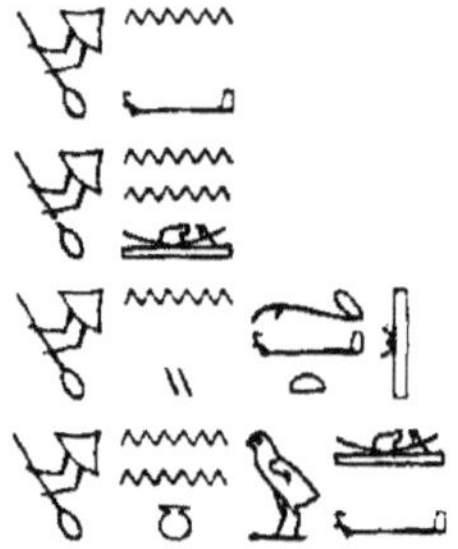

to ferry across a stream, to transport by water, to row, to paddle.

khent  a passage, a journey.

khenen 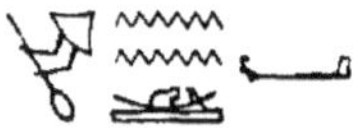 sailor.

khenȧ 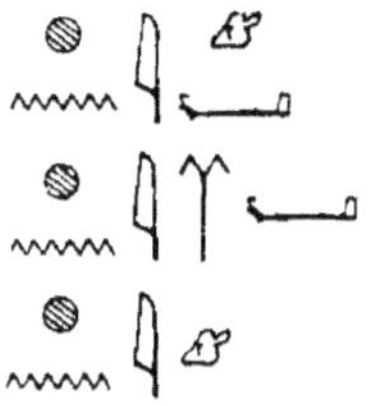 to lock up, shut up, keep in captivity.

khenp  to draw out, pluck out.

 a tearing; 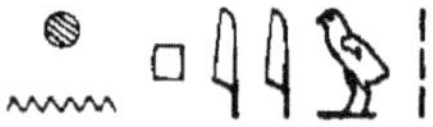 tearers, renders.

khenf 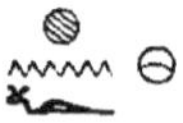 a bread-cake.

khenem  jasper, carnelian.

khnem  to form, join up or together.

Khnem the god Khnemu, the Potter-god.

Khnemu-Ḥeru-Ḥetep the name of a god.

khnem well; a proper name (?).

Khnemet-urt a proper name.

Khemet-em-ānkh-ȧnnuit the name of one of the Seven Cows.

henem to snuff the air, to smell, scent out.

henemti nurse, servant, companion.

henemu . . . .

henem-nefer a proper name?

khenemem  to smell, feed upon (?).

Khenememti  the two ministering goddesses, Isis and Nephthys.

khenemes 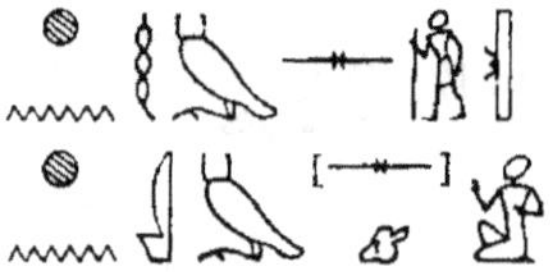 protector, friend.

khennu  those who cry out.

khennu 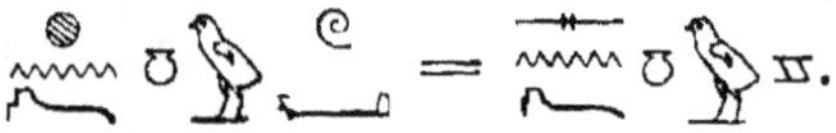

khennu  injury, evil hap.

khenrà  to shut in, imprison.

khenrà 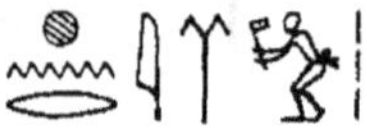 fiends.

khenrit 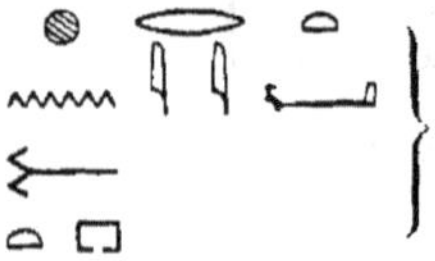 prison.

khens  to stride about, to journey, travel.

Khensu  "traveller", a name of the Moon-god.

Khensu-p-åru-sekheru em Uast 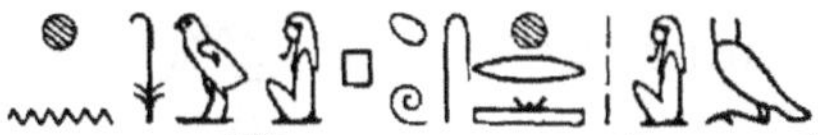  Khensu, worker of destinies in Thebes.

Khensu em Uast Nefer-ḥetepi  Khensu in Thebes, Nefer-ḥetep.

khent 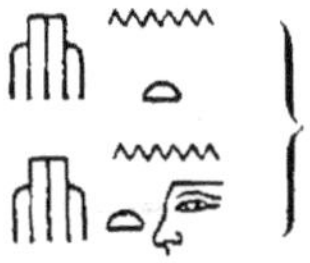 the nose.

khent  the fore part of anything, the front, in front of, before.

khenti  he who is in front, or at the head, chief, governor.

Khenti Åmenti  He who is at the head of Åmenti and of those who are therein; a title of Osiris.

Khenti Āḥa he who is chief of the fighting.

Khenti-aḥāt .

Khenti-āt-ȧment a title of Osiris.

Khenti-Un a title of Osiris.

Khenti-Peḳu a title of Osiris.

Khenti-menȧtuf a title of Osiris.

Khenti-Naȧreṭ-f a title of Osiris.

Khenti-nut-f a title of Osiris.

Khenti-nep a title of Osiris.

Khenti-n-merti (?) a title of Horus.

Khenti neter ḥet "Chief of the god-house".

Khenti neter seḥ "Chief of the god-hall".

Khenti Re-stau "Chief of the funerary corridors"; a title of Osiris.

Khenti-hetut-f "Chief of his fire".

Khentiu ḥensekti "Chiefs of long hair and beards".

Khent ḥeḥ a title of Osiris.

Khenti Ḥeq-ȧnṭ a title of Osiris.

Khenti ḥespu the name of the bows of the magic boat.

Khenti-khas a name of a god.

Khenti-Khati, ***Khent-Khaṭti*** "the dweller in the belly"; a title of Horus.

Khenti-Suten-ḥenen a title of Osiris.

Khenti-Sekhem a title of Horus of Letopolis.

Khenti-seḥ-ḥemt "chief of the house of the wife"; a title of Osiris.

Khenti-seḥt-kaut-f "chief of the house of his cows"; a title of Osiris,

Khent-she (or ***mer***)-***Āa-perti*** "chief of the Lake of Pharaoh"; a title of Osiris.

Khenti-Tenent a title of Osiris.

khent abode, the private portion of a palace or temple; plur. , , .

khent, ***khenti*** to sail upstream, usually to the south; .

khentiu sailors.

khenti a mineral colour.

khenṭ to travel, journey.

khenṭi traveller.

khenṭi to ascend.

khenṭ thigh, haunch.

Khenṭ-Ḥepiu name of the steering pole.

khentch to travel.

kher a preposition, with, before, etc.; under the Majesty of, in the reign of.

khert the things of, the affairs of, property of; the affairs of the country; the business of the Two Lands.

kher under, beneath; things or beings who are below.

under the favour of.

before.

kheri low-lying land, the earth as opposed to the sky; plur.

kheru  men and women in subjection, serfs, vassals, or perhaps the tillers of low-lying lands.

kher  to have, hold, possess. 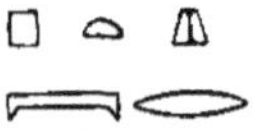

"heaven hath thy soul, earth hath thy form".

khert 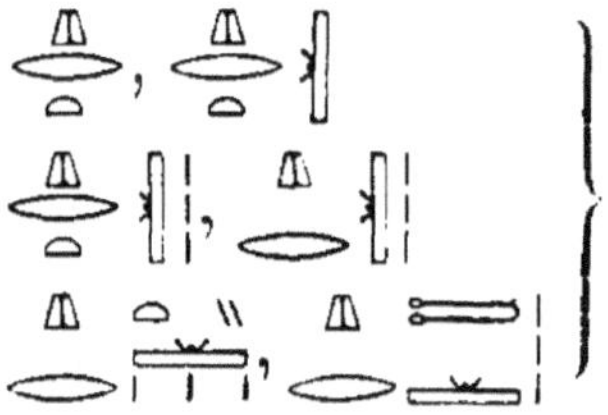 goods, possessions, share, portion, lot, what belongs to someone, property, wealth, products of.

khert hru  the things of the day, what belongs to the day, daily round or routine.

 every-day matters.

kher
kherui  testicles.

kher 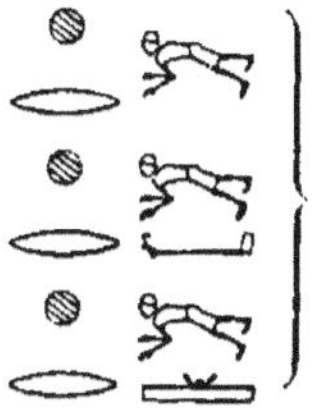 to fall down, to happen.

kheri 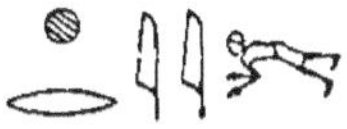 fallen one, foe.

kherit 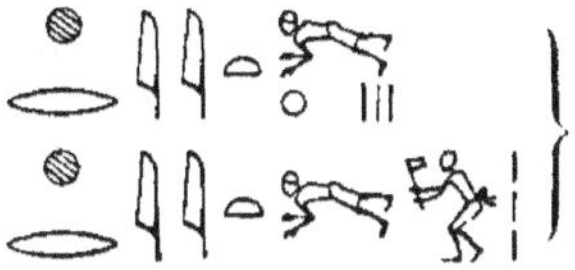 the dead, the damned.

kherit 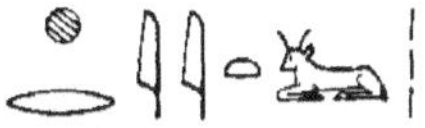 victims for sacrifice.

Kher  the name of a god.

Kherȧ  a proper name.

kheru 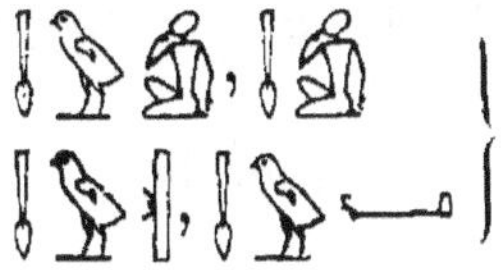 voice, word, speech, sound; plur. 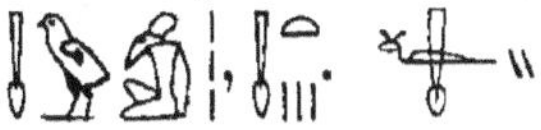 reading unknown.

 loud-voiced.

 a man's voice.

 multiplying the sound of words, *i. e.*, talking overmuch.

kheriu enemies, hostile attacks.

Kher-āḥa a city near the site of the modern Fusṭâṭ, or Old Cairo.

kherp to be chief or master, to direct, be in command, to present an offering.

Kherp Prince, Chief; plur.

Kherp-nest title of a priest.

kherpu steering pole.

kherefu two Lion-gods.

kher ḥeb the priest who recited religious compositions and the Liturgy.

Kherserȧu a proper name.

khersek to destroy;

Khersek-Shu a proper name.

khert course.

khertu it is said, speech.

khert̤ child; plur.

a title of the scribe Nebseni.

khekh to run.

khekh
khekhi throat.

khekhu darkness.

khes to slay.

khesu ritual, a book.

khesbet̤ blue stone, lapis-lazuli;

real lapis-lazuli as opposed to blue paste.

blue-eyed.

khesef to meet, to oppose, to drive back, repulse; repulse; irresistible.

khesef-ā

kheseft repulse.

khesefu adversaries, foes; hostile faces.

bowings down before.

Khesef-aṭ a proper name.

Khesef-ḥer-āsh-kheru a proper name.

Khesef-ḥer-khemiu the name of the herald of the Seventh Ārit.

Khesem  Letopolis.

khesṭeḥ  to destroy.

khet 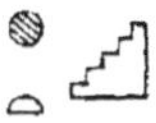 steps, throne.

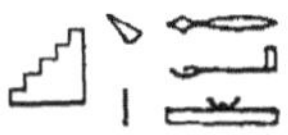 great stairs of Osiris.

khet  fire, flame.

khet  wood, tree, stick, staff, sceptre, board;  planks of a ship; 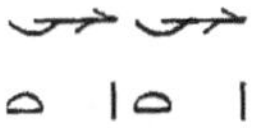 rod.

khet 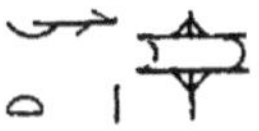 mast.

khet 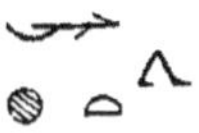
khetkhet  } to retreat, go back.

khet  back, behind.

 behind, in the following of.

 followers.

het 
hetu 
 } to write, to cut on wood or stone; ,  cut, engraved.

khet things, affairs, cases, goods, property.

everything.

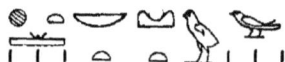

all sorts of bad things.

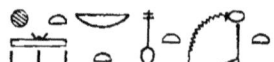

everything beautiful and pure.

all most beautiful things.

sweet things.

everything bad and evil.

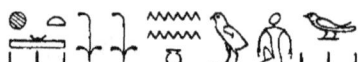

weak things.

things about Osiris.

things on the altars.

things of Horus (*i. e.*, offerings, property of).

things (offerings) of the night.

things of the festal altars.

things of his father Osiris.

things of the Eye of Horus.

things of the Boat.

their personal things.

khetu . . . .

khetita fiends, devils.

khetem to shut in, to seal, close the door on;

khetemiu those shut in.

khetemit closed place, prison.

kheṭ to float down stream.

kheṭebet

S.

s her, she, its;

sa person, man, one.

everyone, everybody.

set  woman.

sa  son.

 son of Rā.

 firstborn son.

sat  daughter.

 daughter of Rā.

sati  the two divine daughters, *i. e.*, Isis and Nephthys.

Sa-mer-f  "Son loving him"; title of a priest.

Sa-pa-nemmȧ  a proper name.

Sa-ta 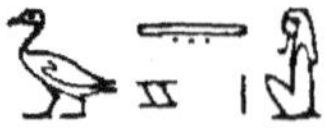 "son of the earth"; the name of a serpent.

sa  side, back.

 in the side.

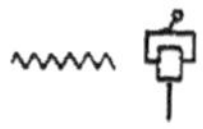 afterwards.

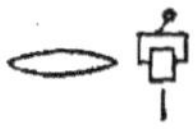 behind.

after.

by the back.

sa chamber (?).

sa to protect, a thing which protects, amulet; plur. , as a protection. See .

sa to perceive, know, recognize.

knower of hearts, trier of reins.

sauu wise man.

Sa

Sau the god of knowledge.

Sa-Àmenti-Rā a proper name.

Saau-ur a proper name.

Saa "shepherd"; a name of Osiris.

21*

sau 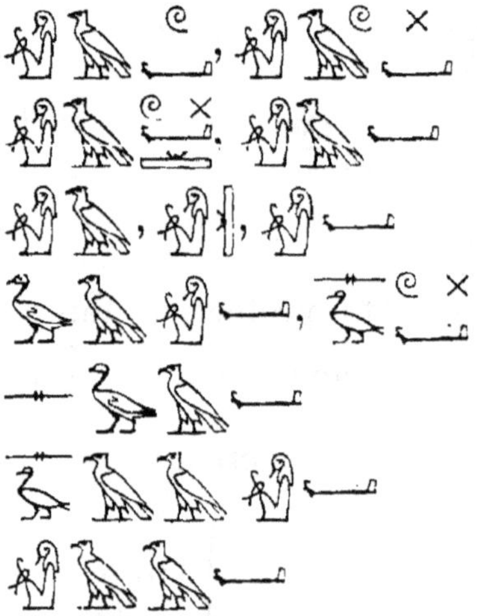 to watch, keep guard over, protect, keep in restraint; to tend sheep.

sau, sai  watcher, guardian, shepherd

 plur. of preceding.

 people in fetters.

 watchers, warders, fetterers, fetters.

sait 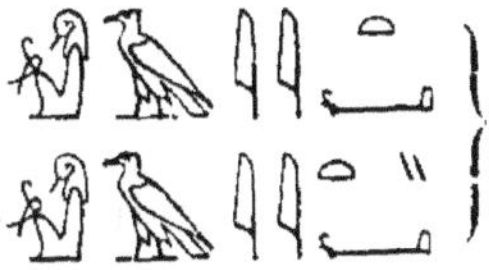 restraint, ward.

sau  corruption.

Sau  the city of Saïs.

 Upper Saïs.

 Lower Saïs.

saāiu 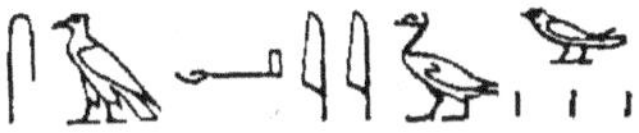 evil ones (?).

s-au  to make glad, to provision.

 wide goings, journeyings.

sauṭ  to transfer.

sab  making to cease.

sab  jackal; plur. .

Sab (?)

Sabȧ  the name of a god.

Sabes  the herald of the Second Ārit.

sam  to consume, burn up.

Samiu		a group of gods or fiends.
samiu		the gods with hair.
samut		hair.
samit		tresses, hair.
Saneḥem		the city of grasshoppers.
saneḥemu		grasshoppers.
Sar	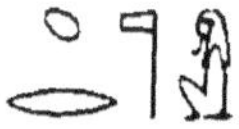	Osiris.
saru		order of dismissal (?).
sariu		evilly disposed persons.
saḥ	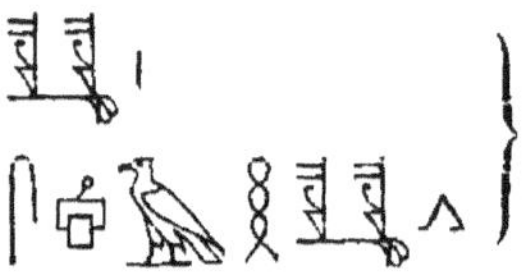	to journey, to travel.
saḥt	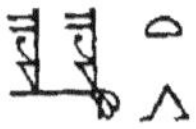	journey.
saḥ		an estate, farm, homestead.
saḥ	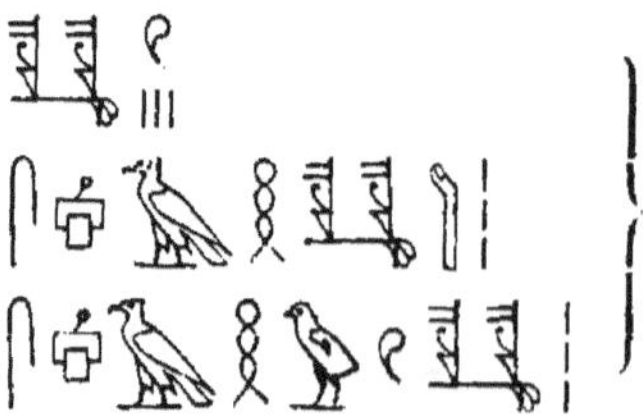	fingers, toes, claws.

Saḥ  Orion.

Saḥ-en-mut-f 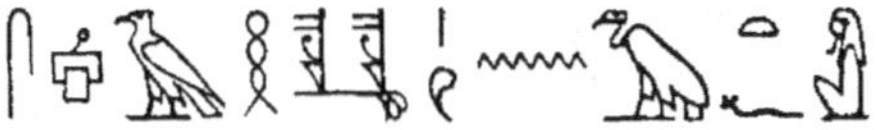 a proper name.

saq  to collect, gather together.

Saq-baiu 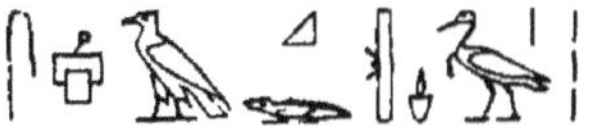 "collector of souls"; the name of a boat.

Saqnaqat  a proper name.

ṡat 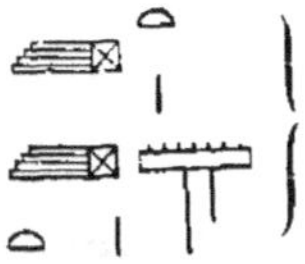 apparel, garment, robe, dress.

ṡat  to think scorn of the god.

ṡat  evil, evil one.

ṡatu  wall, building.

ṡat  earth, ground, floor of a chamber.

ṡati  threshold.

Satiu  the city of Siut, the modern Asyûṭ.

saṭu  terrors.

Sȧ  the name of a town and of a god.

Sȧa  the god Sa.

Sȧa  the name of a town and of a god.

Sȧu  to cry out.

sȧat  to encroach, attack.

Sȧatiu   slaughterers.

; plur. 

sȧu  to drink water.

sȧbit  animals for sacrifice.

sȧb-kui 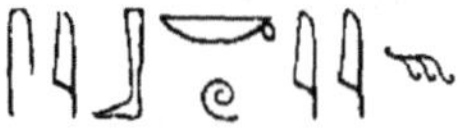 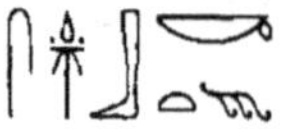 to make to weep.

sȧp  to judge, decide, compute, reckon up, examine, inspect, inquire into; , 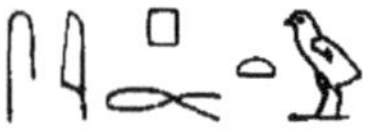 judged, computed.

sȧpu  judge, judgment; plur. .

sȧp 
 account, reckoning, a list of goods, property.

sȧpti 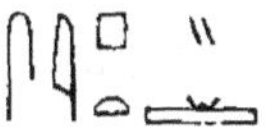

Sȧp 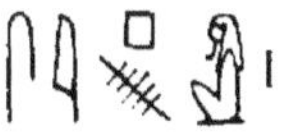 the name of a god.

sȧpt  abode of the god Sȧp.

sȧm (***sȧam***)  to shew kindness.

sȧn  length, extent.

sȧn 
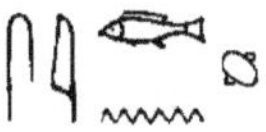
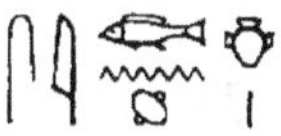 to be kind, do good to, benefit, nourish; 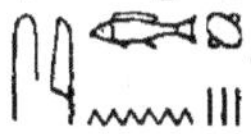 things which benefit.

sȧn 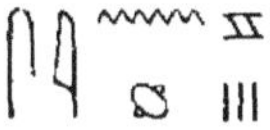 clay.

sȧn  to walk, march, pass along.

sȧn 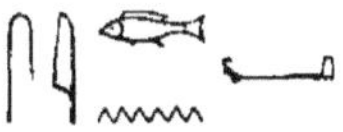 to pull, draw.

sȧn 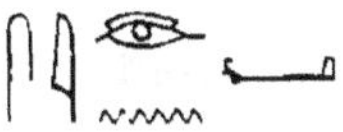 to be in good case.

sȧs 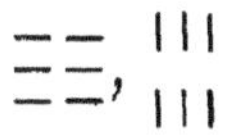 six; 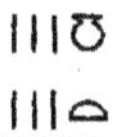 sixth;  = 1/6;  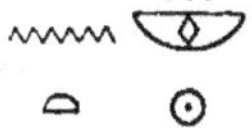 the festival held on the sixth day of each month.

Sȧsȧ  the name of a city =  .

sȧka 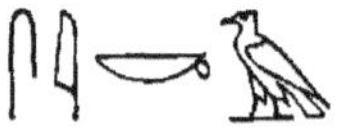 to afford relief.

sȧqer  to make strong, or perfect.

Sȧti  the name of a city.

sȧtti (?)  executioners.

sȧṭi  headsman, executioner.

sȧṭen  to transfer.

sāa 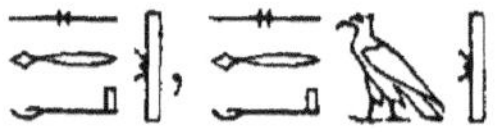 to magnify.

sāam  to slay.

sāb (**suāb**) 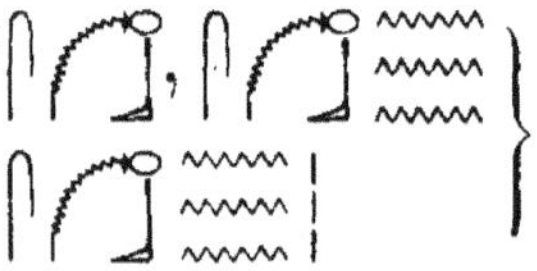 to wash, purify, cleanse.

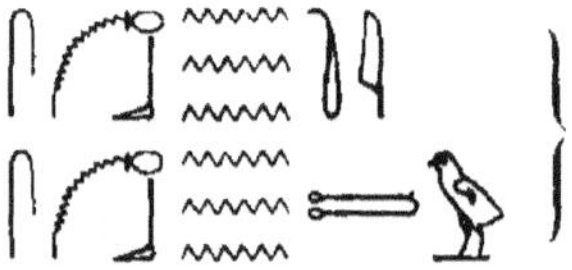 washed, plated.

sāba  to make to enter, force an entrance.

sām — to make to eat or drink, to swallow.

sāmiu — eaters, devourers.

Sām-em-senf — "drinker of blood"; a proper name.

Sām-em-ḳesu — "eater of bones"; a proper name.

sām — flowers, plants.

sāma — . . . .

sānkh — to vivify, keep alive, to support life, to feed, give sustenance to, "vivifier of hearts"; a title of Osiris.

sānṭ — to make strong.

sār — to make to come, to introduce.

sārt 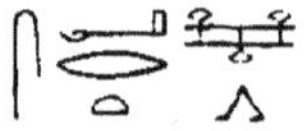 approach, introduction.

sāriu  introducers.

sāḥ, **sāḥu**  the spiritual body of a man, later the mummy; plur. . Mentioned with the  and the .

sāḥ 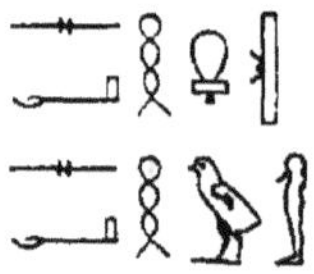 to become a *sāḥ*, 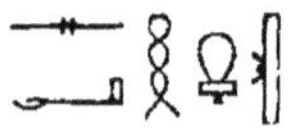 endowed with a *sāḥ*.

sāḥ 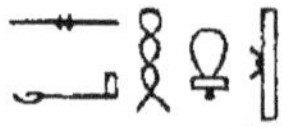 honour.

sāḥā 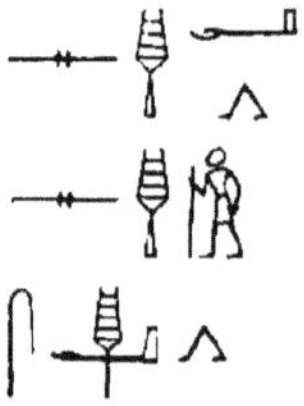 to set up, make to stand up.

 set up a pillar.

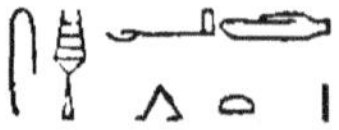 set up the Ṭeṭ.

su  he, him: 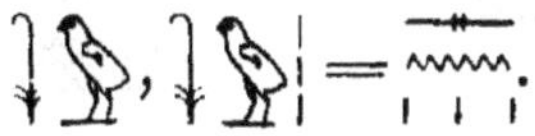

su tchesef  he himself.

sua 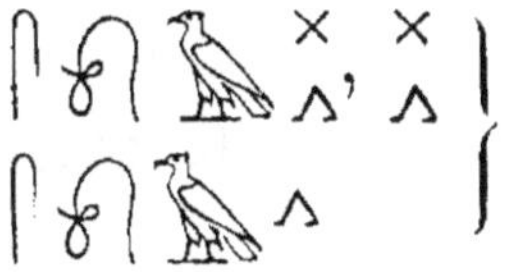 to pass by.

suash 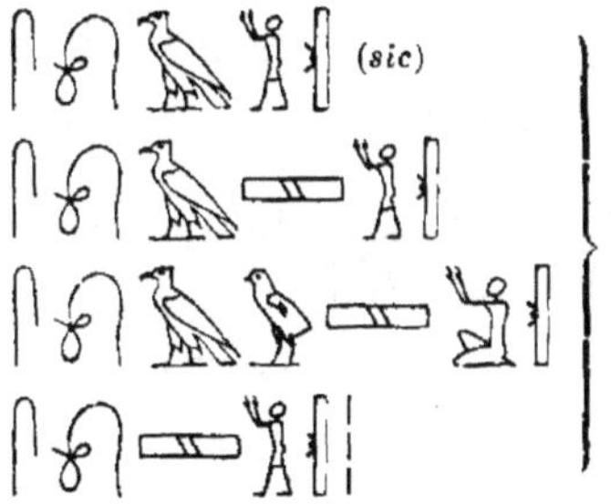

suatch 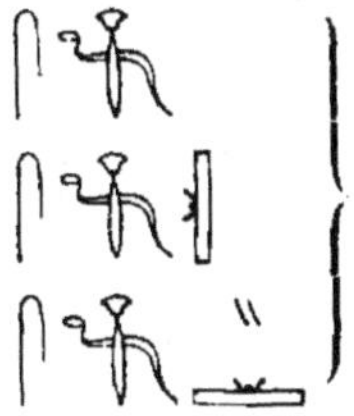 to be green, vigorous, flourishing.

suȧs  decay.

sui  crocodile.

sun 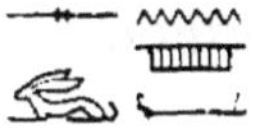 to open.

sun  to be destroyed.

sun 
sunen  pool, lake, any large collection of water.

sunȧt  unguent.

Sunnu 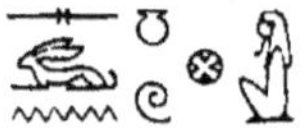 the city called by the Greek Syene. Heb. סְוֵנֵה.

surȧ   to give to drink, to drink.

suriu  drinkers.

surṭ 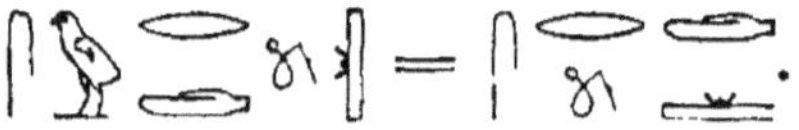

suha  to supplicate.

suḥ 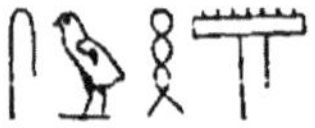 a garment.

suḥt  egg;  testicles (?).

sukha  evil recollection.

sukheṭ  to embalm, mummify.

suser 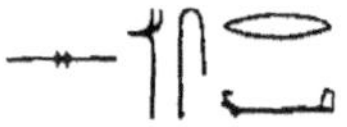 to strengthen.

susekh  to make broad, to make wide (*i. e.*, long) the steps.

Sukaṭi  the name of a god.

sut  he, it, himself, they, them.

sut  hair.

Sut 
Suti  the god of darkness and night, and of physical and moral evil.

Suti-mes  a proper name.

suten , ,  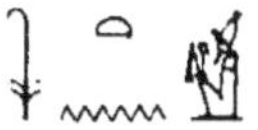 king;  king of the gods.

 the reigning king.

 kings.

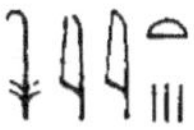,  sovereignty, kingship, reign.

sutenit  to reign, sovereignty.

suten bȧti  King of the South and North.

suteniu bȧtiu   plur. of preceding.

suten bȧt Ȧsȧr  Osiris, king of the Two Egypts.

suten ḥeḥ  "king of eternity"; a title of Osiris.

suten Ṭuat  "king of the Ṭuat"; a title of Osiris.

suten ḥemt  "king's woman", *i. e.*, queen.

suten sesh  "king's scribe", *i. e.*, royal scribe.

suten . . . . 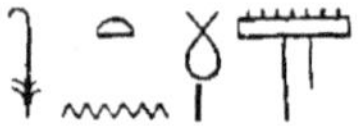 byssus; plur. .

suten ṭā ḥetep  an ancient formula meaning "may the king give an offering", dating from the time when the king sent gifts for the funeral feasts of his loyal servants. At a later period its use was purely conventional in funerary texts.

Suten-ḥenen (or ***Ḥenensu***)  Herakleopolis, the חָנֵס of Isaiah XXX. 4. The Copts called it ϩⲛⲉⲥ, or ϩⲛⲏⲥ, or ⲉϩⲛⲏⲥ, and its Arabic name is اهناس.

sutennu 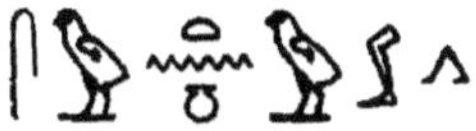 to extend, walk with long strides.

suṭekh  to treat with medicaments, to embalm.

sutcha / ***setcha***  to set out on a journey, to go, travel.

sutcha / ***setcha***  to be strong, sound, well, to make strong and happy.

i  it, its, them.

i  fulness, satiety.

ia 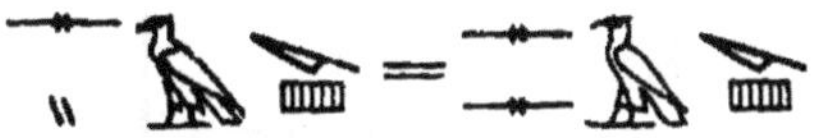 to cut, engrave.

eb (***Ḳeb?***) 
ebu (***Ḳebu***)  the Earth-god.

 the abode of Seb (or Ḳeb).

b 
bbi  to guide, to lead, to pass by or through a place; 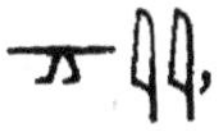, 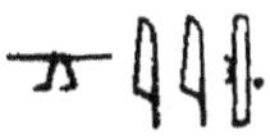.

 passage.

sba  star, Star-god; plur. 

sbaiu  stars.

sba 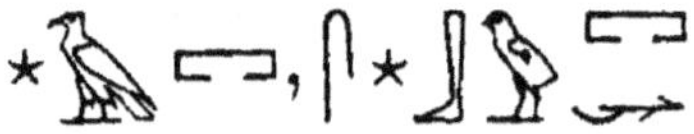

sbau  door, gate, pylon; the forms   also occur.

sbau 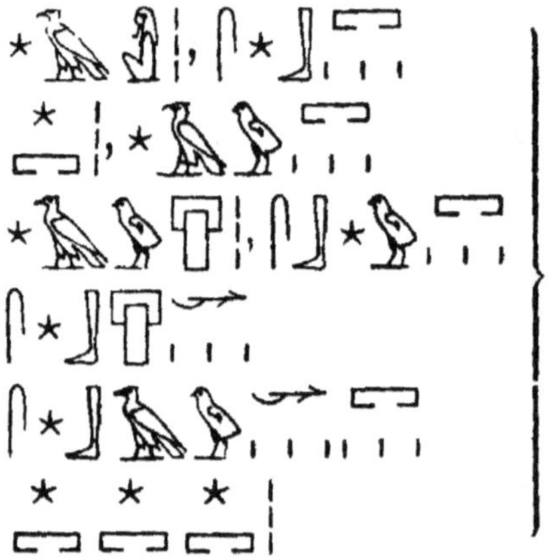 plur. of preceding.

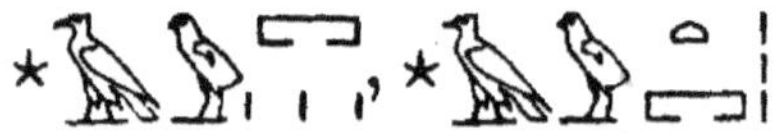 doors of the Other World.

sba  to instruct.

sbaut  to rebel.

sebaḳi  helpless one, inert, weak.

Sebȧ  the name of a goddess.

sebȧ 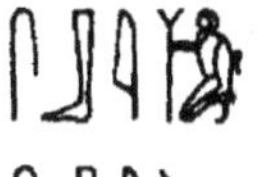 to be an enemy of some one.

sebȧ  enemy, fiend.

sebȧu  plur. of preceding.

eben  to retreat, depart.

ebeḥ 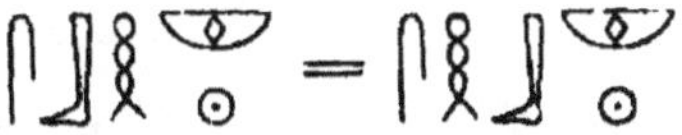 to keep a festival.

ebeḥ  to call upon someone, to invoke.

ebḥet, **ebḥit** 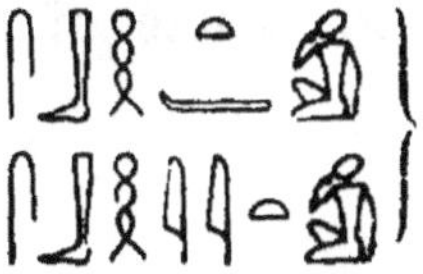 invocation, praise.

sebekh be master of, have power over (?).

sebkhet gate, pylon.

plur. of preceding.

sebekhbekht to scatter (?).

Sebek the Crocodile-god, who was a form of the Sun-god.

Sebeku the Crocodile-gods.

sebeq leg, thigh.

Sebeq-en-Shesmu a proper name.

Sebeq-en-Tem a proper name.

Sebeḳ, ***Sebḳa***, ***Sebaḳu*** the name of a god.

sebt  to be pleased (?), laugh, laughter.

sebt  walls.

sep  season, luck, fate, occasion, opportunity, circumstance, case, etc.; plur. 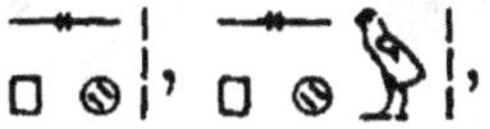 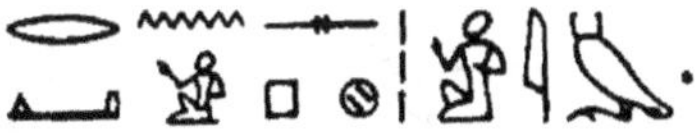.

 a right case, a just trial.

 ill luck, a bad time.

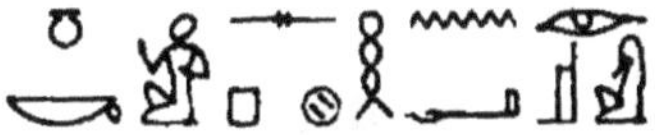 I am Fate and Osiris.

 a prosperous time.

 the occasion of the night.

 likewise, at the same time.

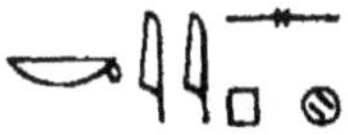 another time or opportunity.

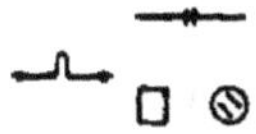 at no time, never.

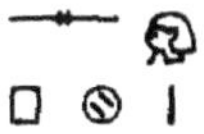 primeval time, when the world began.

sep 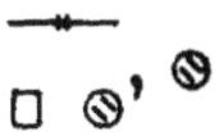 time;  twice;  four times;  millions of times.

sep sen	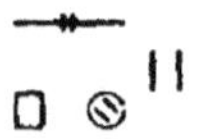	duplicity.
sep		to pass sentence.
sep		crown (?).
Sep		the name of a god.
Sepa	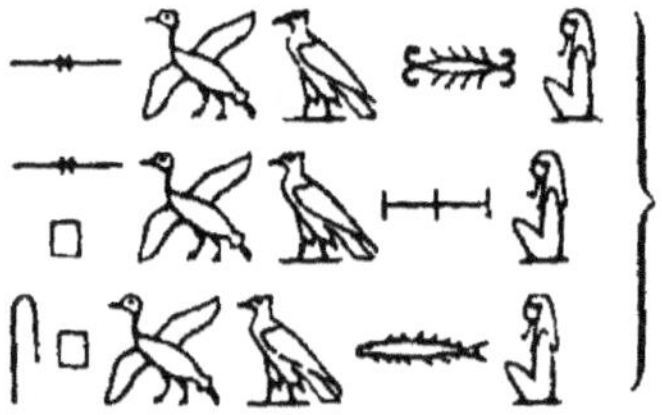	the name of a god.
seppi / ***sepi***	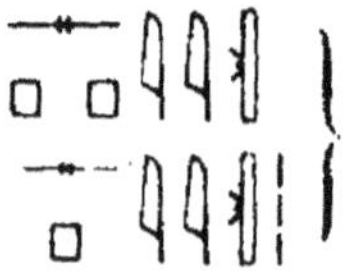	remainder.
seppu	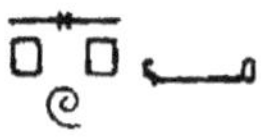	omission.
sper		to come to a place, to arrive at;  comers.
sper		to speak to, address.
speh	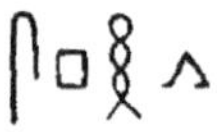	to make to arrive at.
sepeh	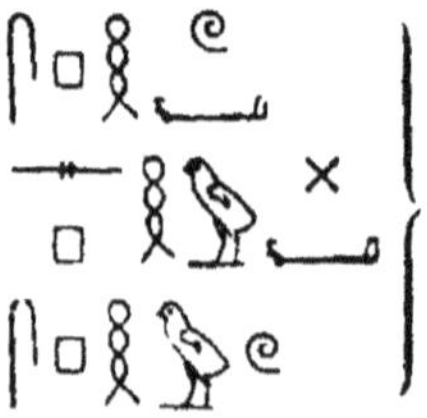	to tie with a rope, to fetter.

sepḥer  to design, make a plan, draw, write.

sepḥer  to make to revolve.

Sepes 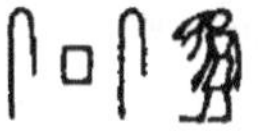 a proper name.

sept  lip ;  edge of the water.

 the two lips.

sept  nome; plur. .

 the nome of Maāti.

Septu  a god of the Eastern Delta; a form of Horus.

Sepṭ  the star Sirius.

sepṭ  to be ready to do or use something, prepared; to be provided with.  provided.

 prepared for the moment.

having horns ready to strike.

ready of face, keen, alert (?).

sept a kind of wood.

sept leg.

Sept-kheri-neḥait-ȧmi-beq a proper name.

Sept-mast-ent-Reruti a proper name.

sef yesterday;

sef maāt . . . .

sef ḥer to be gracious, longsuffering.

sefi babe, child.

sefekh seven.

sefekh to untie, undress, set free;

Sefekh-neb-s a proper name.

seft		to slay.
seft		knife, sword.
seft	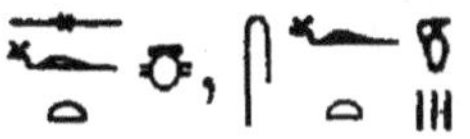	pitch, unguent.
sem		a priest (also setem ).
sma		loin.
sma		to join together, to unite with.
		union, assembly.
smat (?)		a burial place.
sma.ta		union with the earth, *i. e.*, burial.
		day of burial.
		to unite the Two Lands, *i. e.*, Egypt.
sma		to kill, slaughter.
		slaughterer, butcher.

sma — cow or bull bound for sacrifice.

smaui — to renew, remake.

smaȧr — to oppress.

smau — branches.

poles of a bier.

smaiu — branches.

smaiu — slaughterers, fiends.

plur. of preceding.

butchers of Set.

god of slaughter.

Smait 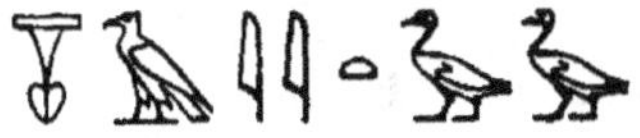 two goddesses of slaughter.

smaā  to pay what is due, make an offering.

smaāiu  slayers.

smaā-kheru  to justify, to make triumphant, to proclaim blessed.

smam  to slay, sacrifice.

smam  butcher.

smamiu  slaughterers, fiends.

smam  a bull for sacrifice.

smamu  cattle for sacrifice, victims.

Smam  the name of a god.

Smam-ur  the name of the Soul of Seb (Keb).

Smam  the name of a lake.

smamu  foliage or branches of a tree.

smamu clouds.

smat bows of a boat (?).

smatu torture chambers, shambles.

Smati a proper name.

Smamti a proper name.

smaṭ festival of the half month.

smȧ to report, announce, bear a message; reporting;

smȧ, ***smȧiu*** herald, announcer.

smȧ, ***smȧt*** report.

smȧ leather.

smȧu pieces of leather.

semu herbs, pasturage.

semiu devourers.

semi to entreat.

smemā to burn up.

smen to stablish, be stablished, fixed, made firm.

fixed head.

smen a kind of goose.

smenkh to repair, re-establish, beautify, make perfect.

smert eyelids.

smer to inflict or cause pain.

smeḥ to flood, to submerge, water fields.

smeḥit flood.

semkheṭ . . . .

semes to make to be born, produce.

semsu eldest, firstborn.

Semti (?) a king of the 1st dynasty. This name was formerly read Ḥesepti.

smet to listen.

smetmet (?) to pry into.

Smetu the warder of the First Ārit.

smet woven with, or shot with (of cloth).

Smet-āqa the name of a rudder.

Smeti-āqa name of a part of the magic boat.

Smetti a proper name.

smetru	to investigate, search out, find the truth.
semṭet	servant, serf.
sen	they, their, them.
sen	two; second, fellow, equal, companion, like, equal; two breasts.
sen	to smell, breathe.
sen ta	to smell the earth, to pay homage.
sen	house, abode (?).
sen	brother; dual ; plur.
sent	sister.
	two sisters, pair of sisters.

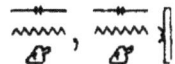

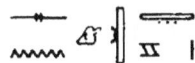

seni  companion, fellow.

sen  to pass away, depart, to walk.

sen  to slit, to cut.

Senu 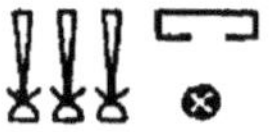 a city near Panopolis.

senȧ 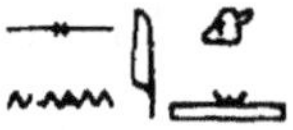 adoration.

senȧha  injury, misery.

senā  restraint.

senāāt 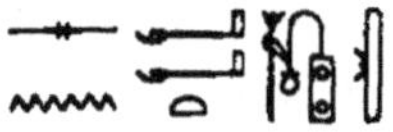 to beautify (?).

senb  to be well, strong, healthy.

senbȧ  health, soundness.

senb 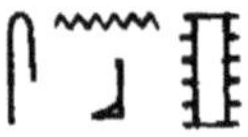 wall; plur. 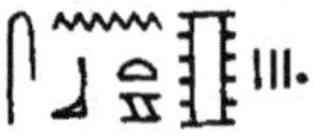.

senbet  libation vessel.

senpu  slaughterings.

senf blood.

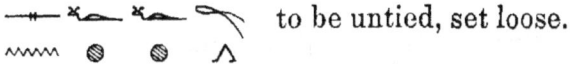

senfekhfekh to be untied, set loose.

senem abundance.

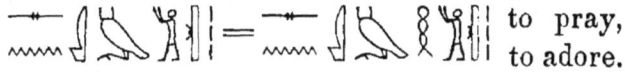

senem to pray, to adore.

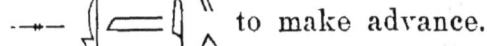

senemȧi to make advance.

Senemti a proper name.

senemem hair.

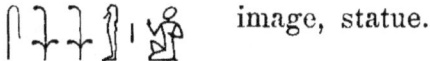

senen image, statue.

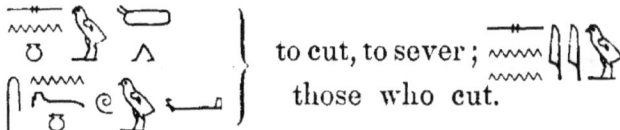

sennu to cut, to sever; those who cut.

sennit . . . .

sennu to gather (?).

sennu cakes, bread-offerings.

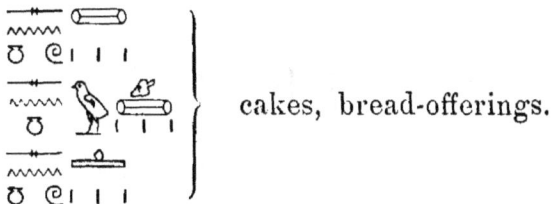

sennȧu  to fail.

sennuṭ  carrier.

senni 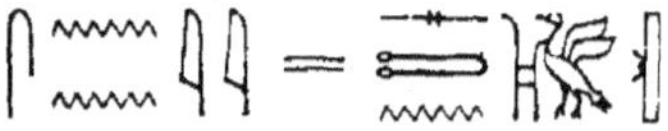

Sen-nefer  a proper name.

senneshni  storm.

seneh  to be in servitude.

senehep 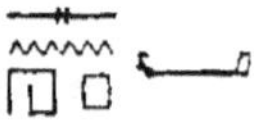 to be strong.

Seneh-paqarha  the name of a city.

Senehaparḳana 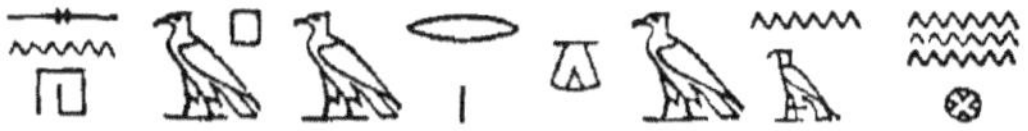 the name of a city.

seneḥem  to deliver.

senkha  to disembark (?).

senekhekh 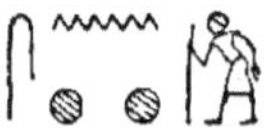 to grow old.

senes 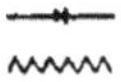
sensi 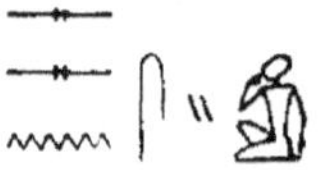 } to praise.

sensu  to cry out, invoke.

Senseneb  the name of the mother of Nu.

sensenni 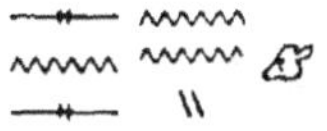 to breathe, snuff the air.

sensen 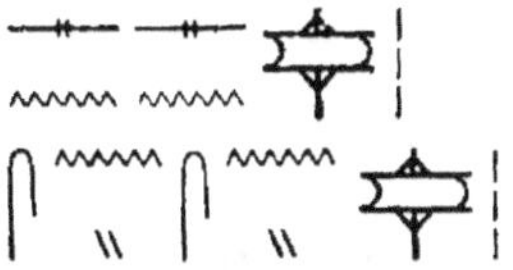 breathings, breaths.

sensen 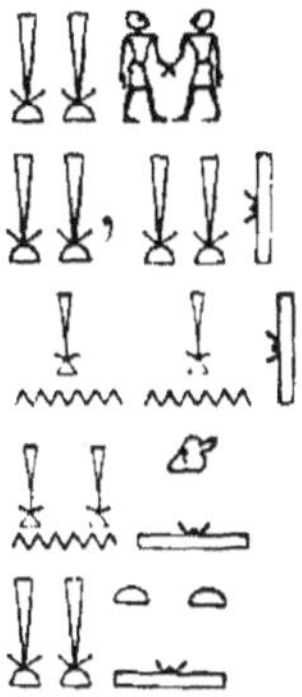 to become friendly with some one, to fraternize; to smell.

sensen 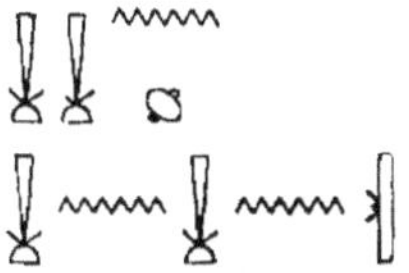 to have a bad smell, to become corrupt, to decay.

senesh 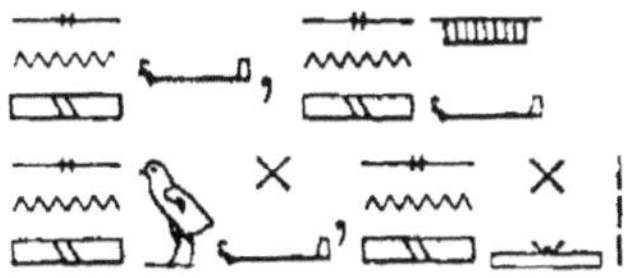 to unbolt, unbar, open.

senshu  bolts (?).

seneshni  storm, hurricane.

Senk	a proper name.
senket	light.
Senket	the name of a city.
senk-àb	strong-willed.
senq (?)	to suckle.
senqet	to suckle.
sent	labourers, builders.
sent	foundation.
sent	draughtboard, game of draughts.
sent	to pass away.
sent	decay.
sentu	enemies.

Sent-Rā 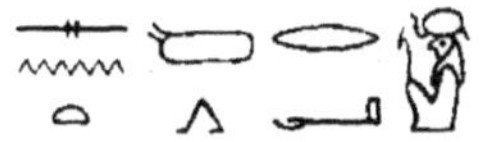 a proper name.

senter
senther 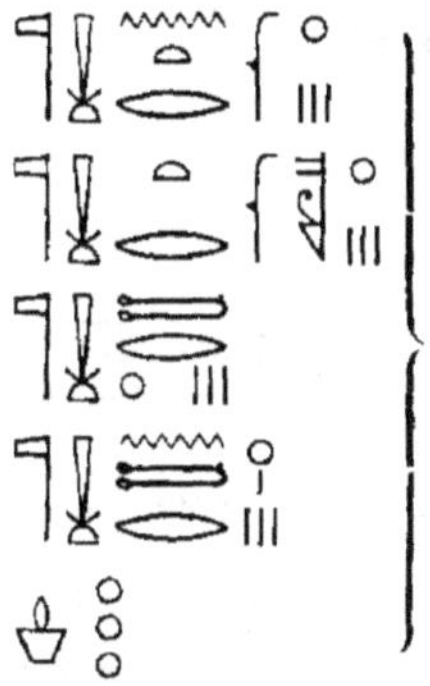 incense offered to the god; 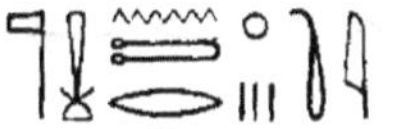 censed;  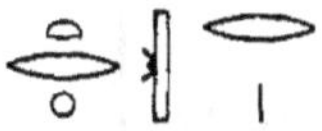 to cense the mouth.

senteḥ 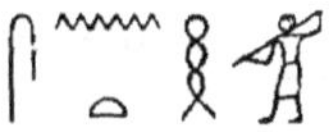 to have power over.

Sent.....  the brother-gods Horus and Set.

senṭ  to fear, be afraid.

senṭ ȧb 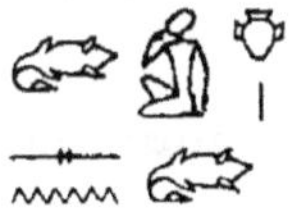 timid.

senṭ  fear.

senetchem 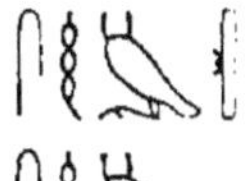 to make glad or happy.

 pleasure.

 ease.

senetchem 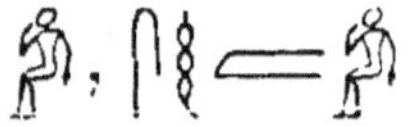 to sit.

sentchert  restraint.

ser 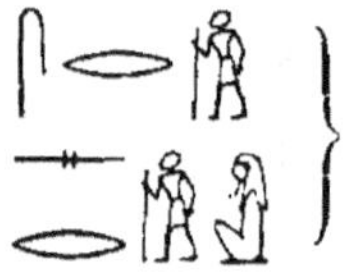 prince, chief;  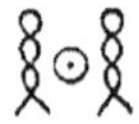 everlasting prince;  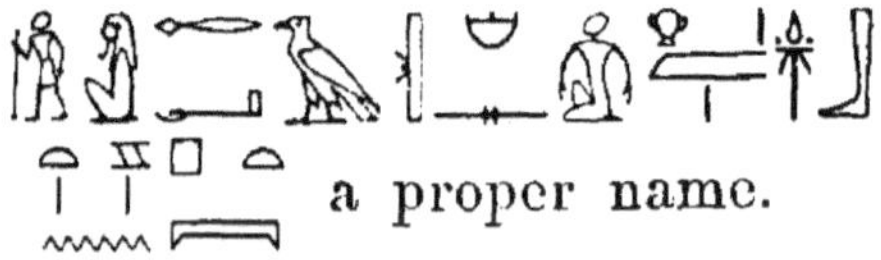 a proper name.

 plur. of preceding.

ser 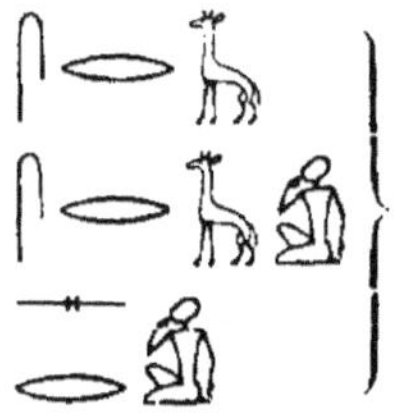 to give orders or directions, to announce, give tidings; 

sert  order, announcement.

Ser-kheru 

Serȧ-kheru  the name of one of the Forty-two Judges in the Hall of Osiris.

Serȧt-beqet  the name of a sacred cow.

seru  grain, barley.

seru — geese of a special kind.

serui (?) — flame.

serukheṭ — to treat with medicaments, embalm.

seruṭ — to make to grow, to flourish, to perpetuate.

seref — to be hot, flame, fire.

serem — to make to weep.

serenp — to make young.

serḥu (?) — (?) to overthrow.

serekh — to make to know, to inform.

serekh — a funerary building, a cognizance.

Serekhi — the name of one of the Forty-two Judges in the Hall of Osiris.

seres — to be awake, to watch.

— watch, watching, watcher.

Seres-ḥer "watching face"; the name of a god.

"watching faces"; a class of divine beings.

serqaȧu to be refreshed, to breathe.

Serqet the goddess Serqet.

Sert a city in the Seventh Ȧat.

sert "goad"; the name of a part of the magic boat.

sert̩ =

Sert̩iu the name of one of the Forty-two Judges in the Hall of Osiris.

sehep lawgiver.

seher, **seherr** to make quiet, subdue.

sehert carnelian.

seḥ  hall;  the chamber of the embalmment of Osiris.

seḥap  to hide.

seḥuā  to confuse, disarrange.

seḥui  to gather together, collect.

seḥurȧ  to curse.

seḥeb 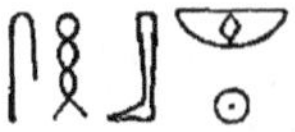 to keep a feast, to make festival.

seḥem  to turn back.

seḥeptet  name of a boat (?).

seḥen  to order, arrange (?).

seḥer  to drive away.

 driver away; plur. 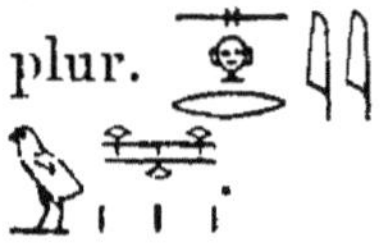

seḥes 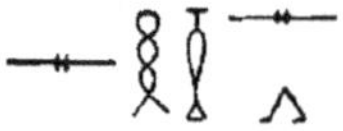 to make to meet.

seḥset 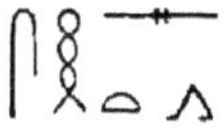 a meeting.

seḥeq  to cut off, hack in pieces.

seḥeq  to appoint to some office.

seḥeqer  to cause to hunger, to keep hungry.

seḥetep 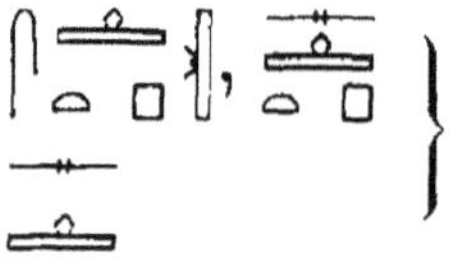 to make to be at peace, to propitiate, to pacify.

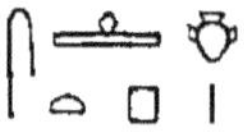 to quiet the heart.

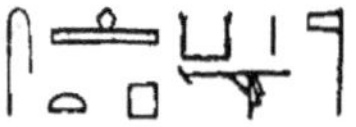 to propitiate the divine Ka.

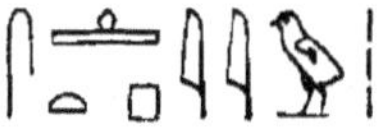 peacemakers.

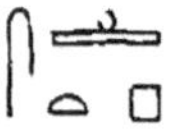 pacification.

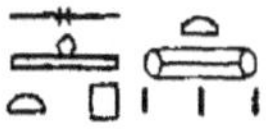 offerings which bring peace.

Seḥetep-taui 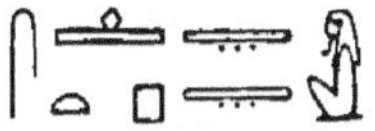 "pacifier of the Two Lands"; a proper name.

seḥetem  to destroy.

Seḥetemet-Au-ā-em-ābet 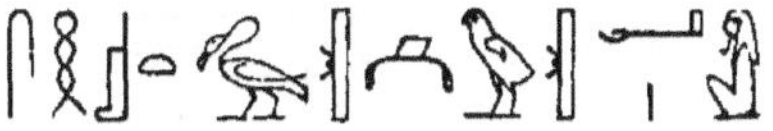 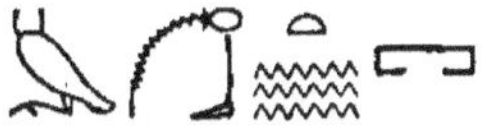 the name of the banks of a river.

Seḥtet 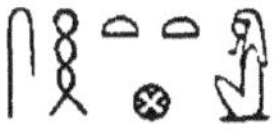 a proper name.

seḥetch  to emit light, illumine, to shine.

 light, radiance, brilliance.

Seḥetch-ur 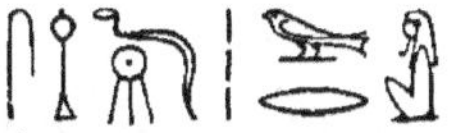 "Great Light", *i. e.*, Rā.

sekh 

sekh 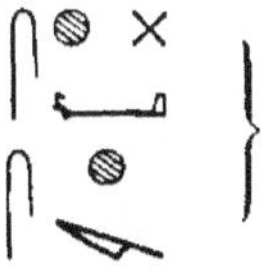 to break, strike, cut, wound.

sekha  to have in mind, to commemorate, to remember.

 remembrance for good.

 memorial services.

 remembrance of evil.

sekha  to be deaf.

Sekhai  a Cow-goddess.

sekhabui  eaters (?).

sekhap 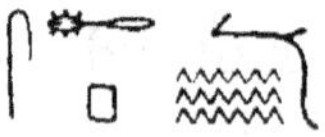 to swallow.

sekhar  to milk.

sekharu  to plate, to mould.

sekhakeru  to ornament.

Sekhat-Ḥeru  a Cow-goddess.

Sekhāi  to make to rise or appear, to crown.

Sekhiu  the name of a double serpent god or fiend.

sekhu 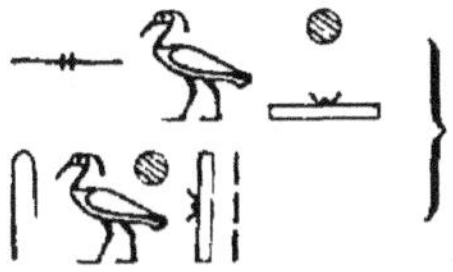 to praise, glorify.

sekhu  praise.

sekhun  to revile, curse.

sekhuṭ  to fortify.

sekheb  see 

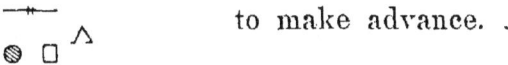

sekhep 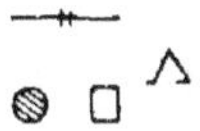 to make advance. .

Sekhepti 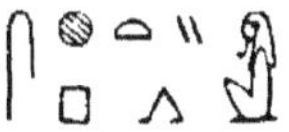 a proper name.

sekheper 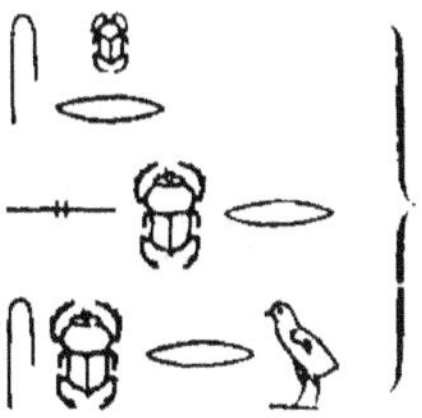 to make to become, to create, fashion, form.

sekheperu 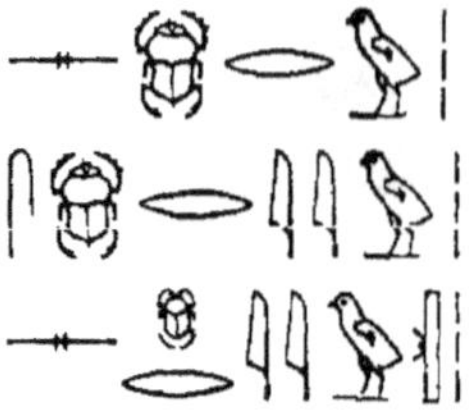 those who cause things to be.

sekhef 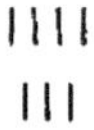 seven; 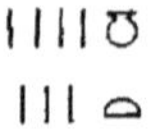 seventh.

sekhem 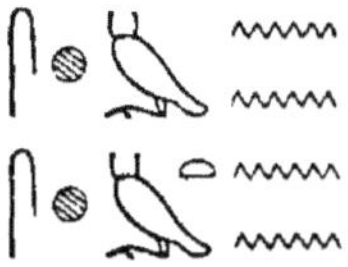 to forget, forgetfulness.

Sekhem 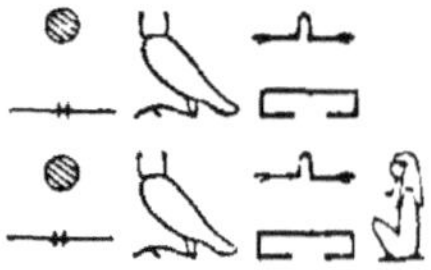 shrine, sanctuary.

 gods of the shrine.

 the city of Letopolis.

sekhem  to recite, to read.

sekhem 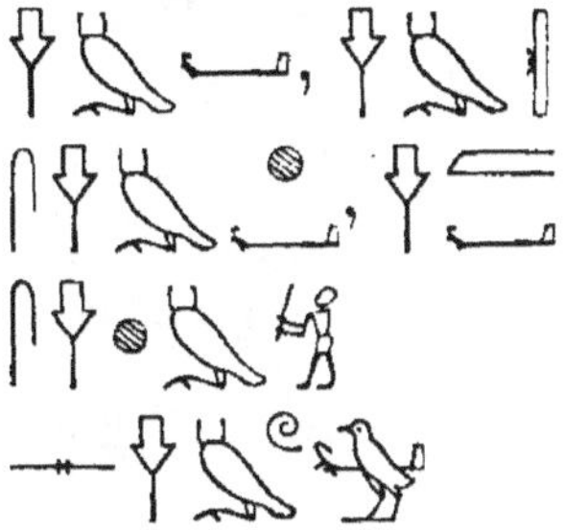 to be strong, mighty, to prevail over, to gain the mastery, show oneself strong, might, power.

 bold man, victor.

 brave in heart.

 weak.

 mighty one, strong.

Sekhem  the natural power, vital power of a man, any power spiritual or physical.

Sekhemu  the Powers;  the Double Power.

Sekhem-ur  "great Power"; a proper name.

Sekhem-em-àb-f  "strong in his heart"; a proper name.

Sekhem-nefer "good Power"; a proper name.

Sekhmet-ren-s-em-ḥemut-s the name of a sacred cow.

***Sekhmet* (*Sekhet*)** name of a goddess.

Sekhmet-Bast-Rā a solar triad.

sekhen to direct (?).

sekhen to embrace.

"great embracer"; a proper name.

sekhni to make to alight.

sekhenen to become rotten, to decay.

sekhensh to make to stink, to calumniate.

sekhent to make to advance.

sekhent  pillars.

sekher 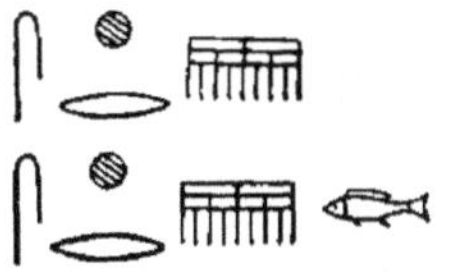 to offend.

[***sekher***  plan, device, counsel, arrangement.]

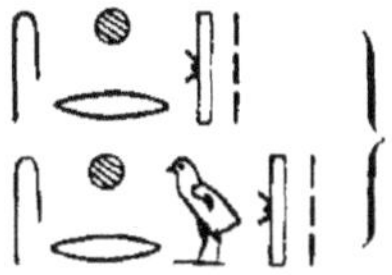 plur. of preceding.

 a plan of triumph, or blessedness.

 celestial designs, ordinances of heaven.

sekher 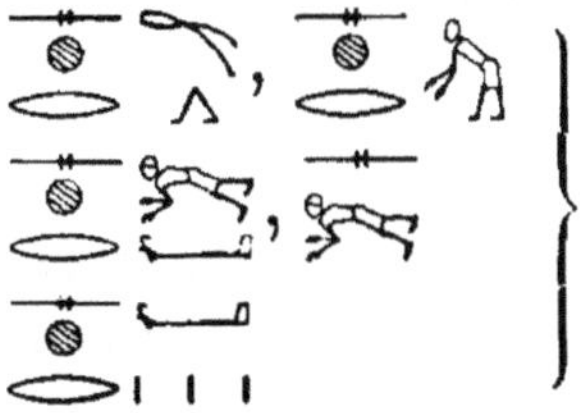 to overthrow.

 fallen.

 overthrow.

Sekher-āṭ  the god of the Sixth Ārit.

Sekheriu 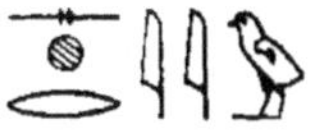 the name of one of the Forty-two Judges in the Hall of Osiris.

Sekher-remu  a proper name.

sekhekh  to straighten.

sekhes  to run.

sekhes 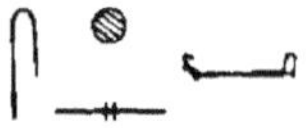
sekhsekh  } to fasten, make firm.

sekhesef 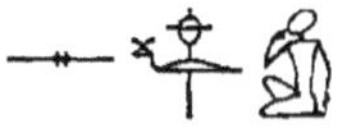  } to meet with hostility, to repulse, to contradict, give evidence against.

sekhet  to net, to snare, spread out a net.

sekhtu 
sekhtiu    } snarers, hunters, fowlers, fishermen.

sekhet 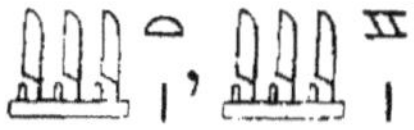 field, meadow; plur. 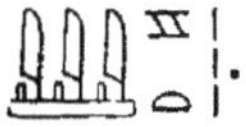.

sekhtiu  the divine field labourers.

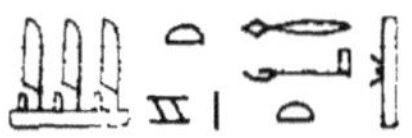 "Great Field", *i. e.*, heaven.

Sekhet-Åanru (or ***Åaru***) 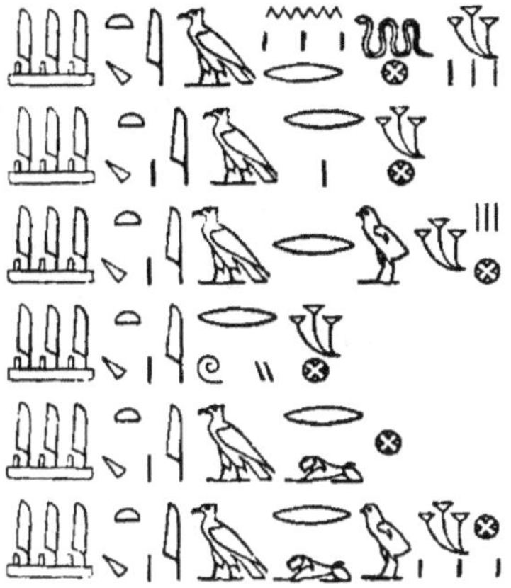 the "Field of reeds", *i. e.*, the Elysian Fields.

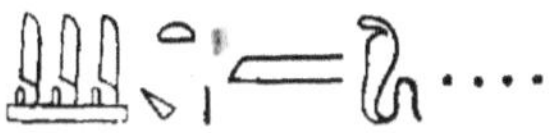 a proper name?

Sekhet-neḥeḥ  "Field of Eternity".

Sekhet-neteru 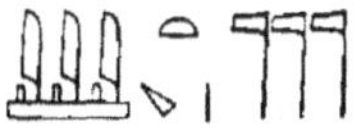 "Field of the gods".

Sekhet-Rā 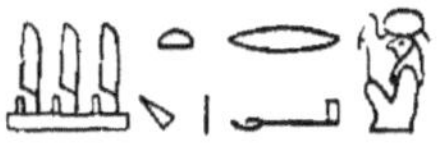 "Field of Rā".

Sekhet-ḥetep 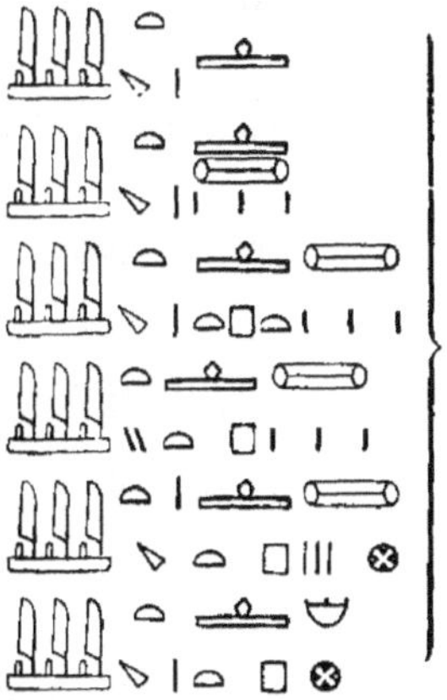 the "Field of Peace", or "Field of Offerings"; a name of the Elysian Fields.

Sekhti-ḥetep 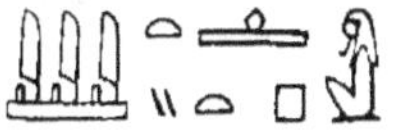 the god of the Field of Peace.

Sekhet-sanehemu "Field of the Grasshoppers".

Sekhet-Sȧsȧ "Field of Fire".

sekhettu plants.

sekhet } to turn upside down, invert, stand on the head;

sekheṭ

Sekheṭ-ḥer-āsh-ȧru "inverted face, of many forms"; the name of the porter of the First Ārit.

sekhṭu to hunger.

sesu times, days.

sesun to destroy.

sesunṭ to destroy.

seseb to slay.

sesen } to snuff the air.

seska 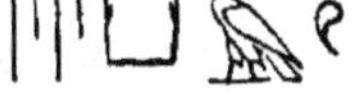 body.

seset 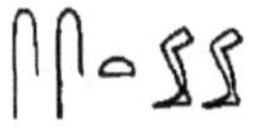 legs.

seset  to burn up.

sesh 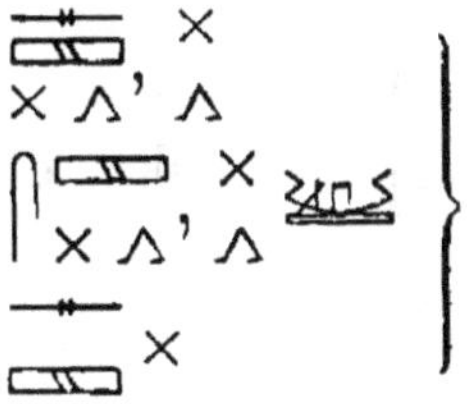 to pass, journey, travel.

 passage.

 impassable.

sesh 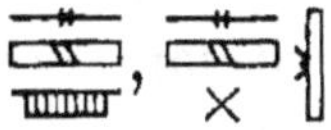 to open, unbolt.

sesh 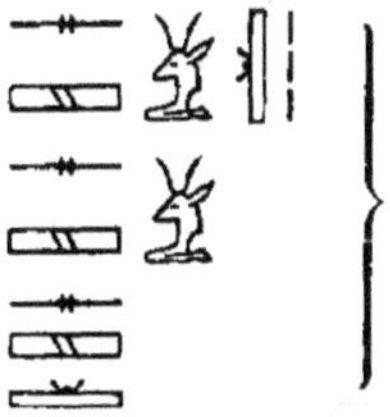 to be wise, skilful, knowledge.

sesh 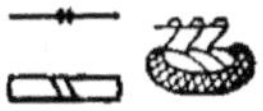 nest; plur. .

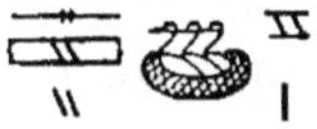 birth-place.

 two nests.

Seshet  name of a town and its god.

sesh 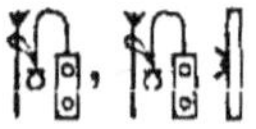 to write, draw, copy, make a plan.

seshu 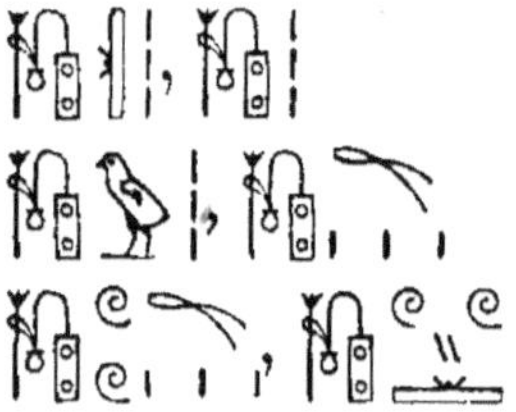 writings, decrees, documents, archives, books, copies of books, etc.

sesh  scribe, copyist.

 accomplished scribe.

 veritable scribe (as opposed to a titular scribe).

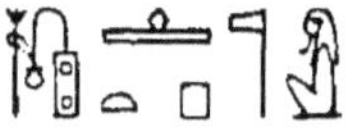 scribe of the temple property.

 scribe and draughtsman.

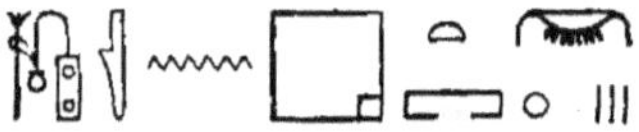 scribe and draughtsman of the house of gold.

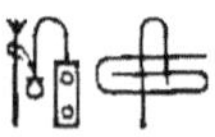 scribe and designer.

seshai  skilled, able, competent.

seshu		to be empty.
seshep	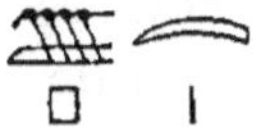	the measure of a palm.
seshepu	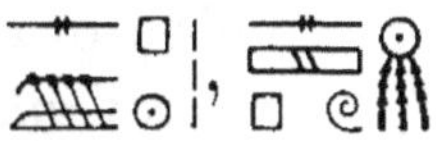	light, radiance; see SHESEP.
seshem		to lead, guide, conduct, guidance.
seshem		guide, leader.
		plur. of preceding.
seshmet		advance, guiding, guidance.

 gratification (?).

Seshemit  "conductress"; the name of a goddess.

Seshmu-ḥeḥ  "guide of eternity"; a proper name.

Seshmu-ta  "guide of the earth"; a proper name.

Seshmu-taui  "guide of the Two Lands"; a proper name.

Seshem  divine image, statue.

seshem  figure, design, image, form, similitude.

seshen 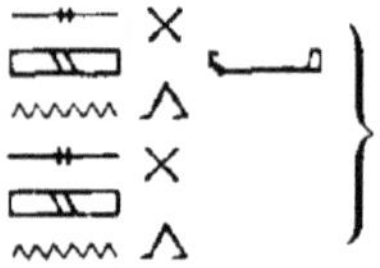 to scatter, destroy.

seshen  . . . . . .

seshen 

seshennu 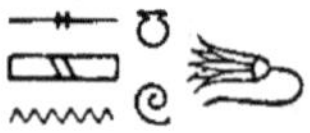

senshen 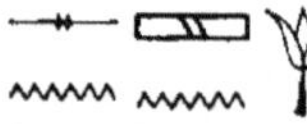

seshesh 

lily.

seshru  garments, apparel.

seshert a cake, loaf.

seshet (?) fire; plur. ; gods of fire .

Sesheta the goddess of architecture.

sesheta to be hidden, mysterious, incomprehensible.

sesheta , hidden things, mysteries, secrets.

of invisible forms and shapes.

hidden of name.

very great mysteries indeed.

great secrets of Ȧmenti.

seshetu fiends (?).

seshet̤ bandage, bandlet, tiara, girdle, fillet for the head.

seshet-t 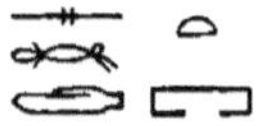 a chamber with a window or opening in it.

sek  to decay, perish; 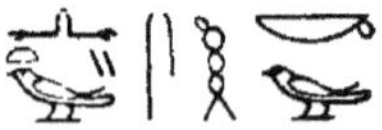 incorruptible.

sek 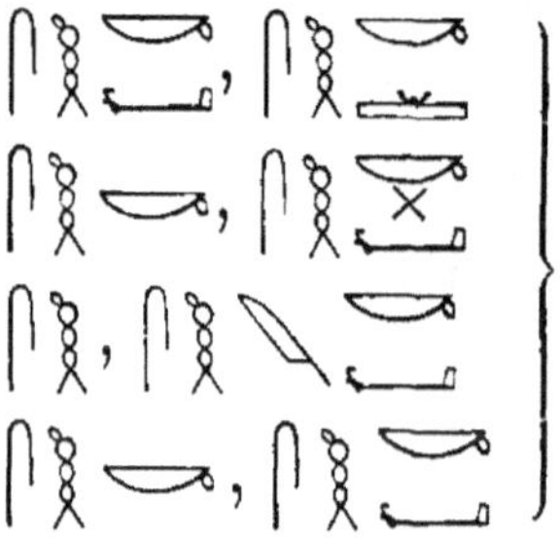 to break through, fight a way, to fight, destroy; to advance.

seksek

sek-re 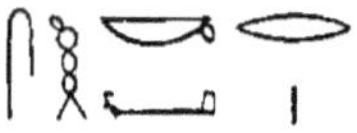 to direct.

Sek-ḥer 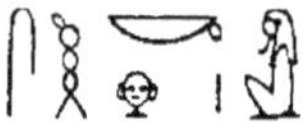 a proper name.

Seku  (with *àkhemu*) a class of gods.

seka 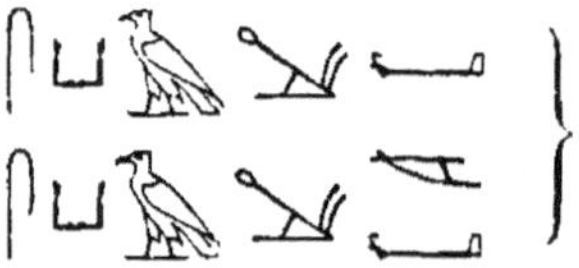 to plough.

sekemiu  grey or white hair.

Seker 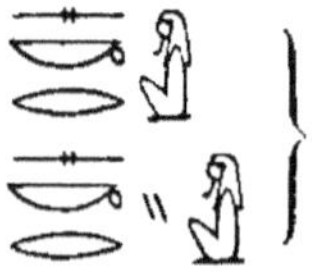 the ancient god of the Other World of Ṣaḳḳârah.

Sekri

 Seker in his secret place.

Seker ***Sekri***		the town of Seker.
Sekri		the festival of Seker.
Seker		the sacred bark of Seker.
Seksek		the name of a fiend.
sektiu		to fetter.
Sektet	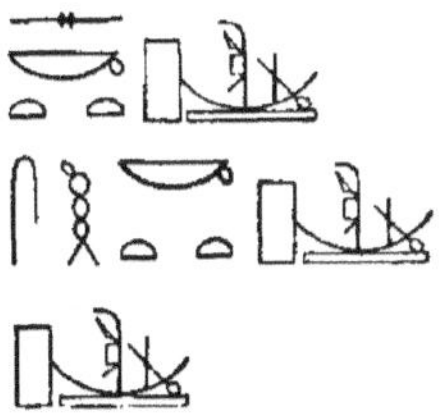	the boat in which the sun travelled from noon to midnight.
seq	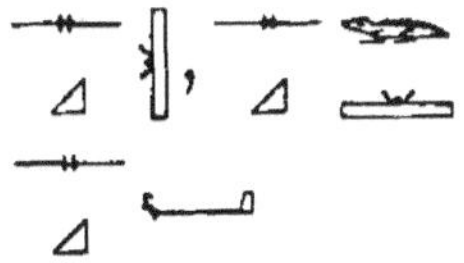	to collect, gather together.
seqa	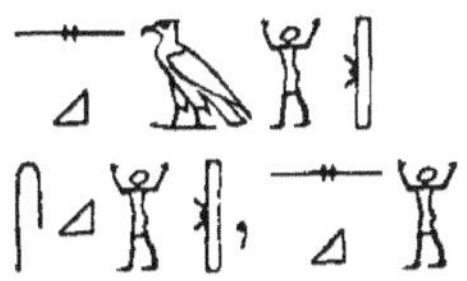	to exalt, to lift up.
seqai		exalted one.
		plur. of preceding.

seqeb 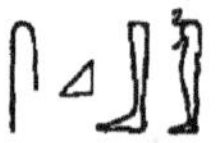 image (?).

seqebb 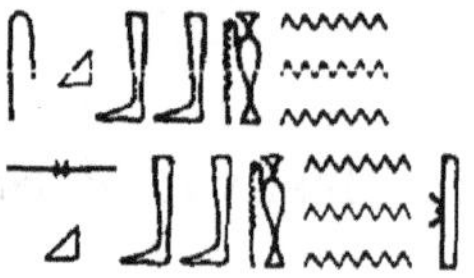 to cool, refresh oneself.

Seqebit 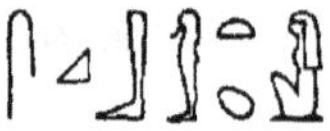 name of a goddess.

seqer  to smite, take prisoner.

 smiter.

seqeṭ 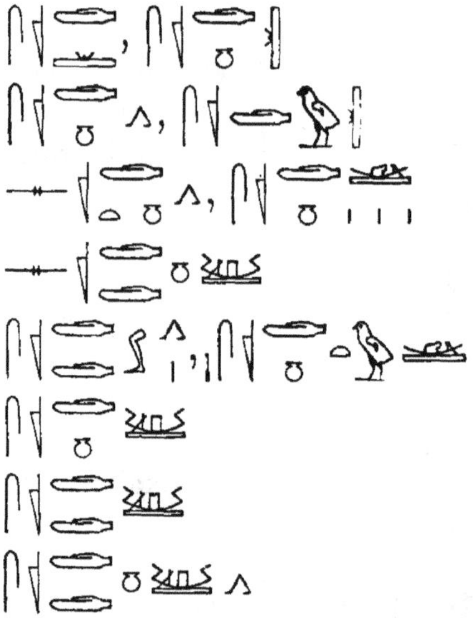 to sail in a boat, to journey, make a voyage;  encircled.

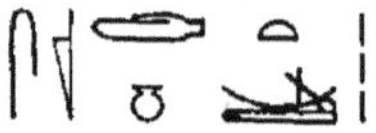 voyages, sailings.

 sailors, boatmen.

seqeṭ  dispositions.

Seqeṭ-ḥer 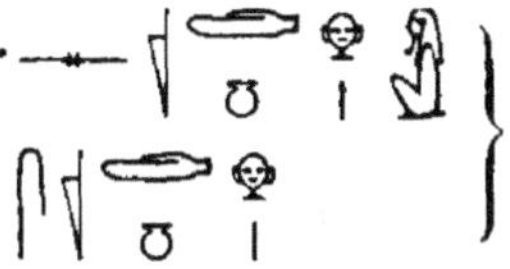 warder of the Second Ārit.

seḳenniu  helpless ones, weak.

seḳer  to put to silence, make quiet.

seḳert  silence.

set 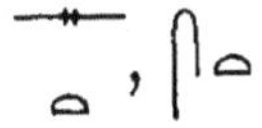 she, it, its.

set 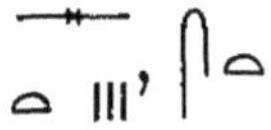 they, them, their.

set (?)  to break.

set 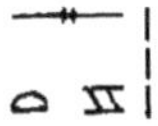 ground.

Set  the god of physical and moral evil; see Suti.

set (***semt***)  mountain; plur. 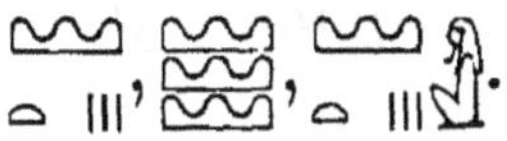.

set	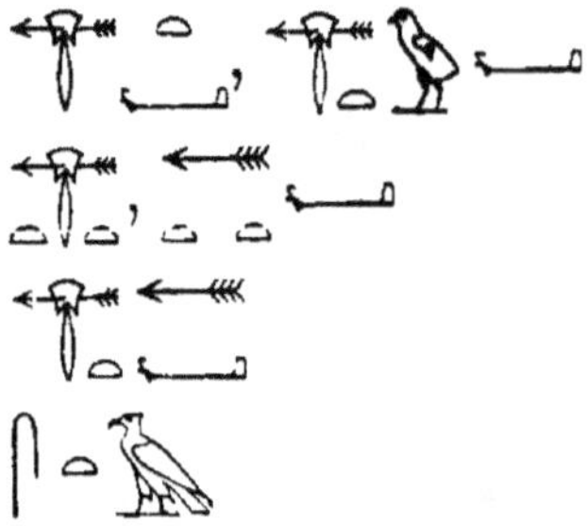	to shoot arrows, to hurl stones.
set		to sow seed.
setit		seed, progeny.
setut	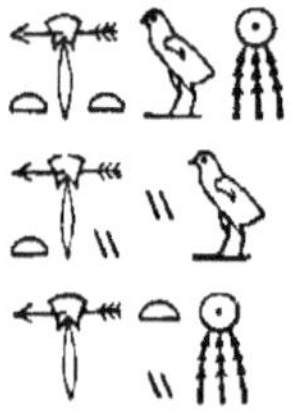	arrows or beams of light, rays, radiance.
setau	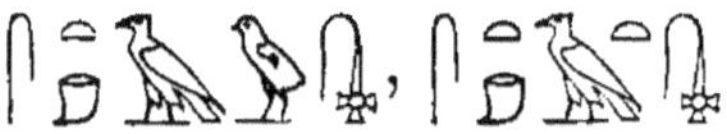	to light a fire, to burn, flame.
seti		burning, burner.
setit		adversaries (?).
Sett		the name of a goddess of the First Cataract.
Sett		an Asiatic woman.
Set-ṭemui		a proper name (var.  ).

Sta  a proper name.

sta, stat
stau 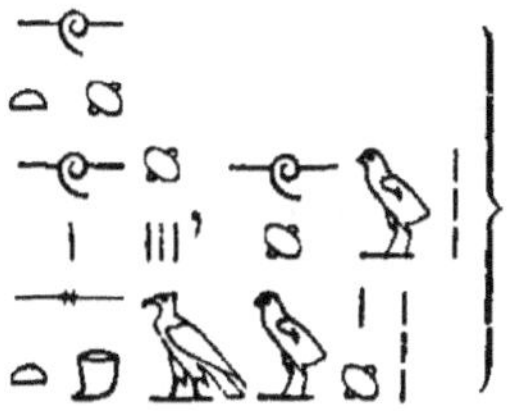 filth, dung.

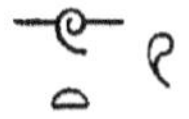 a portion of the body.

stat  filthy ones, fiends.

sta  to tow a boat, drag along, bring carry.

stau  those who tow, bearers, carriers.

stau 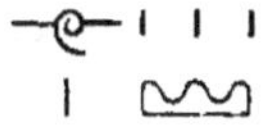 see  RE-STAU.

stat 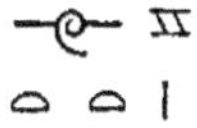 a measure of land.

sti 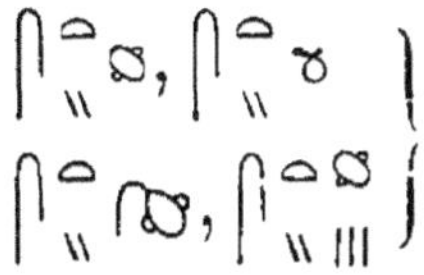 smell, odour.

sti	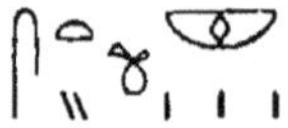	festal perfume.
Sti		"land of the bow"; a name of Nubia.
setua		to make or ascribe praise.
setut (or ***sutet***)		to walk about.
setut		to symbolize, typify.
seteb		captives.
setep	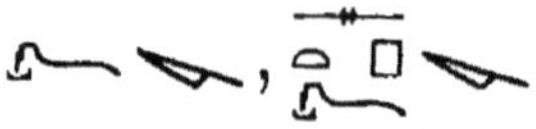	to cut.
setep	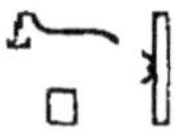	to chose, chosen.
setepu		choice cuts of meats.
setep sa		to work protection on behalf of someone.
setem		to hear; obey;  hearer.
		—what is heard, listener.

setemiu  listeners.

Setem-ḥeri 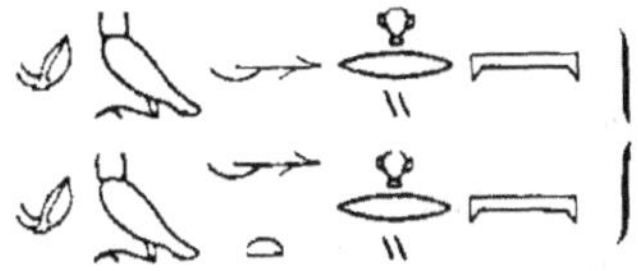 the name of the upper hinge.

Setem-kheri  the name of the lower hinge.

Setem-ȧnsi  a proper name.

seṭennu 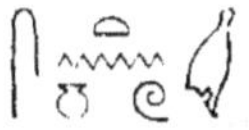 to be distinguished.

setentit  distinctions.

setenem 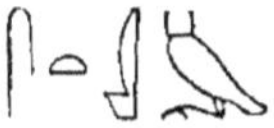 to make to walk.

seter  wooden tablet (?).

setḥu  to open.

set-ḥemt  woman, wife.

seteken 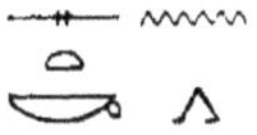 to make to enter.

 invaders, those who make to enter.

seṭ 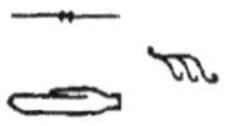 hair, foliage.

seṭ 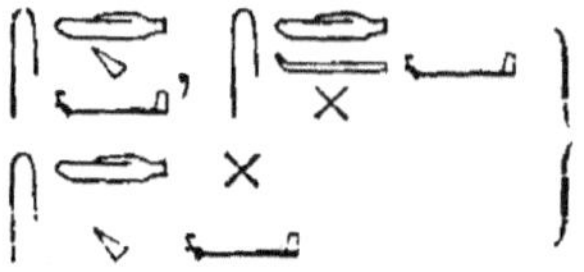 to break, split.

Seṭ-qesu (or, ***Seṭ-qersu***) 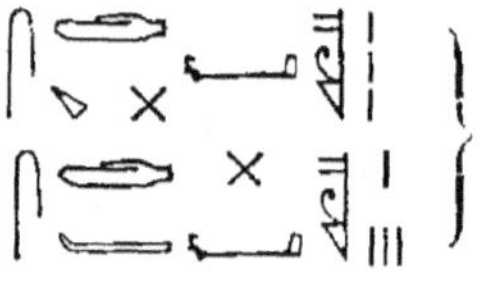 "bone-breaker"; the name of one of the Forty-two Judges in the Hall of Osiris.

seṭ 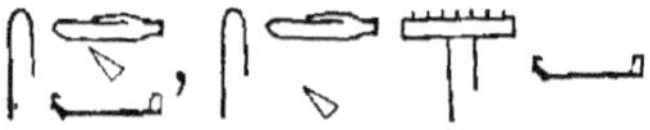 to clothe, to dress.

 a garment.

 those who clothe.

seṭa  to tremble, quake, trembling, terror.

seṭui  to defame.

seṭu  . . . .

seṭeb 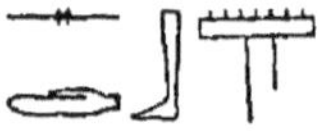 garment, hangings of a shrine.

seṭeb 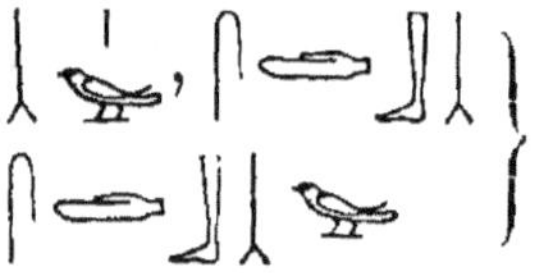 obstacle, disaster, calamity, misfortune.

 plur. of preceding.

seṭebḥ  to be ready, equipped.

seṭemu  edicts for slaughter.

seṭen  distinguished.

Seṭeḳ 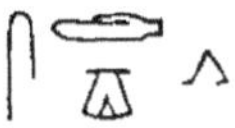 a proper name.

seṭeḳa  to cover.

seṭeḳaut  sleep.

seṭet 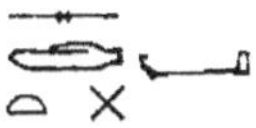 to break.

seṭeṭ 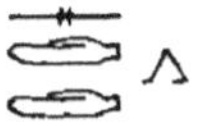 to travel.

seth 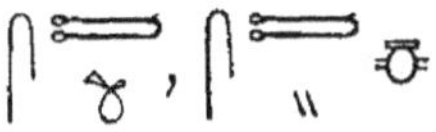 scent, unguent.

sethen  distinctions.

sethenem 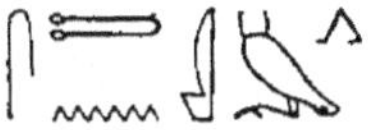 to make to walk.

sethes 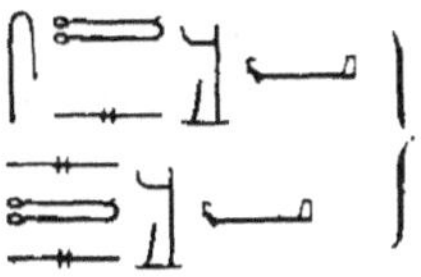 to raise up, lift up.

sethes 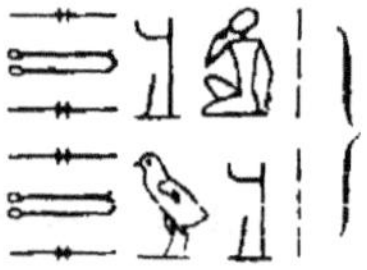 to praise, extol, "lift up", or "raise", a song or hymn, praisings.

sethesu  props, supports.

sethesu  supporters.

sethes Shu  what Shu raises up, *i. e.*, the sky.

sethesu Shu  the supports of Shu, *i. e.*, the four cardinal points.

sethes 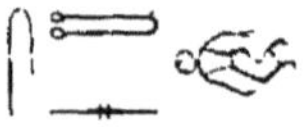 to be laid out.

sethes 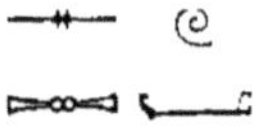 to knit together.

sethesu  libations.

setheken  to have sexual union.

setcha  to make to set out, travel.

setchami  to protect (?).

setchit  seeds of a plant (?).

setcheb  to oppose, be in the way of, obstruct.

setchefa  to feed with food celestial or terrestrial.

setcher 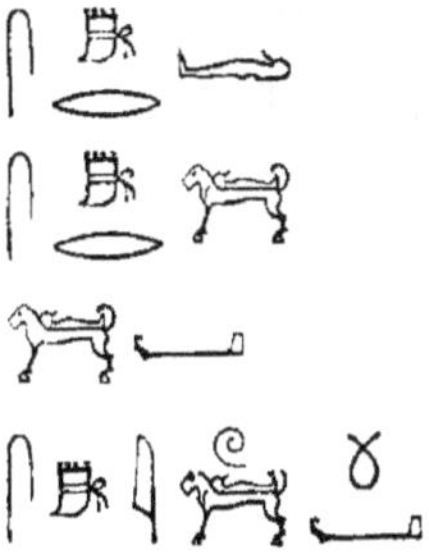 to lie down in sleep or death; dead, dead one;  the dead.

 bier.

setcheser 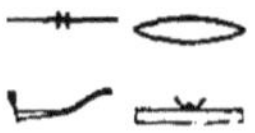 to sanctify.

setcheṭfu  to wound.

SH.

she pool, lake, laver; plur.

She asbiu Lake of flames.

She Aḳeb Lake of Aḳeb, *i. e.*, celestial ocean.

She Åqer Lake of Åqer, *i. e.*, the per-fect lake (?).

She ur Great Lake.

She Maāti Lake of Maāti.

She em Māfket Lakes of Tur-quoise.

She Nu Lake of Nu.

She en Amu Lake of Fire.

She en Åsår Lake of Osiris.

She en Māat Lake of Māat.

She en Nesersert Lake of Fire.

Lake of Fire.

She neter Lake of the god, *i. e.*, Osiris.

She en Ḥeru Lake of Horus.

She ḥeru Lake of the celestial ones.

She ḥeḥ Lake of Millions of years.

She en ḥesmen Lake of Natron.

She Ḥetep Lake of the god Ḥetep.

She ent ḥetch Lake of Light.

She en khebentiu Lake of the wicked.

She en kharu Lake of the geese.

She en seḥetep Lake of propitiation.

She en seshet Lake of Fire.

Shet Ṭemui Lake of the two knives.

She Tchesert Lakes of the goddess Tchesert.

sha field.

sha  bread-cakes, food.

sha 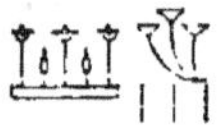 plants.

sha  to destine, predestine, foreordain.

shaȧ  pig.

shaȧs  to travel, journey, go forward.

shaā  one hundred.

shaā  to begin, beginning.

 unto, 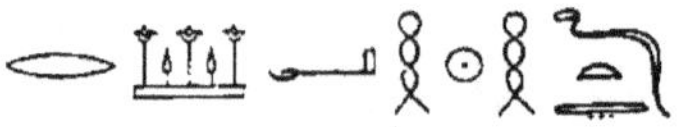 unto all eternity.

Shau  the name of a city or town.

shauabti  the name of the figure inscribed with the VIth Chapter of the Book of the Dead.

shauā  book, writing.

Shai  the god of Luck or Destiny.

Shabu  the name of a god.

shabu  water plants.

shabti  See SHAUABTI.

shabu cakes, food.

Shapuneterȧrka name of an Utchat.

shamu damned (?).

Sharshar... a proper name.

Sharsharkhet name of an Utchat.

Sharshatȧkatȧ a proper name.

shaheb south wind.

shas to journey, travel.

Shakanasa a proper name.

Shaka a name of Ȧmen.

shā sand.

shā (?) book, writing, document.
shāt

Book of praise.

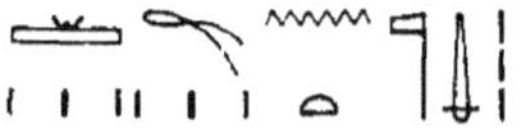 Books of holy words.

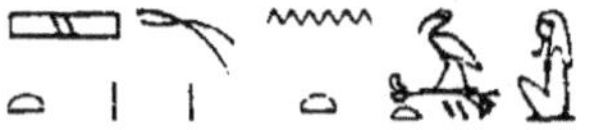 Book of Thoth.

 Book of traversing Eternity.

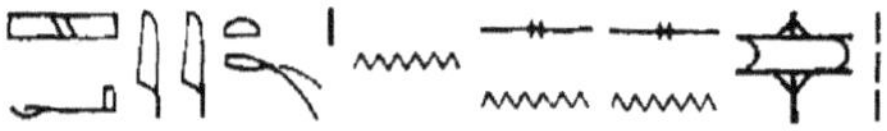 Book of Breathings.

shā  to cut, cut away, cut off.

shāit  knife.

shāmu  decorated (?).

shāt 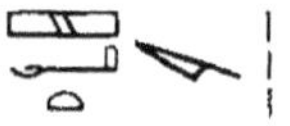 knife, knives.

shāṭ  to cut, to wound, hack off.

shāṭ
shāṭet 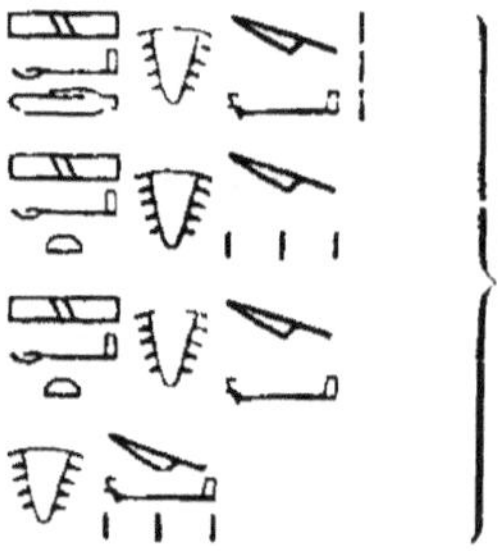 woundings, cuttings, slaughter, knives (?).

 slaughter-blocks (?).

shu  to be dry, hot.

Shu		the god of the air, dryness, light, etc.; the counterpart of Tefnut.
Shut	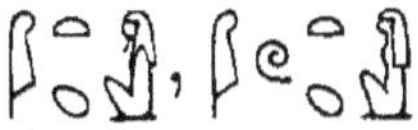	fem. of preceding.
Shuu		the Sun-god.
shuit		light.
shuit		the abode of light (?) sky (?).
shu		to lack, be needy, in want of.
shu		plants, papyrus.
shut		feather.
shuti	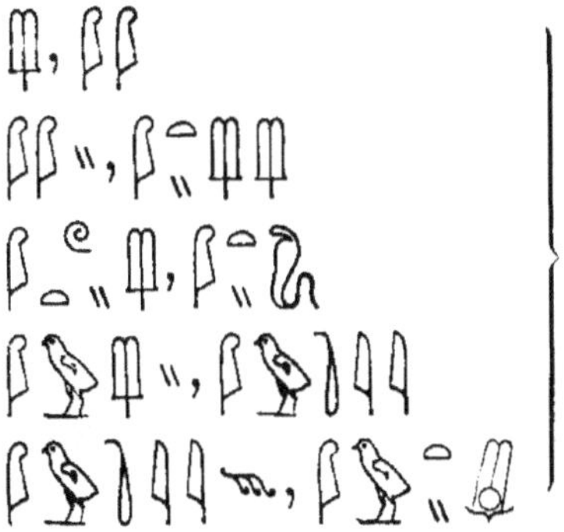	the two-feather crown, *e.g.*, that worn by Åmen.
shut		feathers, plumage.
shuti		merchant.

shutet . . . .

shebu cakes, food.

shebeb throat.

Shebeb en Ḳesti name of a part of a boat.

sheben cakes, food.

shebenu mixed.

shep blind.

shepent vessel.

sheps to be holy, venerable, sacred, worshipful, majestic, awesome.

holy beings.

shept ȧb shame of heart, loathing.

shefu, ***shefut*** boils, blains, insolence, arrogance.

sheft ram (?), strength, power, terror; plur.

terrible of face.

sheft, *shefit* — strength, power, terror.

Shefit, *Shefiti* — the Ram-god, symbol of strength.

Shefshefit — strength, power, might.

shem, *seshem* — to walk, go, travel.

to calumniate, set the mouth in motion against a man.

shemiu, *shemt* — journeys, goings about, travellers.

shemu — the season of summer.

shemem — to be hot.

shemmet — fire, flames.

shemmet — poison.

shemā  to sing, or play a musical instrument.

shemāit  a singer.

shemā  the south; 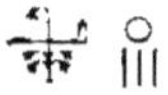 stones of the south.

Shemāit 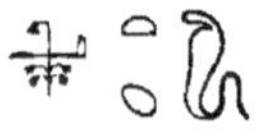 the goddess of the South, *i. e.*, Nekhebit.

shems  to follow, to accompany, be the member of a bodyguard.

shemsi  follower, body-servant.

 plur. of preceding.

 chief servants of Osiris.

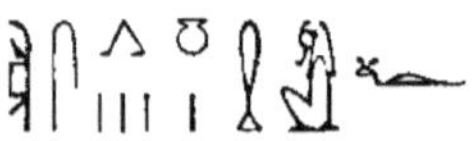 servants of His Majesty.

shen  to revolve.

shen, ***shenit***, ***shenu***, ***shenn*** — circuit, circle, orbit; circuit of the earth.

shen hair.

shenȧ hair.

Shenȧt-pet-utheset-neter the name of a sacred cow.

Shenȧt-sheps-neteru the name of a sacred cow.

shenā granary.

shenā breast, body.

shenā to turn back, repulse.

shenā repulse, violence (?).

shenāāu wayfarers (?).

shenā  to turn back, repulse.

shenstet  wickedness.

sheni 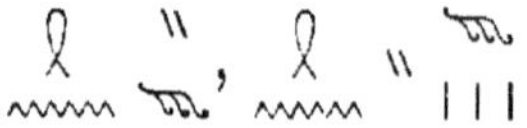 hair, locks.

shenit  storm.

sheniu  chamber.

shenit 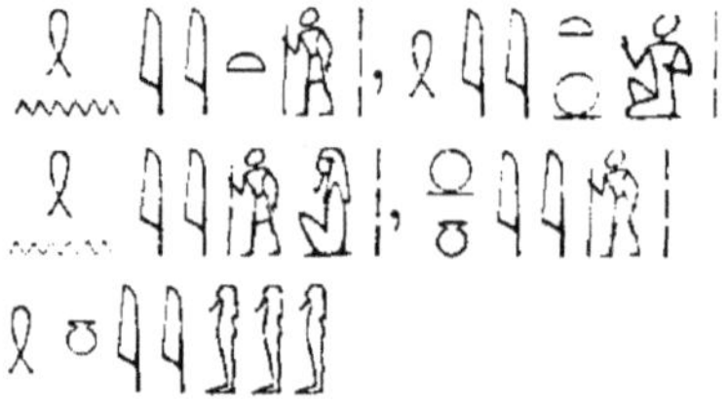 chiefs, princes.

shenbet  body.

shnemi 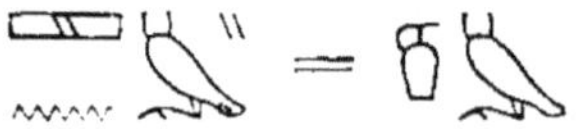

Shenmu  the name of a town.

shennu  a powder of some sort (?).

shennu snares (?).

shennu acacia trees.

Shennu the name of a town.

shens cakes, with shewbread.

shent flesh, skin (?).

shentu to curse, blaspheme.

shenti granary.

shenti heron.

shenti garment.

shentetu curse.

shenṭet a tree, the acacia.

shen-tȧ read .

Shentit the name of a goddess.

sher = and .

[***sherr*** to be little.]

sherràu

sherriu little ones, feeble men or gods.

sheràt

shert little one or thing, something of no value.

shertet

Sherem a proper name.

shersher winds, breath.

shert , nose, nostrils.

shert grain.

shert cake, bread.

shes (?) linen weavers (?).

shes , , linen, a linen garment.

shes linen of the finest quality.

shes maāt "cord of law", *i. e.*, with unfailing correctness and regularity.

shes to be tied up, fettered.

shesui (?) the two eyes (?).

shesep palm, a measure.

shesep to take, undertake, accept, receive.

receivers.

heart's desire.

shesep to shine, be bright.

light. Note the forms and and SESHEP.

Shesep-temesu name of a fiend (?).

shesau skilled, able, intelligent, wise.

Shesmu  the headsman of Osiris.

Shes-khentet  a proper name.

sheta  tortoise.

sheta  to be hidden, secret, mysterious.

 hidden, hidden person or thing.

sheta 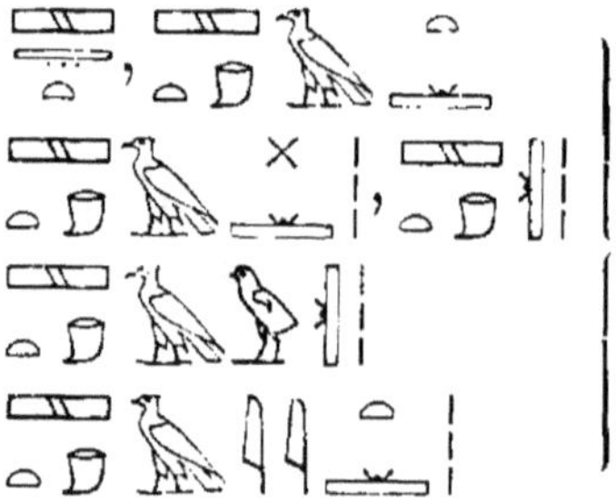 hidden thing, secret, mystery, something invisible and not understood.

 hidden places.

 hidden forms.

 hidden soul.

 hidden faces.

 hidden transformations.

 hidden things.

Shetait — the "hidden place"; a name of the Other World of Seker at Ṣaḳḳârah.

Shetat

Sheta-ḥer — "hidden face"; a proper name.

Shetau-ā̃ — "hidden of arm"; a proper name.

Shetet-pet — a proper name.

sheṭ — to break up the ground, dig out, tear open, to deliver, strengthen, tie, bind up.

sheṭet — lake, pool; plur.

sheṭit — tank, cistern.

sheṭ — to read, recite a book or prayer.

sheṭ — to swathe, to clothe.

a garment.

clothed, or covered, of arms.

sheṭu — leather straps.

sheṭḥu — crushed grapes (?).

Sheṭ-kheru — the name of one of the Forty-two Judges in the Hall of Osiris.

K.

k — thee, thou, thy; with sign of the dual .

ka — the double of a man or god, the personality of a man or god, self, the being of a man which is associated with the heart-soul , and is independent of the spirit-soul ; plur. , .

Ka-ḥetep — a proper name.

kau — food.

ka 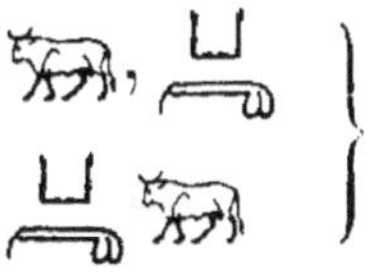 bull.

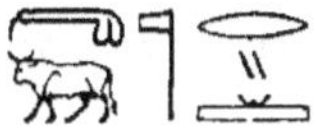 the divine bull.

Ka-Åmentet  "Bull of Amenti"; a name of Osiris.

Ka-ȧn-erṭā-nef-nebȧ-f 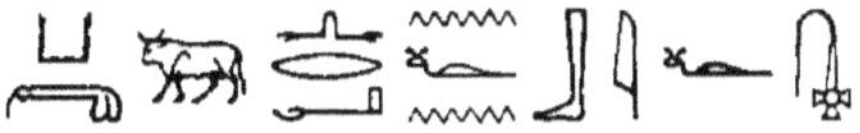 a proper name.

Ka-ur  "Great Bull".

Ka-ṭesher  "Red Bull".

Ka  "Bull husband of the cows".

kaut 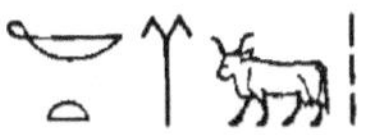 cows.

ka  to think, to cry out.

 thought.

ka  verily, prithee.

Kaa  the name of a god.

kaiu  cries (?), criers (?).

Ka-àri-k  a proper name.

kaui  a class of beings.

kabit  lamentations.

karȧ 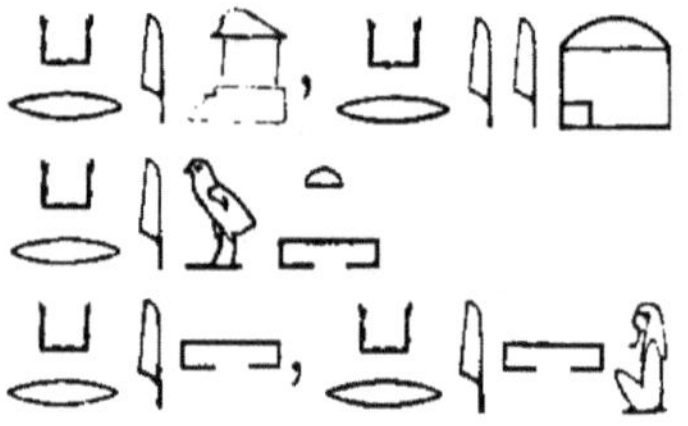 shrine, chapel, sanctuary; 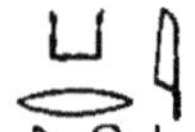  gods of the shrine.

Kaharsapusar-em-ka-ḥerremt   a proper name.

Kasaika 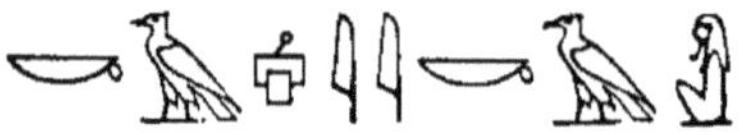 a proper name.

kat  work, works, labours.

ki  verily.

ki  another.  ...  the one ... the other.

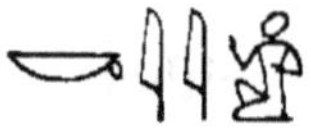 another man.

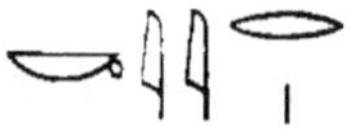 another chapter.

 another person.

another time.

another reading, a variant.

kuȧ I.

kep to hide.

hidden place.

Kep-ḥer a proper name.

kefa to act with violence, expel, drive away.

kefa to remove the clothes, strip, undress. uncover.

kem to make an end of, to finish.

the end.

kem black.

Kem-ur the name of a town and of a lake.

Kemt  the "black" land, *i. e.*, Egypt.

Kemkem  the name of a god.

kenȧ  to speak.

Kenemet  the name of a town.

kenemet  night, darkness.

Kenemti  the name of one of the Forty-two Judges in the Hall of Osiris.

kenḥu (?)  night.

Kenset  Nubia. The correct reading appears to be Sti, *i. e.*, the "land of the bow".

Ker 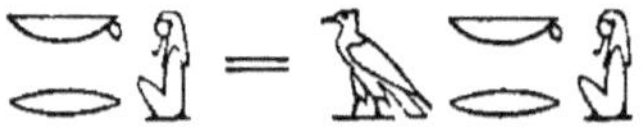 (?).

kerit 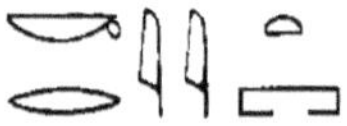 habitation, abode.

Keḥkeḥet  a proper name.

kes  to bow in homage.

kesu  homage, bowings.

Kesemu-enent  a class of divine beings.

kek, kekui 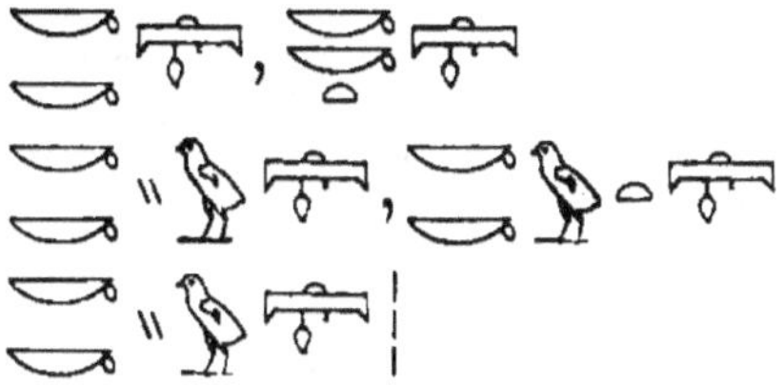 darkness, night.

ket  another.

ketuit 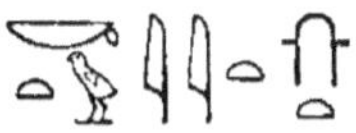 abode, habitation.

ketut  weapons, knives.

ket khu  other things.

ketet  little, bad.

⊿ Q.

qa 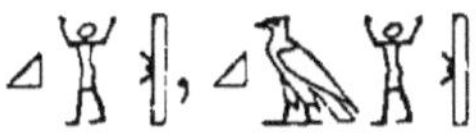 to be high, exalted, height.

 High God.

 Exalted one.

 doubly high, very high.

exceedingly high.

height of heaven.

high, *i. e.*, loud-voiced.

most terrible.

high up on the standard.

the god of the very high plumes.

Qa-ha-ḥetep a proper name.

Qa-ḥer a proper name.

qa high ground, hill, staircase.

qa to be rotten, putrefy.

qa form.

qaat bolts, fastenings.

qaȧ  form, image.

Qai  the name of a god.

qab  the innermost part.

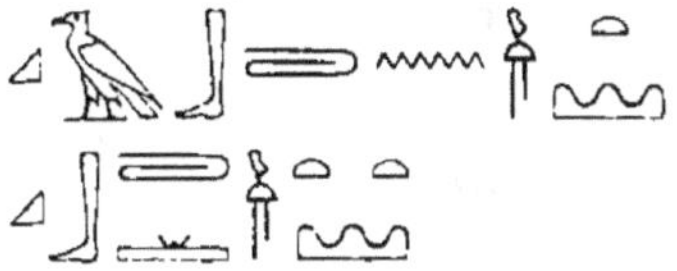 the centre of Ȧmenti.

qabt  a part of the body.

Qabt-ent-Shu-erṭā-nef-em-sau-Ȧsȧr   a proper name.

qamȧi 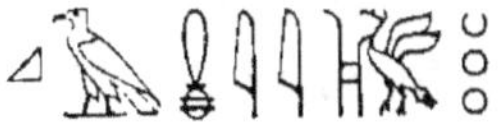 incense, unguent.

qamemt  to weep (?).

qart  a part of the Other World.

qart  bolts, fastenings.

Qaḥu 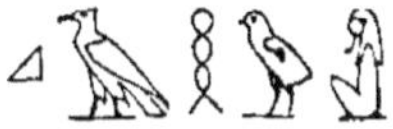 a proper name.

qaḥit  fire (?).

qasu, *qass* 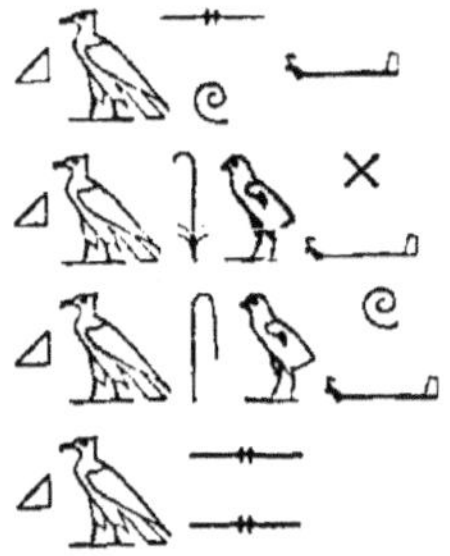 to tie, bind, fetter.

 fetter.

 fetters.

qaqa  hill.

qā 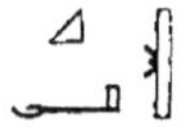 be provided with (?).

qāḥu  arm and shoulder; dual , plur.  

qāḥ 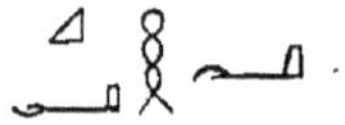 side of (?).

qu  limbs, flesh.

qeb  north wind.

qebbi, *qebti* 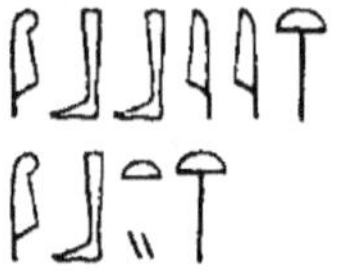 shade, shadow.

qeb 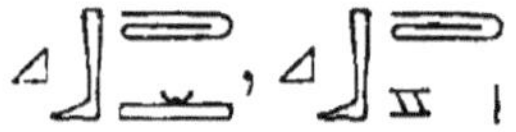, see .

qebḥ 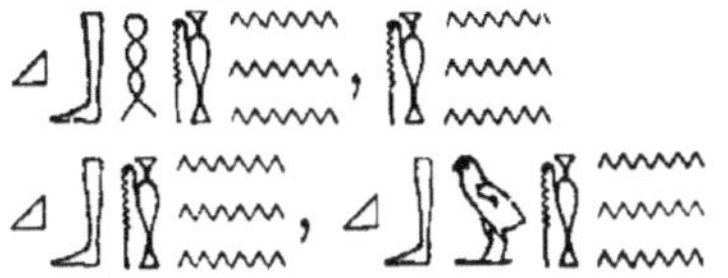 to cool, refresh, be cooled, refreshed.

 place of cooling, the bath (?).

 the cool water of the First Cataract.

Qebḥ  the marsh of water-fowl.

Qebḥ-senu-f 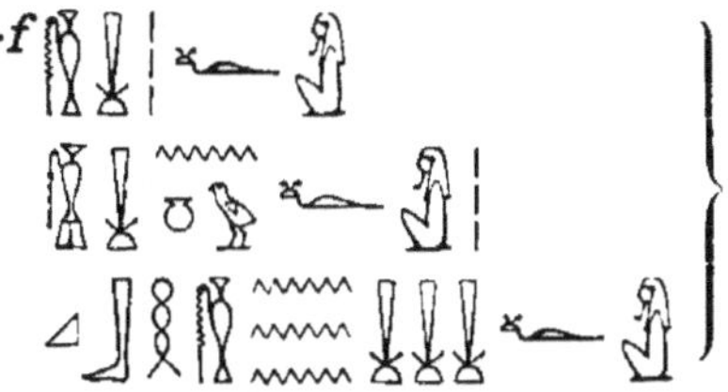 one of the four sons of Horus.

Qebti  Coptos.

qefen 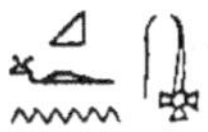 baked cake.

Qefenu 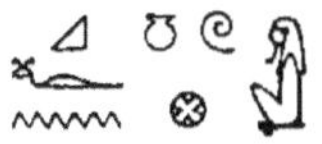 the name of a town.

qefṭenu 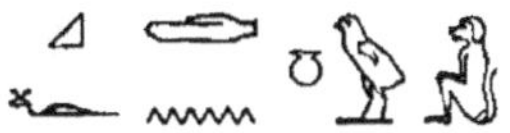 ape.

qema 

qemama  to create, to fashion, to form.

qemam, ***qemamu*** 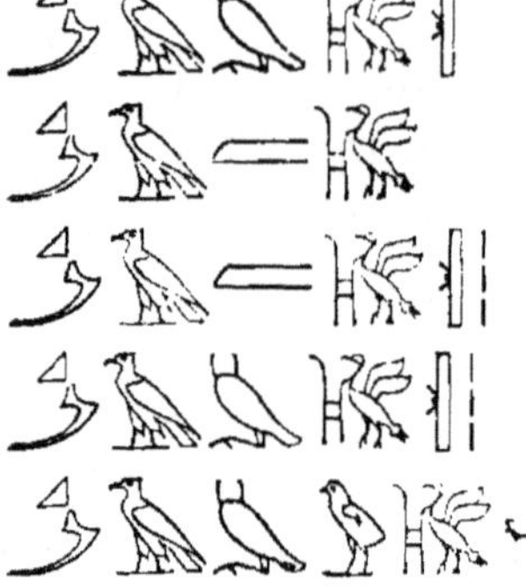 to create, to fashion, to form.

 creatress.

 god of creation.

qemḥ 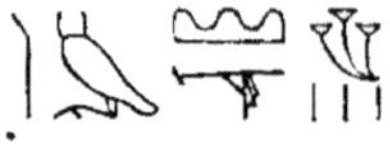 leaves of a tree.

qem-tu  to overturn.

qemṭu  to say, repeat.

Qen  a proper name (?).

qen 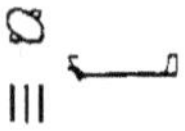 fat.

qen  to do evil, be evil.

qen  to be strong, bold, brave.

qenȧ  to embrace, embrace.

qenȧt  a kind of incense.

qeni 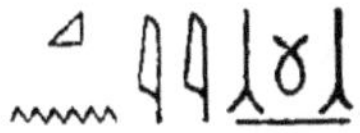 a kind of linen.

qenu  strong.

qenbet 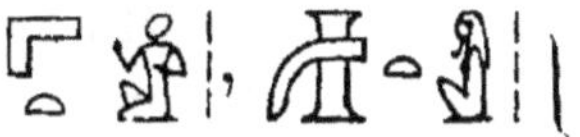
qenbit  a class of officials, human or divine.

Qenna  a proper name.

qenert  grain (?) fruit (?).

qenqen  to beat, to strike.

qenqen 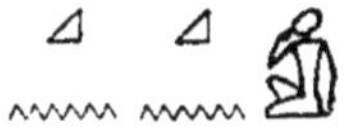 to feed, eat.

Qenqentet  the name of a lake in Sekhet-Åaru.

qer  the north wind.

qerȧ  storm, thunder, a proper name.

qerȧs 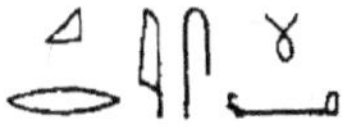 sepulture, burial.

qerfi 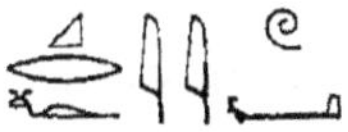 to tie, be tied.

Qernet  the name of a town.

qert, qerrt  cave, cavern.

qerti  the name of the two caves near Philae wherein the Nile rose; the name of one of the Forty-two Judges in the Hall of Osiris.

qeres 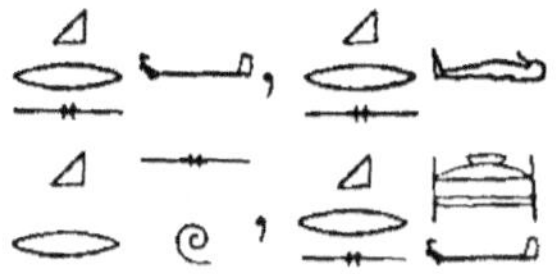 to bury; dead body.

qersu 
qerset 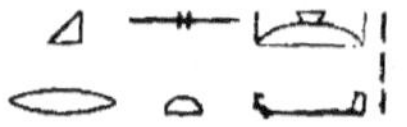 coffin, sarcophagus.

qerset 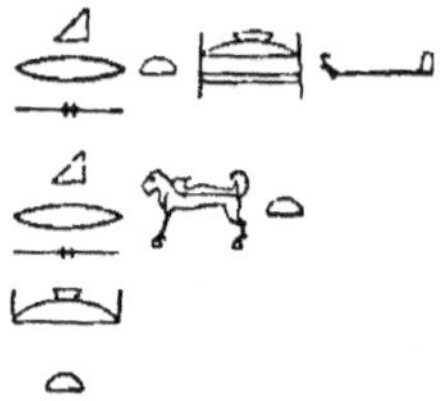 burial.

qerqer 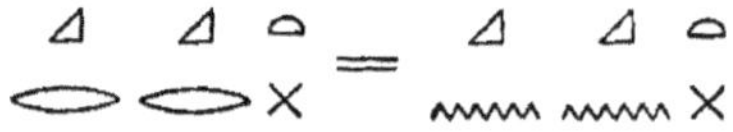

qert  bolt, fastening; 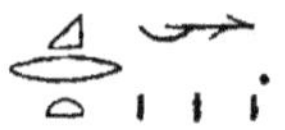.

qeḥḥtum (?)  castrated animals for sacrifice (?).

qes  burial (?).

qesu (for ***qersu***) — bones.

qesu (***qersu***) — preserves (of birds).

Qesi — Cusae, the capital of the XIVth nome of Upper Egypt.

qesen — to be evil, bad.

qeq — see ÀM to eat.

Qetetbu — a proper name.

qeṭ — to build.

qeṭ, ***qeṭu*** — to draw, sketch, make a plan or design; work of the artist.

qeṭu — sailors, mariners, crew of a boat.

Qeṭu — a fiend.

qeṭ  orbit, circle, like, similitude, character, dispositions.

 likewise, also, totality.

qeṭt 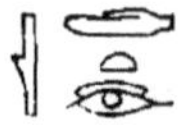 slumber.

 Ḳ.

ḳa  to besiege.

ḳa  filth, dung.

ḳa  to stink.

ḳaut 
ḳau  calamity, calamities, misery, to suffer want, to lack something or anything.

ḳai  lake.

ḳau  a substance offered to the gods.

ḳauasha  to break.

ḳab  to depart (?).

ḳabti  the hair of some portion of the body.

ḳaf		ape; plur. .
ḳas		chamber.
ḳast (?)		. . . .
ḳat		claw, limb.
ḳatu		thoughts, meditations.
ḳuat		to besiege.
Ḳeb		
ḳeb		the celestial ocean.
ḳeba		to suffer, be in misery.
ḳeba		to cast an evil glance (?).
ḳeba		some wooden object.
ḳem		to find, discover.
		something found.

ḳemḳem to discover, find out.

Ḳem-ḥeru a class of divine beings

ḳemut weak, evil beings.

ḳemḥ to see.

ḳemḥet eye.

Ḳemḥu the name of a god.

Ḳemḥusu a proper name.

ḳemḥut hair (?).

ḳen, ***ḳenn*** weak, feeble, helpless.

ḳenu cattle.

Ḳem-ur, ***Ḳen-ur***, ***Ḳer-ur*** a proper name.

ḳenut deeds, documents, records

Ḳenḳenur the name of a god.

ḳent  slit.

ḳer  moreover.

ḳert 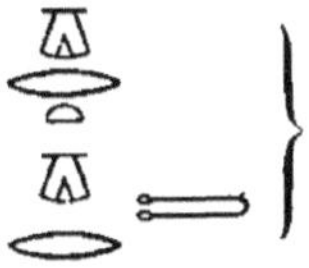 but.

ḳer  to be silent.

ḳerḥ 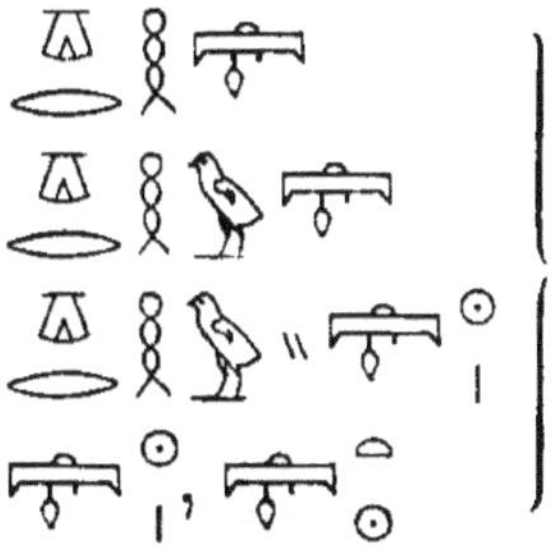 night, darkness.

Ḳersher,  a proper name.

ḳer[*ḳ*]  to have, to hold, possess.

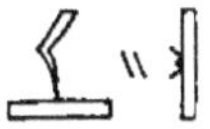 possessor.

 possessions.

ḳer[*ḳ*]  lie, falsehood, deceit.

 lie, falsehood, deceit.

Ḳer[ḳ]et  the name of a town.

ḳeḥ  weak, helpless, wretched.

ḳes  one half.

ḳes  side; dual 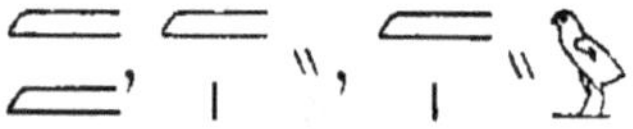 both sides; plur. .

 left side.

 right side.

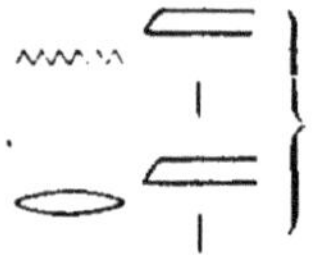 near, by the side of.

ḳesu  to anoint, ointment.

Ḳesui 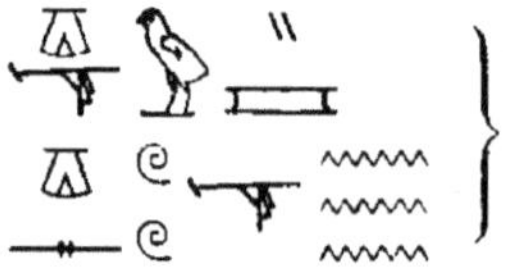 the name of a canal (?).

Ḳestȧ 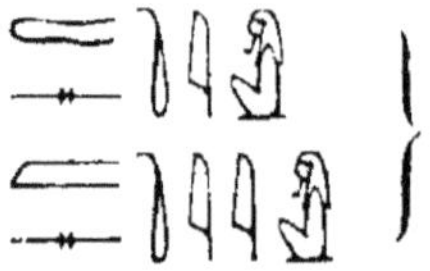 one of the Four Sons of Horus.

ḳestȧ		scribe's palette.
ḳesh	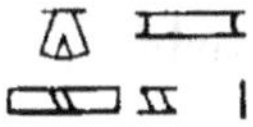	pool, lake.

T.

t	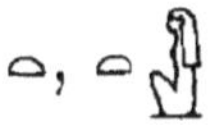	thy.
ta		the;  what is his, his.
ta	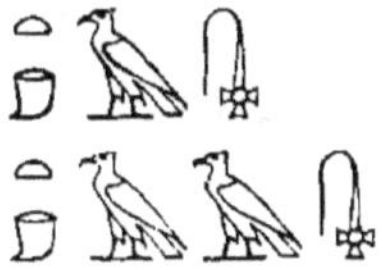	to be hot, to burn.
tau		flame, fire, hot, angry.
Ta-reṭ		the name of one of the Forty-two Judges in the Hall of Osiris.
ta	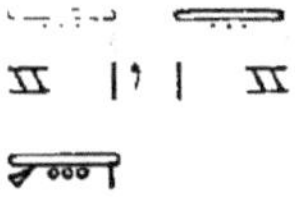	land, ground, country, the earth, the world.
taui		the "Two Lands", *i. e.*, Upper and Lower Egypt.

taiu 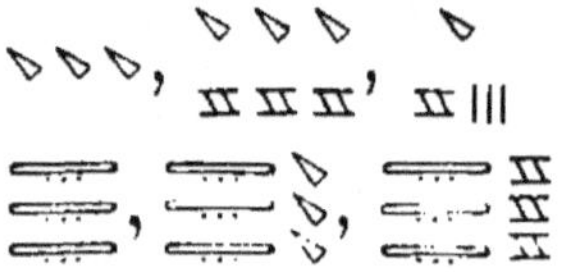 lands, countries, the world, all lands.

 the regions of the Other World.

 earth-gods.

Ta āb  "pure land", *i. e.*, the Other World.

Ta ānkhtet  "land of life", *i. e.*, the grave.

Ta ur  "great land"; a part of Abydos.

Ta en Manu  "land of Manu", *i. e.*, the West.

Ta en Maāt  "land of Law", *i. e.*, the Other World.

Ta en maākheru 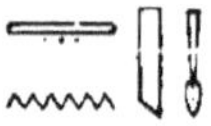 "land of triumph", *i. e.*, the Other World.

Ta Merȧ  "land of Merȧ", *i. e.*, Upper and Lower Egypt.

Ta Meḥ 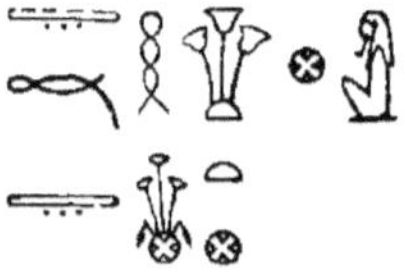 "land of the North", the Delta.

Ta mes tchetta  "land of eternity", *i. e.*, the Other World.

Ta Nefer 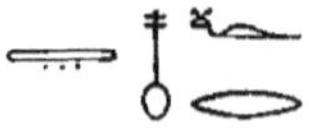 "beautiful land", *i. e.*, the grave.

Ta Nent  a portion of the Other World.

Ta neḥeḥ  "land of eternity", *i. e.*, the Other World.

Taiu nu neteru 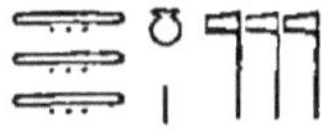 "lands of the gods", *i. e.*, heaven.

Ta remu  "land of fish".

Taui Rekhti 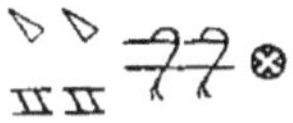

Taiu Rekhti 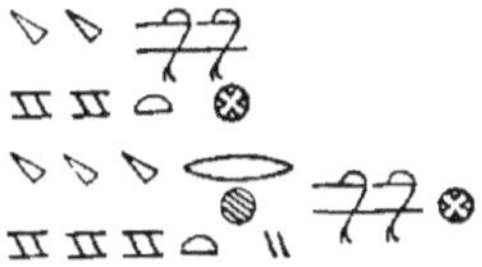

"lands of the Rekhti", *i. e.*, Isis and Nephthys.

Ta kharu  "land of the *kharu* geese".

Ta Sekri 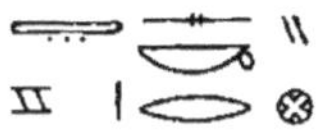 "land of Seker", *i. e.*, the Other World of Memphis.

Ta She  "land of the Lake", *i. e.*, the Fayyûm.

Ta shemā 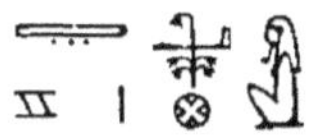 "land of the South".

Ta sheta  "land of mystery", *i. e.*, the Other World.

Ta Sti 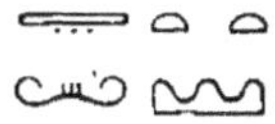 "land of the bow", *i. e.*, Nubia.

Ta qebḥ  "land of cool water", *i. e.*, the Cataract region.

Ta Ṭuat  "land of the Ṭuat", *i. e.*, the Other World.

Ta Tchesert  "holy land", *i. e.*, the Other World.

Ta en tchetta  "land of eternity", *i. e.*, the Other World.

ta  bread, cakes.

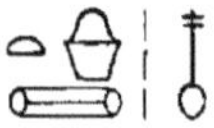 cakes made of fine flour.

 white bread.

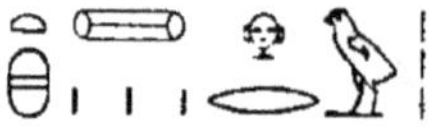 celestial bread.

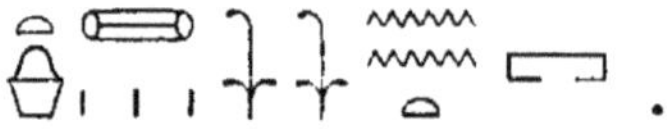 bread of Nenet (?).

 . . . . . .

Tait 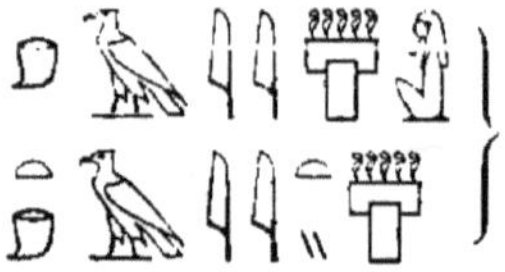 a proper name.

tait  sail.

Tait  the name of a goddess.

Tar  the name of a fiend.

taḥenen  to dip in water (?).

Ta-ḥer-sta-nef 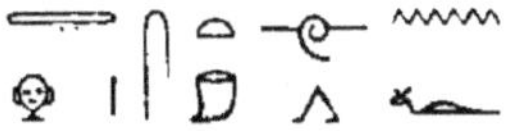 a proper name.

Tatunen 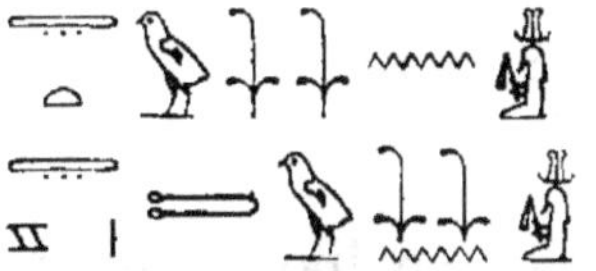 the name of a god.

tȧt  emanation; plur. .

tiu 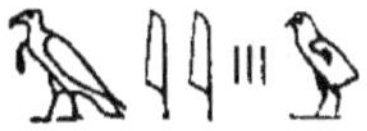 adorers.

tini 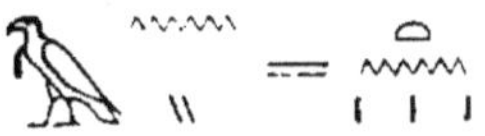 (?).

tu  a demonstrative particle.

tua  to adore.

tuȧ  I.

tui  a demonstrative particle.

tui  . . . . . .

tui  . . . . .

tuf  his.

tuni  . . . . . .

tur 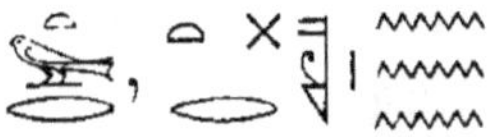

turȧ 

to cleanse, purify, be pure, clean.

tuk  thou.

tuḳ  apparel.

tut  to be like, similar.

tut  type, form, image, statue, portrait figure.

 as, like, similar.

tut  to arrange, group together.

tebu  to be shod, sandal (?).

teb  sandal.

tebi, tebt 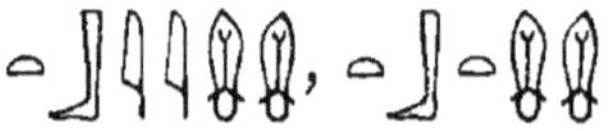 pair of sandals.

Tebu 
Tebti  } the name of a city.

tebteb  to walk.

tebtebti 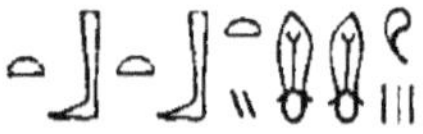 the soles of the feet (?).

tep  head, the tip, point, or top of anything.

tep  upon.

tepi 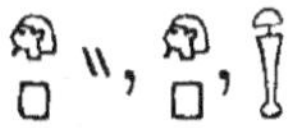 he who is on, the first, best, or finest of anything.

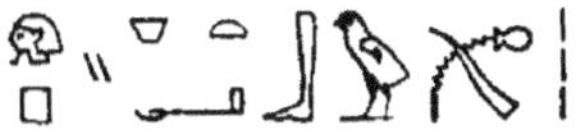 the best of the offerings.

 the finest linen.

 the choicest flowers.

 the earliest hour of every day.

 the earliest dawn.

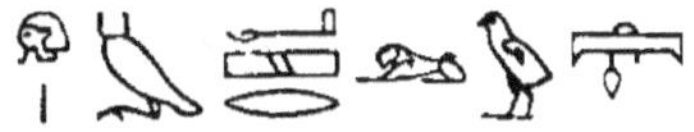 the earliest twilight hour.

 the greatest happiness.

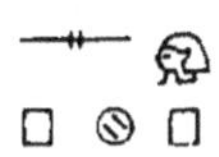 primeval time.

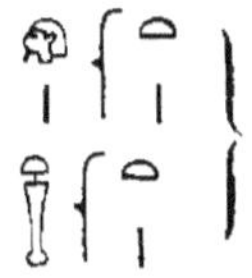 New Year's Day.

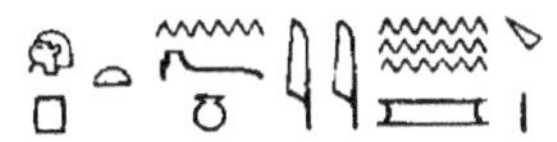 the best water in the lake.

 the original state of anything.

tep ā 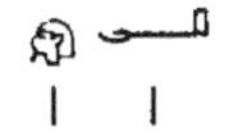 straightway.

tep ā 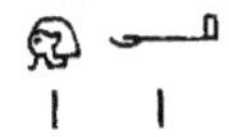 he of olden time, ancestor.

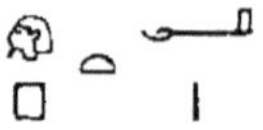 she of olden time, ancestress. plur.  ancestors, forebears.

ṭep re / *tepi re* 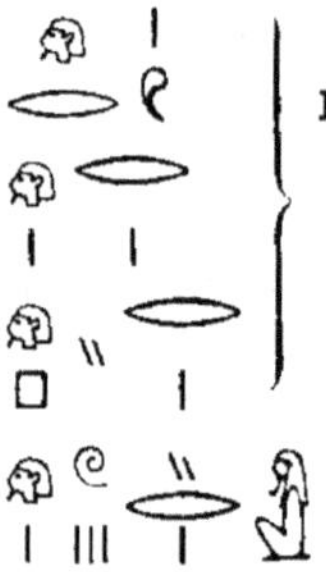 mouth, then what comes from the mouth, speech, voice, utterance; plur. .

tep reṭui 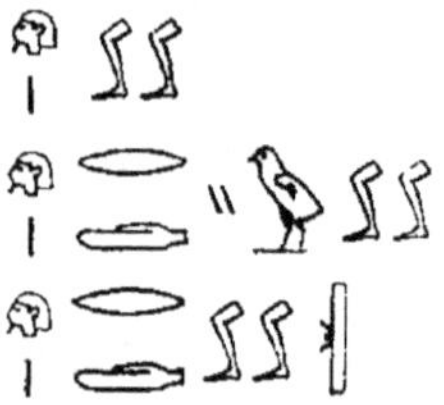 prescription, precept, command, chapter.

tep 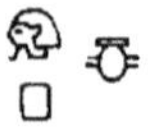 unguent of finest quality.

tep  a kind of goose.

tept  uraeus crown.

Tep-ṭu / *Tep-ṭu-f* 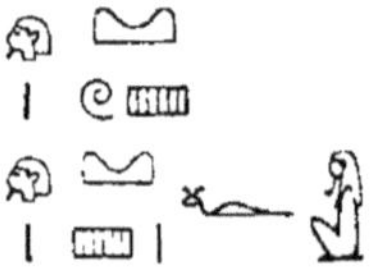 "he on the hill, or his hill"; a name of Anubis.

Tepa  the name of a cow.

tepȧ  to snuff the air, breathe.

tepḥet — cavern, cave, den, hole in the ground; plur.

tef — father.

tefa — that.

Tefnut — the name of a Water-goddess.

tem — to come to an end.

temt, *temtu*, *temti* — all, entirely; wholly and entirely.

tem, *temem* — to be complete, whole, entire.

tem — a particle of negation, no, not, without.

Tem, *Temu* — Tem, the "father of the gods".

Tem Harmakhis.

Tem Kheperà.

temam — basket (?).

temamu — stations (?).

temaāu(?) — winds.

temu, *tememu* — all people, mortals, mankind.

temem — part of a sledge.

tememu — parts of a net.

Temem-re — a proper name.

Tem-sep — the name of one of the Forty-two Judges in the Hall of Osiris.

temt 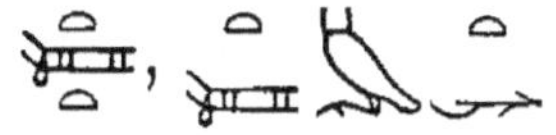 sledge.

ten  this.

ten 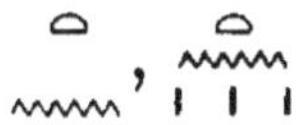 ye, you.

Teni  an ancient city near Abydos.

ten 

teni 

tenu  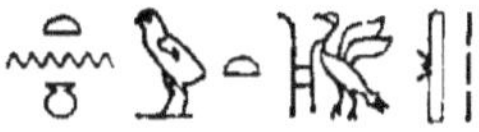

what kind of? what manner of? whence? where?

ten  to be or become great, great, distinguished.

tenait  light.

tenu  to divide, separate.

tenem 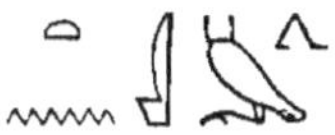 to turn back.

Tenemit  a proper name.

ter 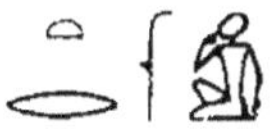 a particle, then, etc.

ter  time, season; plur. 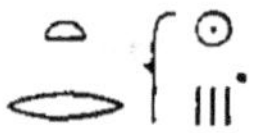.

terui  the two seasons, *i. e.*, morning and evening, or sunrise and sunset; .

teriti 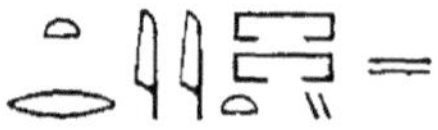 = 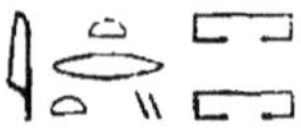 the northern and southern halves of the sky.

teru  stream.

teh 
teha  to march against, attack.

tehami  strider.

tehenen 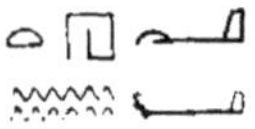 to appoint, raise up.

tiḥṭut 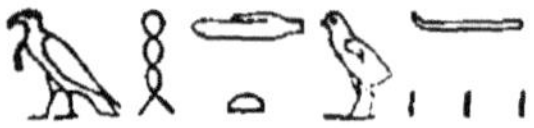 prayers, offerings.

tekh  the pointer or tongue of a balance;  "the pointer of the place of truth".

tekhni  hidden.

tekhtekh 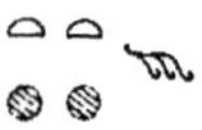 to shake out the hair.

tesh 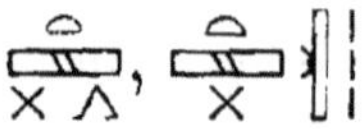 to depart, to go.

Teshtesh		an image which was dressed up as Osiris.
teka		fire, flame, lamp.
tekau		fire, flame, lamp.
tekat		fire, flame, lamp.
Tekem		the name of a god.
tekem		to approach.
teken		to enter, go in.
		those who enter.
tektek		to pass, walk, go.
teḳa		to be hot, to kindle.
teḳas		to walk, march.
tetbu		to smear.

 Ṭ.

ṭa		to pass away.
ṭa		emission.
ṭaṭa		to pollute oneself.
ṭaȧu		the name of a garment.
ṭaȧr		restraint.
ṭā ṭāṭā ṭāṭāu	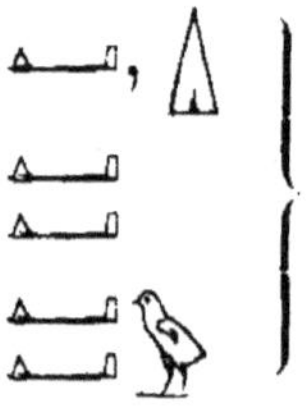	to give, grant, set, place, ascribe.
	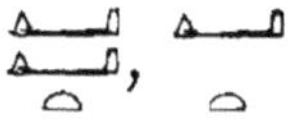	gift.
		giver, giving, placing.
	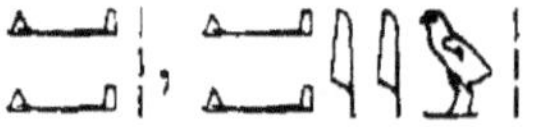	givers.
ṭāt ȧb	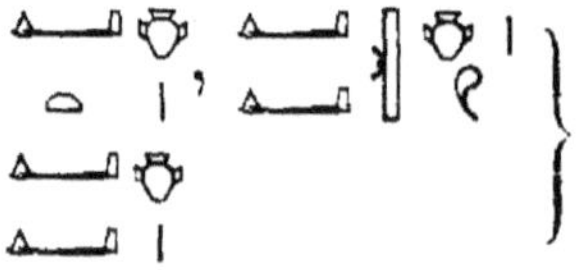	heart's desire.
ṭā		as auxiliary:
		make to fear.

	cause to do.
	cause to be.
	cause to become, etc.
Ṭāṭāu	the city of Busiris or Mendes.
ṭit	gifts.
ṭu	evil, evil thing, sin, fault, wickedness, sinner.
ṭut	
	sin, evil.
	wickedness.
ṭuu	
Ṭut	
Ṭuṭu	the name of one of the Forty-two Judges in the Hall of Osiris.
Ṭuis (?)	the name of the rudder in the magic boat.
ṭuȧu	ale (?), drink.
ṭu	mountain; plur.

the two mountains.

two great high mountains.

Ṭu-en-Bakha Mount Bakha, the Mountain of Sunrise.

Ṭu-en-Neter-khert Mountain of the Other World.

Ṭut-f (?).

Ṭu-menkh-rerek a proper name.

ṭu-ā to put forth the hand (?).

ṭua five; fifth.

ṭuau to do something early in the day.

ṭuat dawn, daybreak, to-morrow.

ṭuait dawn, daybreak, to-morrow.

ṭua to praise, worship, adore; praise.

praisers.

neter ṭua  to offer up thanksgiving.

Ṭuamutef  one of the Four Sons of Horus.

Ṭuat  The Other World.

 the everlasting Ṭuat.

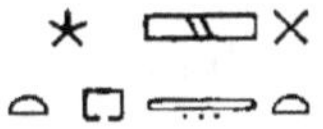 the hidden Ṭuat.

 the god of the Ṭuat.

 the beings of the Ṭuat.

ṭun  to lift up or stretch out the legs.

Ṭun-peḥti 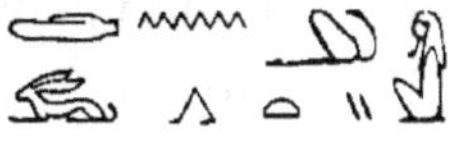 the porter of the Second Ārit.

ṭur 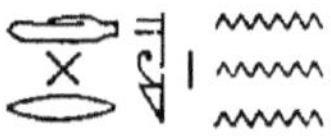 to be clean.

ṭurt  . . . .

ṭeb  horn; dual 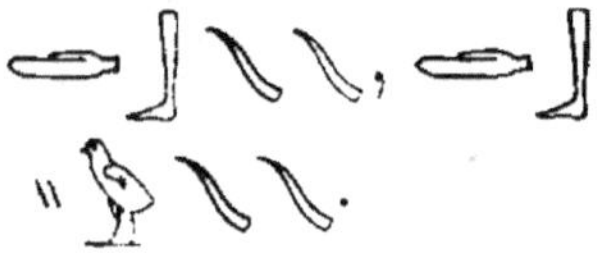.

ṭeb  tomb (?).

ṭeb  to be furnished or equipped.

ṭeb  to wall up, to box in.

ṭebt  box, coffer, coffin, chest, tomb; plur. 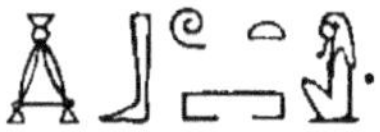.

ṭebu  frame, framework of a net.

Ṭeb-ḥer-kehaat  the herald of the Fifth Ārit.

ṭeben, *ṭebenu*  to revolve.

ṭebḥ  to pray, make supplication.

ṭebḥu (?)	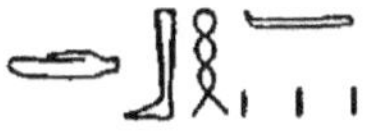	prayer, petition, supplication.
ṭebḥet		
ṭebḥu	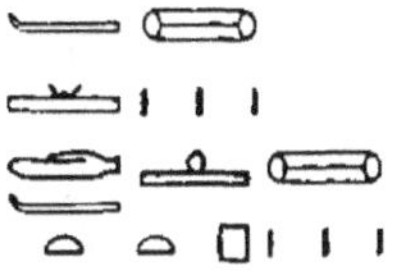	offerings, cakes, bread, etc.
ṭebḥu		funerary furniture.
ṭebḥ	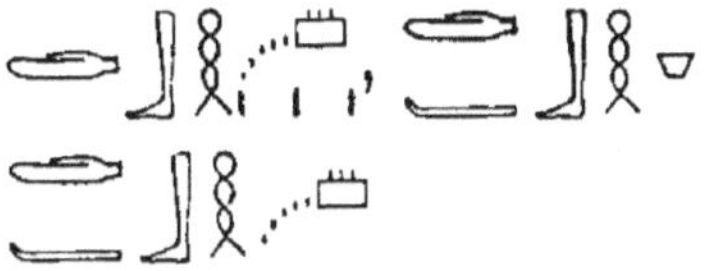	a grain measure.
ṭebt		block, slab, brick.
Ṭep	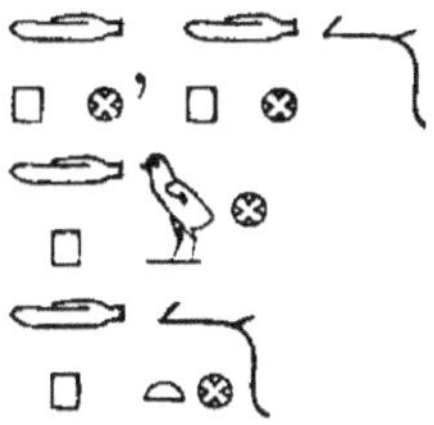	one half of the city of Buto,
ṭept	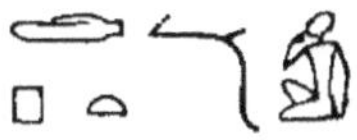	taste.
ṭepu		oar, paddle.
ṭept		boat.
ṭem		to cut, stab.
		with  a piercing voice.

ṭem, *ṭemt* — knife, sword; plur.

two-edged knife, or sword (?).

Ṭem-r(?)-khut-pet . . . . . .

Ṭem-ur — a name of Osiris.

ṭemamt — a hairy covering, two locks.

ṭemam — to make an end of.

ṭemam (*sic*)

ṭemȧ, *ṭemȧi* — to unite, be united, touch, join.

ṭemȧ — city; plur.

ṭemi — shore, bank.

ṭemem — entire, totality.

ṭemṭ
ṭemtch  to collect, gather together, unite, all, entire.

 all, totality.

Ṭemṭiu  a class of divine beings.

ṭen  to cut off, or away.

ṭen  to place.

Ṭenȧ  the name of a god.

ṭenȧ  to separate.

ṭenȧt  bank of a canal, piece of land.

ṭenȧt 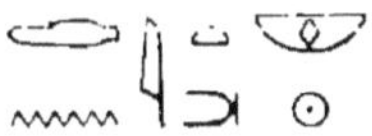 the weekly festival.

ṭenȧ  the name of a chamber.

ṭenȧ 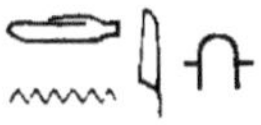
ṭenȧt 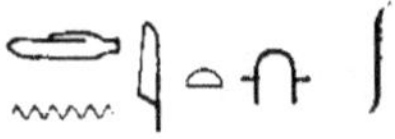 basket.

ṭenȧu  lot, share, division.

ṭeni  vessel.

Ṭeni	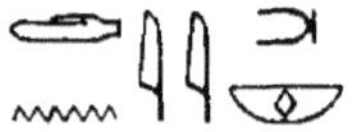	the name of one of the Forty-two Judges in the Hall of Osiris.
Ṭeniu	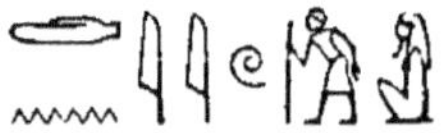	the god of old age.
ṭenu		to be distinguished.
ṭenb		to gnaw.
Ṭenpu		a proper name.
ṭenem		worms.
ṭenḥ		wing.
ṭenḥui	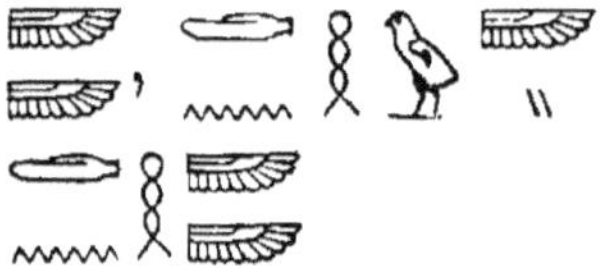	pair of wings.
ṭenḥṭenḥ		to fly.
ṭens		weights.
ṭent		abode.
ṭenṭ		slaughter.
ṭenṭen	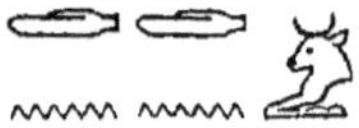	might, violence, valour.
ṭer	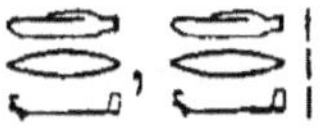	to destroy.

ṭerp — to offer.

ṭeref — wisdom, skill, book of wisdom.

ṭehant — forehead.

ṭehen — to salute humbly.

ṭehen — to place the forehead on the ground in token of homage.

ṭehen ta — to place the forehead on the ground in token of homage.

Ṭehent — "brow of a hill"; a proper name.

Ṭeḥuti — the god Thoth, scribe of the gods, dweller in Khemenu.

Ṭeḥuti-Ḥāpi — Thoth-Ḥāpi.

Ṭeḥutit — the Thoth festival.

ṭeḥer — hair, feathers, foliage.

ṭeḥerȧu — injury, harmful person, sickness (?).

ṭes — vase.

ṭes to cut, smite.

ṭes flint knife; plur. , .

ṭeser sacred, holy.

Ṭesert-tep a proper name.

Ṭesher the name of a town and of its god.

ṭesher to be red, become red, red, ruddy.

red ones, men or devils.

ṭesheru gore, blood, redness (of clouds).

ṭesher blood.

Ṭesher the red land, *i. e.*, the desert.

ṭeshert red flame.

ṭeshert the Red Crown, *i. e.*, the Crown of Lower Egypt.

ṭeqer 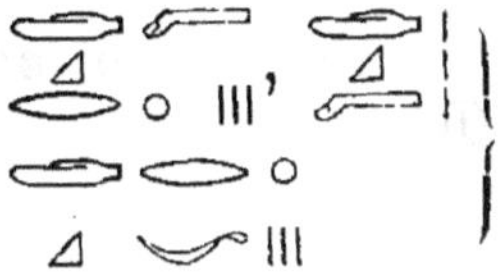 seeds, fruits.

ṭeḳa  to see.

 seeing.

 appearance.

ṭeḳaȧu  seeds, fruits (?).

ṭeḳ, ṭeḳeḳ  sight.

ṭeḳa  to hide.

ṭeḳa  plants.

ṭeḳas  to run, walk towards.

ṭetrit 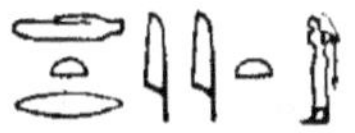 . . . . . Chap. XCIX, 12.

ṭet 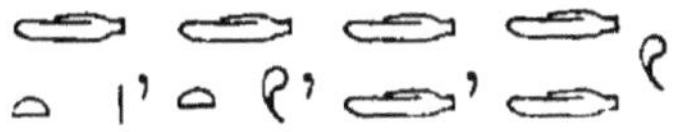 hand.

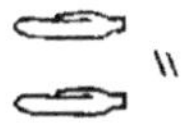 the two hands.

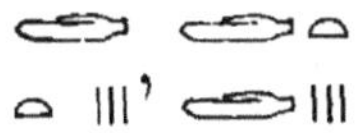 hands.

Ṭet-ent-Ȧst  a proper name.

ṭeṭ, *ṭeṭṭeṭ* 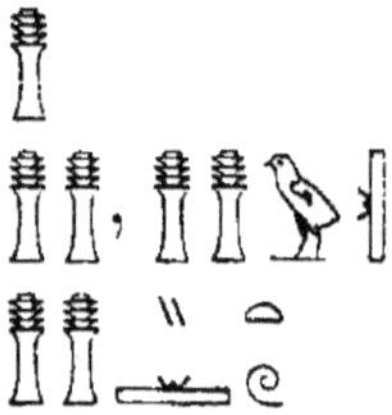 to stablish, be established, stable, permanent.

ṭeṭ  an amulet.

ṭeṭ 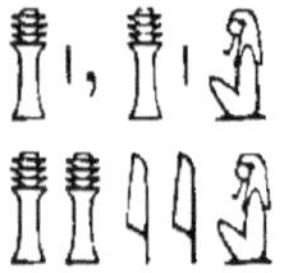 a figure, image, or tree trunk which was "set upright" during the festival of Osiris.

ṭeṭ 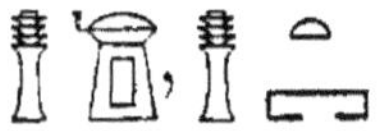 a building.

Ṭeṭu  the city of Busiris.

Ṭeṭt 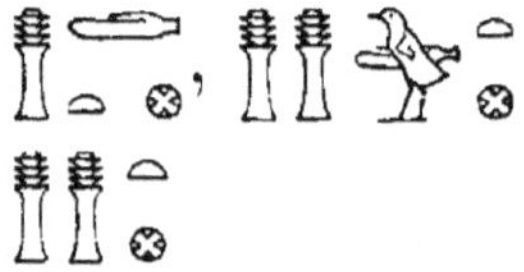 the city of Mendes.

TH.

th	thee, thou, thy,
thȧ (*tȧ*)	with verbs, etc.
Thȧnasa (*Tȧnasa*)	a proper name.
thȧthȧ	thighs.
thu	thou.
thut ȧs	behold!
thui	. . . .
theb (*teb*)	sandals.
Thefnut	the name of a goddess.
thepḥet	storehouse, cave, cavern, hole.
themes	decree, writing.

	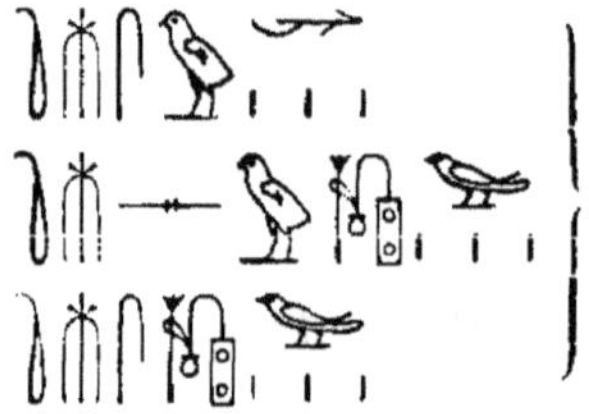	decrees.
then		this.
then	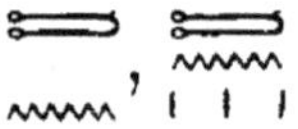	ye, you, your.
then		to be great, exalted, distinguished, worthy.
then		that.
Thena		a proper name.
Thenemi		the name of one of the Forty-two Judges in the Hall of Osiris.
Then-reṭ	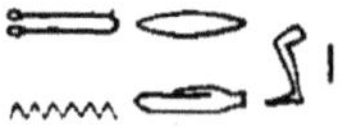	the name of one of the Forty-two Judges in the Hall of Osiris.
thentchat		throne chamber.
therem		to make to weep.

thert  a kind of tree.

theh 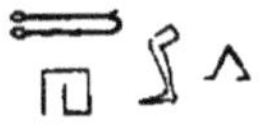 to attack.

theḥenu 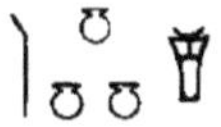 unguent.

Theḥenu
Teḥenu 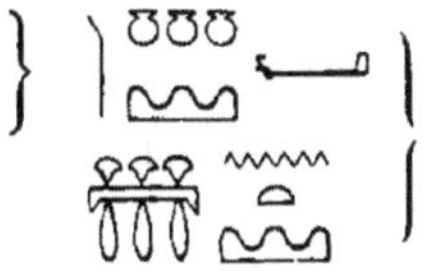 the name of a country, Libya.

theḥent 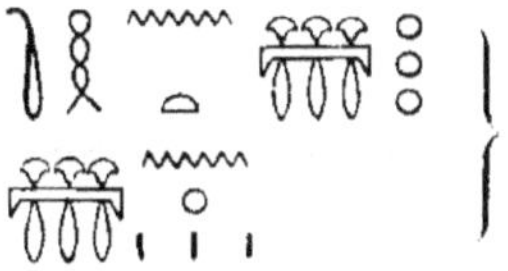 crystal (?), amber (?).

theḥen  to be yellow, or green (?); 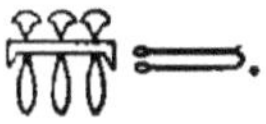.

theḥeḥ  to cry out.

thes  to be strong, give orders.

thes 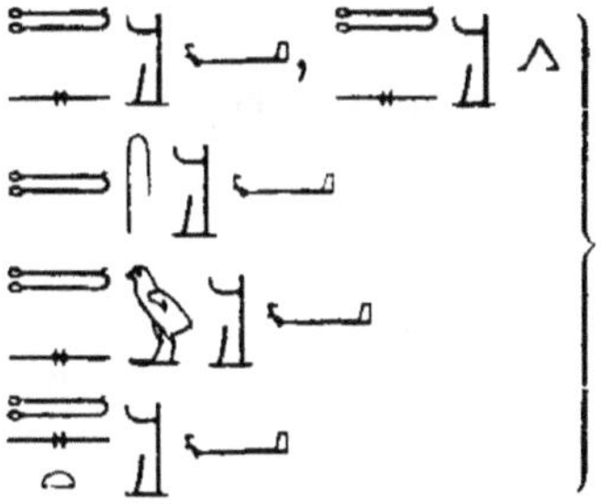 to support, lift up, raise; 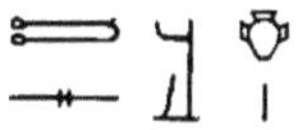 joy.

thesu
thest  supports, props.

thes	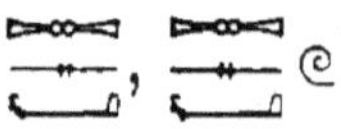	to tie in a knot, knot, fetter.
	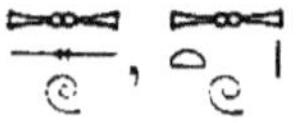	knot.
thes	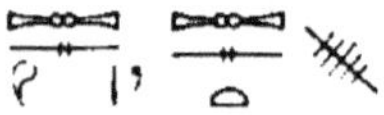	vertebra.
	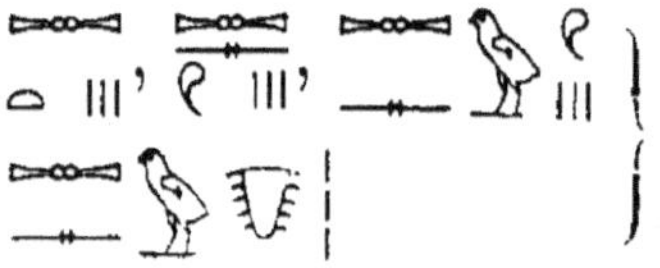	plur. of preceding.
thesu		word, speech, a saying, riddle.
		conversely.
thesȧu	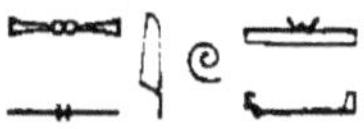	to rule.
Thest-ur		a proper name.
thesem		dog, greyhound.
		plur. of preceding.
thesthes	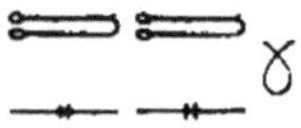	a garment.
Thekem		a proper name.

thet — the name of a red stone, or faïence, amulet.

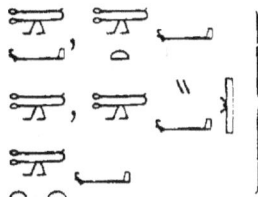

thet — to take possession of, to seize, to carry off, conquer, acquire.

seizers, robbers.

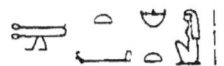

ravisher of hearts.

ravisher of women.

Thet-em-āua — the name of a plank or peg.

thetthet — to destroy.

TCH.

tcha — see ∧.

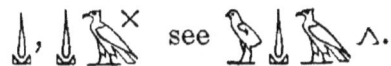

tcha — safe, sound, in good case.

tcha — to split, to cut.

tcha	abyss.
tcha	to transport, to sail with something.
	one who transports.
	transport.
	Great Boat.
tcha	to set out, go forth.
tchaau	hair.
tchau (?)	birds.
tchat	an official.
tcha	to seize, grasp, rob, ravish.
	robber.
	plunder.
	"wing-carrier", fan-bearer.
tcha	male, husband, phallus.

tchau  the west wind.

tchaui  Isis and Nephthys, the "two eagles".

tchaut  twenty;  twentieth.

tchafu  flames.

Tchafi  the souls of Horus and Rā.

tchai  fiend.

tchaitiu  slaughterers.

tcham  papyrus.

tchamet  coverings, garments.

tchart 

tchat   strength, strong.

tchat 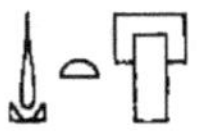 measure.

tchat  knife.

tchaut  foul things, filth.

tchaua 

tchauu  amulet.

tchatcha  "head"; the name of the upper post.

tchatcha 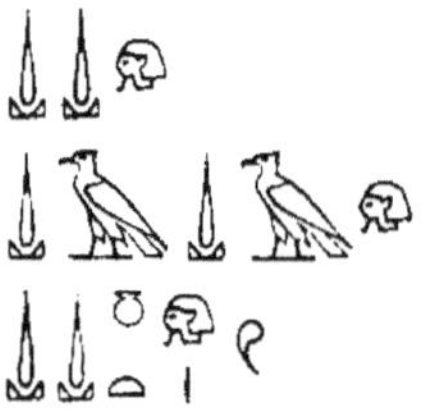 head, top of anything, summit.

tchatchat 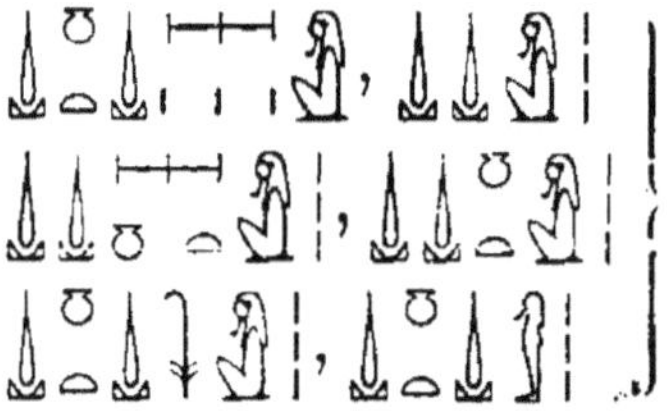 the "Heads", or "Chiefs", *i. e.*, the council of the gods in each great town of Egypt, and in the Other World. Every great god and goddess possessed a company or council of "Chiefs", *e. g.*, Osiris and Rā.

tchatchat  the domain of the cemetery in the hills; plur. 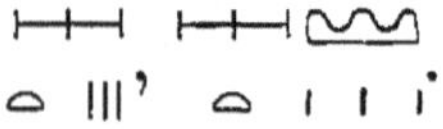.

 the domain of eternity, *i. e.*, the grave.

 the holy domain, *i. e.*, the grave.

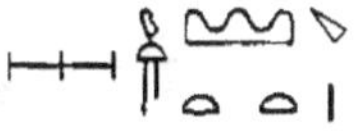 the domain of Ȧmenti, *i. e.*, the grave.

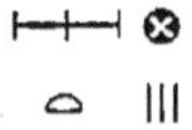 city boundaries.

tchāāu  staves.

tchābet  burning coals.

tchām 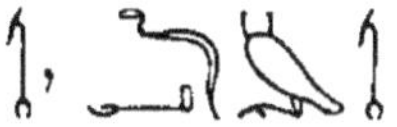 sceptre; plur. .

tchām 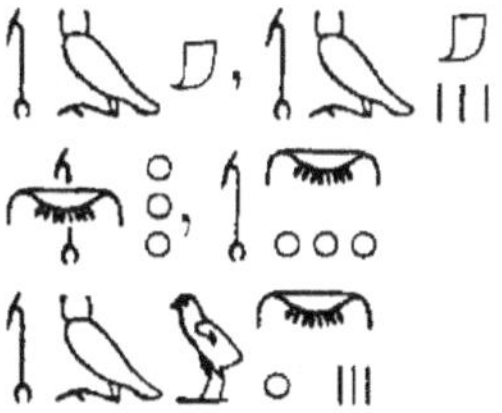 gold with a very large percentage of silver mixed with it, electrum.

tchār 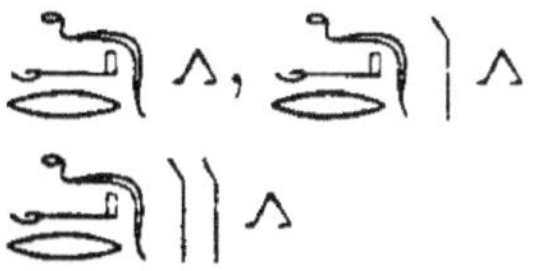 to go about in search of, to pry into.

tchārȧ  fortress.

tchebā  to seal, make a reckoning (?).

tchebā  finger; plur. 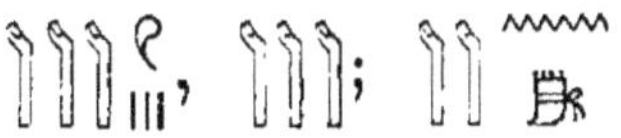 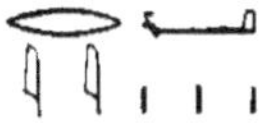 fingers which seize.

Tchebā-en-Sekri  a proper name.

Tchebā-en-Shesmu a proper name.

Tchebāu-en-Ḥeru-semsu name of the paddles in the magic boat.

Tchebāui-en-tepu-ā-Rā a proper name.

tchefa the food of the dead, sepulchral offerings.

Tchefet, ***Tchefit*** a place and a goddess in the Elysian Fields.

tchefetch pupil of the eye.

pupil of the Utchat.

tchefetch to shed.

Tchen a proper name.

tchenḥu beams.

tchentchen to crush, break.

***Tchentche*[*n*]** a proper name.

tcher to break.

tcher since, whilst, when.

tcher-ā straightway.

tcher-enti
tcher-entet } since, because.

to the limit of, all, the whole.

tcher limit, boundary; plur. , boundless.

tcherȧu } to constrain, fetter.

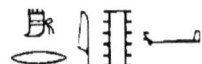

tcherȧ fort, stronghold.

tcherȧu } heel, hoof.

Tcheruu  the god of boundaries.

tcheru  a bird with a shrill voice.

tcheri 
tcherit  } a bird, the incarnation of Isis and Nephthys.

Tcherti  } Isis and Nephthys.

tcheres 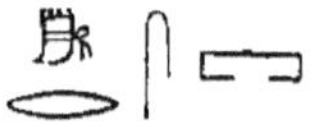 abode, chamber (?).

Tcheḥes 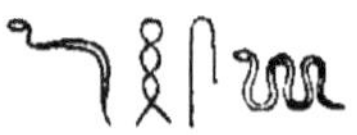 the name of a serpent.

tches 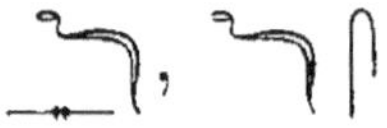 self; 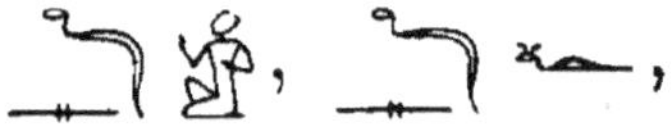 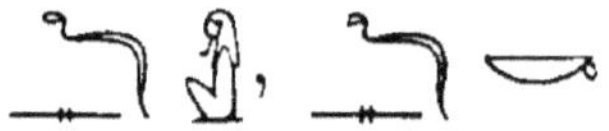 myself, himself. thyself, 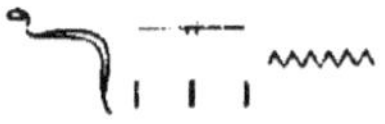 themselves.

 with his own fingers.

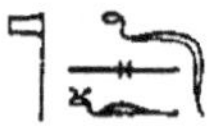 the god himself.

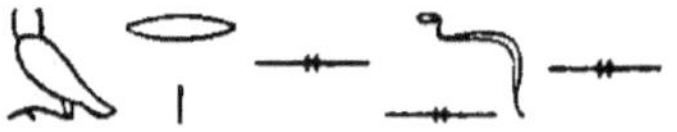 with her own mouth.

tchesef 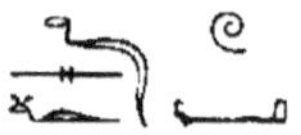 to snare.

 fowler.

tcheser 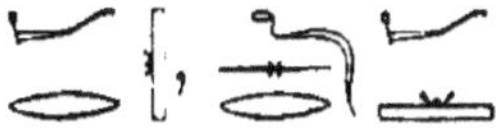 to make clear the ways, to put in good order, to be or make holy.

tcheseru  holy or beautiful things.

 glorious, splendid.

Tchesert  the beautiful mountain, *i. e.*, cemetery.

Tchesert  a proper name.

Tcheser-tep 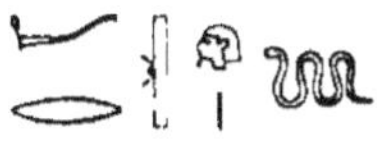 the name of one of the Forty-two Judges in the Hall of Osiris.

tchet 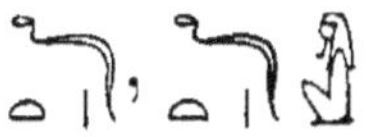 body, person;  my own self.

tchet  house, chamber; 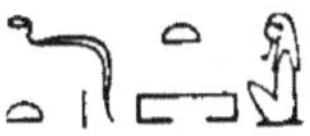 the Ṭuat(?).

tchetta  eternity, everlastingness.

 the god of eternity.

 eternity and everlastingness.

tcheṭ	to say, speak, declare, recite words, converse.
em tcheṭ	saying, introducing a quotation.
tcheṭu	to declare, speak, etc.
tcheṭ-t	words, orders, things said.
tcheṭu	words, orders, things said.
tcheṭ meṭu	"shall be recited" [the following].
	"another reading".
tcheṭ neḥes	negro speech, or language.
tcheṭfet	reptiles.
tcheṭḥu	a place of restraint.
tcheṭḥu	to shut in, imprison.
tchetch	an instrument or standard.

Words and signs of uncertain reading.

 Chap. CXLV, IV, l. 16.

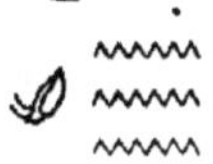 Chap. CX, l. 5.

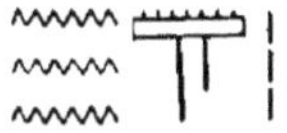 Chap. CX, l. 35.

 Chap. CXXXI, 5.

 Chap. XCIX, l. 38.

ENGLISH INDEX.

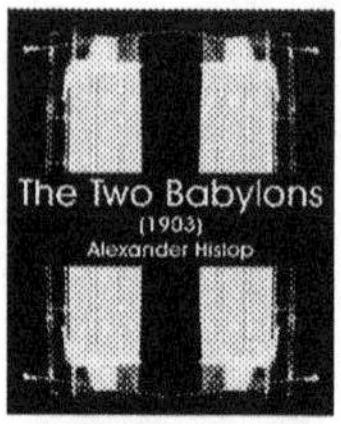

The Two Babylons
Alexander Hislop

QTY

You may be surprised to learn that many traditions of Roman Catholicism in fact don't come from Christ's teachings but from an ancient Babylonian "Mystery" religion that was centered on Nimrod, his wife Semiramis, and a child Tammuz. This book shows how this ancient religion transformed itself as it incorporated Christ into its teachings....

Religion/History **Pages:358**

ISBN: ***1-59462-010-5*** *MSRP* ***$22.95*** ☐

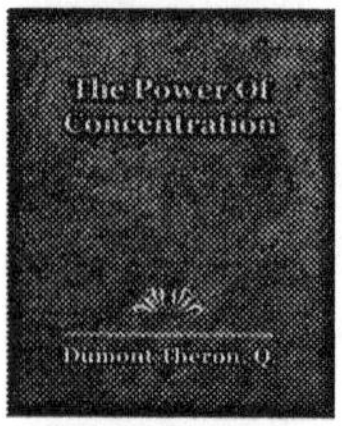

The Power Of Concentration
Theron Q. Dumont

It is of the utmost value to learn how to concentrate. To make the greatest success of anything you must be able to concentrate your entire thought upon the idea you are working on. The person that is able to concentrate utilizes all constructive thoughts and shuts out all destructive ones...

Self Help/Inspirational **Pages:196**

ISBN: ***1-59462-141-1*** *MSRP* ***$14.95*** ☐

Rightly Dividing The Word
Clarence Larkin

The "Fundamental Doctrines" of the Christian Faith are clearly outlined in numerous books on Theology, but they are not available to the average reader and were mainly written for students. The Author has made it the work of his ministry to preach the "Fundamental Doctrines." To this end he has aimed to express them in the simplest and clearest manner..

Religion **Pages:352**

ISBN: ***1-59462-334-1*** *MSRP* ***$23.45*** ☐

The Law of Psychic Phenomena
Thomson Jay Hudson

"I do not expect this book to stand upon its literary merits; for if it is unsound in principle, felicity of diction cannot save it, and if sound, homeliness of expression cannot destroy it. My primary object in offering it to the public is to assist in bringing Psychology within the domain of the exact sciences. That this has never been accomplished..."

New Age **Pages:420**

ISBN: ***1-59462-124-1*** *MSRP* ***$29.95*** ☐

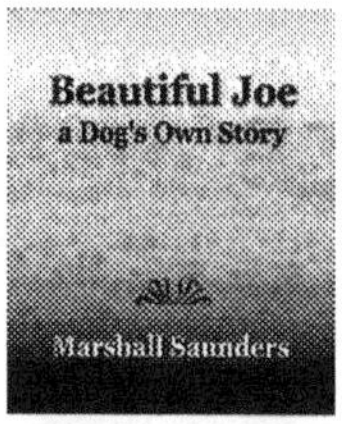

Beautiful Joe
Marshall Saunders

When Marshall visited the Moore family in 1892, she discovered Joe, a dog they had nursed back to health from his previous abusive home to live a happy life. So moved was she, that she wrote this classic masterpiece which won accolades and was recognized as a heartwarming symbol for humane animal treatment...

Fiction **Pages:256**

ISBN: ***1-59462-261-2*** *MSRP* ***$18.45*** ☐

The Codes Of Hammurabi And Moses - W. W. Davies

The discovery of the Hammurabi Code is one of the greatest achievements of archaeology, and is of paramount interest, not only to the student of the Bible, but also to all those interested in ancient history...

Religion **Pages:132**

ISBN: ***1-59462-338-4*** *MSRP* ***$12.95*** ☐

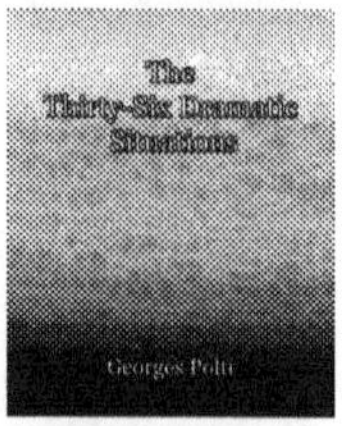

The Thirty-Six Dramatic Situations
Georges Polti

An incredibly useful guide for aspiring authors and playwrights. This volume categorizes every dramatic situation which could occur in a story and describes them in a list of 36 situations. A great aid to help inspire or formalize the creative writing process...

Self Help/Reference **Pages:204**

ISBN: ***1-59462-134-9*** *MSRP* ***$15.95*** ☐

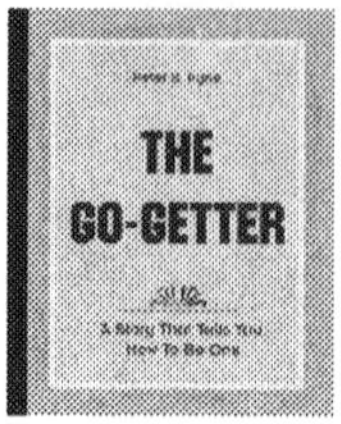

The Go-Getter
Kyne B. Peter

QTY

The Go Getter is the story of William Peck.He was a war veteran and amputee who will not be refused what he wants. Peck not only fights to find employment but continually proves himself more than competent at the many difficult test that are throw his way in the course of his early days with the Ricks Lumber Company...

Business/Self Help/Inspirational **Pages:68**

ISBN: ***1-59462-186-1*** *MSRP* ***$8.95*** ☐

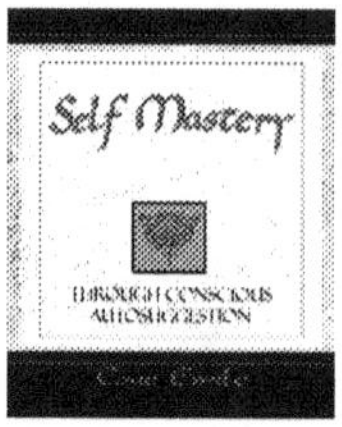

Self Mastery
Emile Coue

Emile Coue came up with novel way to improve the lives of people. He was a pharmacist by trade and often saw ailing people. This lead him to develop autosuggestion, a form of self-hypnosis. At the time his theories weren't popular but over the years evidence is mounting that he was indeed right all along...

New Age/Self Help **Pages:98**

ISBN: ***1-59462-189-6*** *MSRP* ***$7.95*** ☐

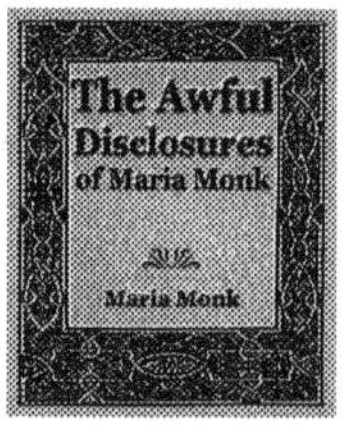

The Awful Disclosures Of
Maria Monk

"I cannot banish the scenes and characters of this book from my memory. To me it can never appear like an amusing fable, or lose its interest and importance. The story is one which is continually before me, and must return fresh to my mind with painful emotions as long as I live..."

Religion **Pages:232**

ISBN: ***1-59462-160-8*** *MSRP* ***$17.95*** ☐

As a Man Thinketh
James Allen

"This little volume (the result of meditation and experience) is not intended as an exhaustive treatise on the much-written-upon subject of the power of thought. It is suggestive rather than explanatory, its object being to stimulate men and women to the discovery and perception of the truth that by virtue of the thoughts which they choose and encourage..."

Inspirational/Self Help **Pages:80**

ISBN: ***1-59462-231-0*** *MSRP* ***$9.45*** ☐

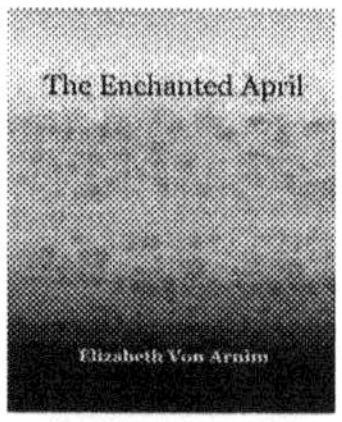

The Enchanted April
Elizabeth Von Arnim

It began in a woman's club in London on a February afternoon, an uncomfortable club, and a miserable afternoon when Mrs. Wilkins, who had come down from Hampstead to shop and had lunched at her club, took up The Times from the table in the smoking-room...

Fiction **Pages:368**

ISBN: ***1-59462-150-0*** *MSRP* ***$23.45*** ☐

Holland - The History Of Netherlands
Thomas Colley Grattan

Thomas Grattan was a prestigious writer from Dublin who served as British Consul to the US. Among his works is an authoritative look at the history of Holland. A colorful and interesting look at history....

History/Politics **Pages:408**

ISBN: ***1-59462-137-3*** *MSRP* ***$26.95*** ☐

A Concise Dictionary of Middle English
A. L. Mayhew
Walter W. Skeat

The present work is intended to meet, in some measure, the requirements of those who wish to make some study of Middle-English, and who find a difficulty in obtaining such assistance as will enable them to find out the meanings and etymologies of the words most essential to their purpose...

Reference/History **Pages:332**

ISBN: ***1-59462-119-5*** *MSRP* ***$29.95*** ☐

Bringing Classics to Life

BOOK JUNGLE

www.bookjungle.com *email: sales@bookjungle.com fax: 630-214-0564 mail: Book Jungle PO Box 2226 Champaign, IL 61825*

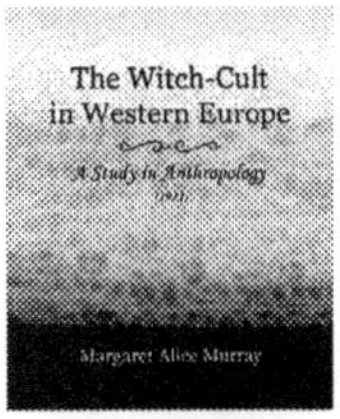

The Witch-Cult in Western Europe QTY
Margaret Murray

The mass of existing material on this subject is so great that I have not attempted to make a survey of the whole of European "Witchcraft" but have confined myself to an intensive study of the cult in Great Britain. In order, however, to obtain a clearer understanding of the ritual and beliefs I have had recourse to French and Flemish sources...

Occult Pages:308
ISBN: *1-59462-126-8* *MSRP* ***$22.45***

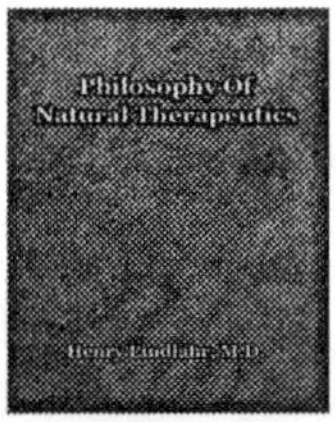

Philosophy Of Natural Therapeutics QTY
Henry Lindlahr

We invite the earnest cooperation in this great work of all those who have awakened to the necessity for more rational living and for radical reform in healing methods...

Health/Philosophy/Self Help Pages:552
ISBN: *1-59462-132-2* *MSRP* ***$34.95***

The Science Of Psychic Healing
Yogi Ramacharaka

This book is not a book of theories it deals with facts. Its author regards the best of theories as but working hypotheses to be used only until better ones present themselves. The "fact" is the principal thing the essential thing to uncover which the tool, theory, is used...

New Age/Health Pages:180
ISBN: *1-59462-140-3* *MSRP* ***$13.95***

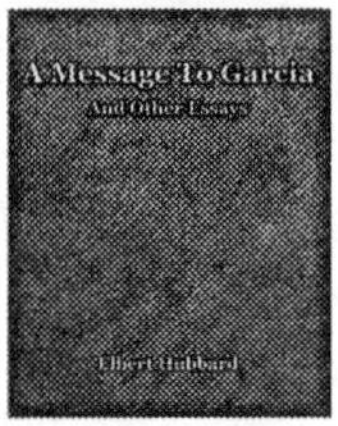

A Message to Garcia
Elbert Hubbard

This literary trifle, A Message to Garcia, was written one evening after supper, in a single hour. It was on the Twenty-second of February, Eighteen Hundred Ninety-nine, Washington's Birthday, and we were just going to press with the March Philistine...

New Age/Fiction Pages:92
ISBN: *1-59462-144-6* *MSRP* ***$9.95***

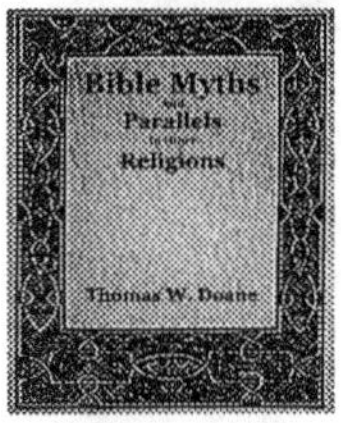

Bible Myths
Thomas Doane

In pursuing the study of the Bible Myths, facts pertaining thereto, in a condensed form, seemed to be greatly needed, and nowhere to be found. Widely scattered through hundreds of ancient and modern volumes, most of the contents of this book may indeed be found; but any previous attempt to trace exclusively the myths and legends...

Religion/History Pages:644
ISBN: *1-59462-163-2* *MSRP* ***$38.95***

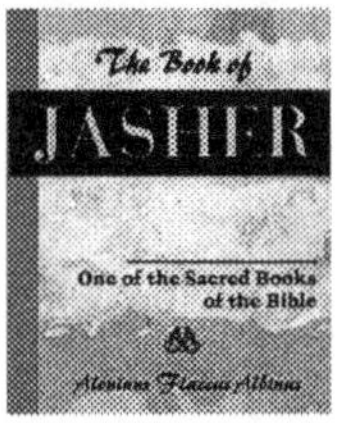

The Book of Jasher
Alcuinus Flaccus Albinus

The Book of Jasher is an historical religious volume that many consider as a missing holy book from the Old Testament. Particularly studied by the Church of Later Day Saints and historians, it covers the history of the world from creation until the period of Judges in Israel. It's authenticity is bolstered due to a reference to the Book of Jasher in the Bible in Joshua 10:13

Religion/History Pages:276
ISBN: *1-59462-197-7* *MSRP* ***$18.95***

Tertium Organum
P. D. Ouspensky

A truly mind expanding writing that combines science with mysticism with unprecedented elegance. He presents the world we live in as a multi dimensional world and time as a motion through this world. But this isn't a cold and purely analytical explanation but a masterful presentation filled with similes and analogies...

New Age Pages:356
ISBN: *1-59462-205-1* *MSRP* ***$23.95***

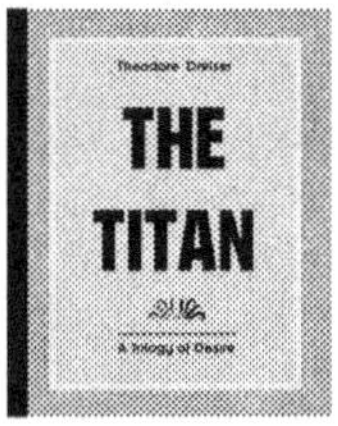

The Titan
Theodore Dreiser

"When Frank Algernon Cowperwood emerged from the Eastern District Penitentiary, in Philadelphia he realized that the old life he had lived in that city since boyhood was ended. His youth was gone, and with it had been lost the great business prospects of his earlier manhood. He must begin again..."

Fiction Pages:564
ISBN: *1-59462-220-5* *MSRP* ***$33.95***

Advance Course in Yogi Philosophy
Yogi Ramacharaka

"The twelve lessons forming this volume were originally issued in the shape of monthly lessons, known as "The Advanced Course in Yogi Philosophy and Oriental Occultism" during a period of twelve months beginning with October, 1904, and ending September, 1905."

Philosophy/Inspirational/Self Help Pages:340
ISBN: *1-59462-229-9* *MSRP* ***$22.95***

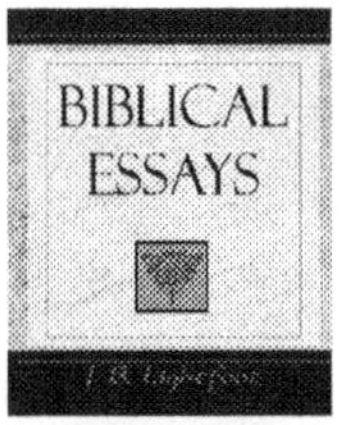

Biblical Essays
J. B. Lightfoot

About one-third of the present volume has already seen the light. The opening essay "On the Internal Evidence for the Authenticity and Genuineness of St John's Gospel" was published in the "Expositor" in the early months of 1890, and has been reprinted since...

Religion/History Pages:480
ISBN: *1-59462-238-8* *MSRP* ***$30.95***

Ambassador Morgenthau's Story
Henry Morgenthau

"By this time the American people have probably become convinced that the Germans deliberately planned the conquest of the world. Yet they hesitate to convict on circumstantial evidence and for this reason all eye witnesses to this, the greatest crime in modern history, should volunteer their testimony..."

History Pages:472
ISBN: *1-59462-244-2* *MSRP* ***$29.95***

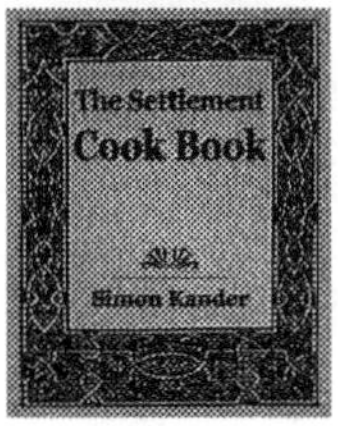

The Settlement Cook Book
Simon Kander

A legacy from the civil war, this book is a classic "American charity cookbook," which was used for fundraisers starting in Milwaukee. While it has transformed over the years, this printing provides great recipes from American history. Over two million copies have been sold. This volume contains a rich collection of recipes from noted chefs and hostesses of the turn of the century...

How-to Pages:472
ISBN: *1-59462-256-6* *MSRP* ***$29.95***

The Aquarian Gospel of Jesus the Christ
Levi Dowling

A retelling of Jesus' story which tells us what happened during the twenty year gap left by the Bible's New Testament. It tells of his travels to the far-east where he studied with the masters and fought against the rigid caste system. This book has enjoyed a resurgence in modern America and provides spiritual insight with charm. Its influences can be seen throughout the Age of Aquarius.

Religion Pages:264
ISBN: *1-59462-321-X* *MSRP* ***$18.95***

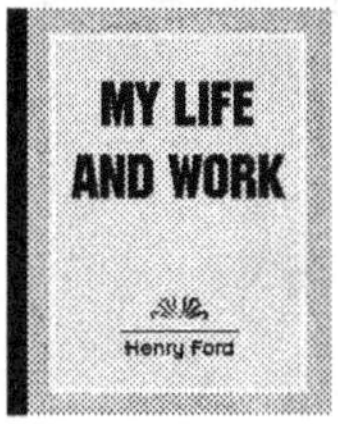

My Life and Work
Henry Ford

Henry Ford revolutionized the world with his implementation of mass production for the Model T automobile. Gain valuable business insight into his life and work with his own auto-biography... "We have only started on our development of our country we have not as yet, with all our talk of wonderful progress, done more than scratch the surface. The progress has been wonderful enough but..."

Biographies/History/Business Pages:300
ISBN: *1-59462-198-5* *MSRP* ***$21.95***

www.ingramcontent.com/pod-product-compliance
Lightning Source LLC
Chambersburg PA
CBHW050239290326
41929CB00048B/2944